A NEW ANTHOLOGY OF VERSE

A NEW ANTHOLOGY OF VERSE

▶ Edited by
Roberta A. Charlesworth
and Dennis Lee

*New and Revised Notes by
Roberta A. Charlesworth*

Toronto Oxford University Press 1989

Oxford University Press, 70 Wynford Drive, Don Mills
Ontario, M3C 1J9

Toronto Oxford New York
Delhi Bombay Calcutta Madras Karachi
Petaling Jaya Singapore Hong Kong Tokyo
Nairobi Dar es Salaam Cape Town
Melbourne Auckland

and associated companies in
Berlin Ibadan

Canadian Cataloguing in Publication Data

Main entry under title:
A New anthology of verse
Bibliography : p. 529
Includes index.
ISBN 0-19-540641-9
1. English poetry 2. Canadian poetry (English).*
I. Charlesworth, Roberta, 1919- . II. Lee, Dennis, 1939- .
PN6101.N49   1989   821'.008   C89-094182-3

1 2 3 4 5 6 7 8 9 — 97 96 95 94 93 92 91 90 89
Printed in Canada by The Bryant Press

Contents

Preface

An Anthology of Verse, the predecessor to this volume, appeared in 1964. It offered Canadian students a selection of classic poems from earlier times, along with a healthy representation of modern and contemporary poems. Twenty-five years later we have updated the selections, while maintaining the principles that have served so many readers. In this revised edition, about forty percent of the contents are new.

The poetry is drawn mainly from England, the United States, and Canada, with a sampling from poets of twenty other nationalities. The poets represent the major periods of English literature, the most generous selection being from the twentieth century. A few major poets of their time are highlighted. One pleasure of this revision has been the chance to represent the female poets internationally, and the Canadian poets, who have emerged with such strength in recent decades.

A New Anthology of Verse offers poetry on a variety of subjects. There are poems about facing your future, relationships with loved (and hated) ones, the anguish of war, the experience of being an immigrant, and dozens of other topics. By the same token, there are long poems and short poems; light verse and weighty ruminations; detached, ironic barbs and vulnerable, emotional outcries. If you open the book anywhere and start exploring, we hope you'll be refreshed by the changes of pace and intensity. The book is meant for reading as much as for classroom study. It's designed to pique readers' interest and imagination so they will keep turning the pages and, in the process, come to their own understanding of poetry.

As you'll see, the logic of the sequence is not purely thematic. Rather, the arrangement of the poems draws the
reader by a constantly changing thread of association from
one poem to the next. For example, a poem dealing with a
particular theme may be followed by another that echoes the
theme in a contrasting form, followed in turn by a poem related in mood. A cluster of serious pieces may end with a
nonsense poem; a pure lyric may lead to a tragic meditation
or a piece of witty invective; love poems may be set off by a
satire on lovers. A grouping may be linked by the use of related techniques, or it may be by one author whose style is
distinctive. Thus the reader is invited to discover the many
ways in which poems speak to one another.

This variety also exposes readers to the major genres of poetry. As well as the various forms of the lyric, they encounter
sustained narratives, excerpts from drama, poetic prose, concrete poems. The poems are indexed by subject, form, and
period (as well as by author and title), permitting thematic,
chronological, or biographical study, and the investigation of
particular forms.

The annotations and biographical notes provide essential
information; they seek to avoid ready-made judgments that
might limit a reader's response. Each natural transition in the
sequence of poems is marked in the notes, and questions are
posed that can be used to illuminate a group of poems or one
or more poems within the group. Notes on the kinds and
techniques of poetry have been expanded beyond mere iden-
tification, since the intent of the anthology is to provide a basis for intelligent appreciation. A short bibliography is also
provided. The two essays, 'Poetry and Ordinary Experience'
by M. L. Rosenthal and 'The Continuity of Poetry' by Elizabeth Drew, are offered as examples of thoughtful enjoyment
of poetry.

A List of the Poems in Numerical Order

Fern Hill

Now as I was young and easy under the apple boughs
About the lilting house and happy as the grass was green,
   The night above the dingle starry,
     Time let me hail and climb
   Golden in the heydays of his eyes,
And honoured among wagons I was prince of the apple
   towns
And once below a time I lordly had the trees and leaves
     Trail with daisies and barley
   Down the rivers of the windfall light.

And as I was green and carefree, famous among the barns   10
About the happy yard and singing as the farm was home,
   In the sun that is young once only,
     Time let me play and be
   Golden in the mercy of his means,
And green and golden I was huntsman and herdsman, the
   calves
Sang to my horn, the foxes on the hills barked clear and
   cold,
     And the sabbath rang slowly
   In the pebbles of the holy streams.

All the sun long it was running, it was lovely, the hay
Fields high as the house, the tunes from the chimneys, it
   was air   20
   And playing, lovely and watery
     And fire green as grass.
   And nightly under the simple stars

As I rode to sleep the owls were bearing the farm away,
All the moon long I heard, blessed among stables, the
    nightjars
    Flying with the ricks, and the horses
        Flashing into the dark.

And then to awake, and the farm, like a wanderer white
With the dew, come back, the cock on his shoulder: it was
    all
    Shining, it was Adam and maiden,   30
        The sky gathered again
    And the sun grew round that very day.
So it must have been after the birth of the simple light
In the first, spinning place, the spellbound horses walking
    warm
    Out of the whinnying green stable
        On to the fields of praise.

And honoured among foxes and pheasants by the gay house
Under the new made clouds and happy as the heart was
    long,
    In the sun born over and over,
        I ran my heedless ways,   40
    My wishes raced through the house high hay
And nothing I cared, at my sky blue trades, that time allows
In all his tuneful turning so few and such morning songs
    Before the children green and golden
        Follow him out of grace,

Nothing I cared, in the lamb white days, that time would
    take me
Up to the swallow thronged loft by the shadow of my
    hand,
  In the moon that is always rising,
    Nor that riding to sleep
  I should hear him fly with the high fields   50
And wake to the farm forever fled from the childless land.
Oh as I was young and easy in the mercy of his means,
    Time held me green and dying
  Though I sang in my chains like the sea.

DYLAN THOMAS

2

There Was a Boy

FROM *The Prelude*

    There was a Boy: ye knew him well, ye cliffs
And islands of Winander! — many a time
At evening, when the earliest stars began
To move along the edges of the hills,
Rising or setting, would he stand alone
Beneath the trees or by the glimmering lake,
And there, with fingers interwoven, both hands
Pressed closely palm to palm, and to his mouth
Uplifted, he, as through an instrument,
Blew mimic hootings to the silent owls,   10
That they might answer him; and they would shout
Across the watery vale, and shout again,
Responsive to his call, with quivering peals,
And long halloos and screams, and echoes loud,
Redoubled and redoubled, concourse wild
Of jocund din; and, when a lengthened pause
Of silence came and baffled his best skill,
Then sometimes, in that silence while he hung
Listening, a gentle shock of mild surprise
Has carried far into his heart the voice   20
Of mountain torrents; or the visible scene
Would enter unawares into his mind,
With all its solemn imagery, its rocks,
Its woods, and that uncertain heaven, received
Into the bosom of the steady lake.

WILLIAM WORDSWORTH

3
A Field of Light

I

Came to lakes; came to dead water,
Ponds with moss and leaves floating,
Planks sunk in the sand.

A log turned at the touch of a foot;
A long weed floated upward;
An eye tilted.

> Small winds made
> A chilly noise;
> The softest cove
> Cried for sound.   10

> Reached for a grape
> And the leaves changed;
> A stone's shape
> Became a clam.

> A fine rain fell
> On fat leaves;
> I was there alone
> In a watery drowse.

2

Angel within me, I asked,
Did I ever curse the sun?   20
Speak and abide.

Under, under the sheaves,
Under the blackened leaves,
Behind the green viscid trellis,
In the deep grass at the edge of a field,
Along the low ground dry only in August, —

Was it dust I was kissing?
A sigh came far.
Alone, I kissed the skin of a stone;
Marrow-soft, danced in the sand.   30

3

The dirt left my hand, visitor.
I could feel the mare's nose.
A path went walking.
The sun glittered on a small rapids.
Some morning thing came, beating its wings.
The great elm filled with birds.

    Listen, love,
    The fat lark sang in the field;
    I touched the ground, the ground warmed by the
       killdeer,
    The salt laughed and the stones;   40
    The ferns had their ways, and the pulsing lizards,
    And the new plants, still awkward in their soil,
    The lovely diminutives.

I could watch! I could watch!
I saw the separateness of all things!
My heart lifted up with the great grasses;
The weeds believed me, and the nesting birds.
There were clouds making a rout of shapes crossing a
     windbreak of cedars,
And a bee shaking drops from a rain-soaked honeysuckle.
The worms were delighted as wrens.   50
And I walked, I walked through the light air;
I moved with the morning.

THEODORE ROETHKE

4

I Taste a Liquor Never Brewed

I taste a liquor never brewed —
From Tankards scooped in Pearl —
Not all the Vats upon the Rhine
Yield such an Alcohol!

Inebriate of Air — am I —
And Debauchee of Dew —
Reeling — thro endless summer days —
From inns of Molten Blue —

When 'Landlords' turn the drunken Bee
Out of the Foxglove's door —
When Butterflies — renounce their 'drams' —
I shall but drink the more!

Till Seraphs swing their snowy Hats —
And Saints — to windows run —
To see the little Tippler
Leaning against the — Sun —

EMILY DICKINSON

5
Depression in Namu, B.C.

The eagle's passage sings there
crossing the sky on a high wire
salmon leap to find their other selves
black bear amble to breakfast at the river
the sun floats thru a blue notch in the hills

There was never a time
I did not know about such a place
to match the imagined place in my mind
— but I have lived too long somewhere else
and beauty bores me without the slight ache
of ugliness that makes me want to change things
knowing it's impossible

AL PURDY

6

Snake

A snake came to my water-trough
On a hot, hot day, and I in pyjamas for the heat,
To drink there.

In the deep, strange-scented shade of the great dark carob-
     tree
I came down the steps with my pitcher
And must wait, must stand and wait, for there he was at the
     trough before me.

He reached down from a fissure in the earth-wall in the
     gloom
And trailed his yellow-brown slackness soft-bellied down,
     over the edge of the stone trough
And rested his throat upon the stone bottom,
And where the water had dripped from the tap, in a small
     clearness,   10
He sipped with his straight mouth,
Softly drank through his straight gums, into his slack long
     body,
Silently.

Someone was before me at my water-trough,
And I, like a second-comer, waiting.

He lifted his head from his drinking, as cattle do,
And looked at me vaguely, as drinking cattle do,
And flickered his two-forked tongue from his lips, and
     mused a moment,

[10]

And stooped and drank a little more,
Being earth-brown, earth-golden from the burning bowels
    of the earth   20
On the day of Sicilian July, with Etna smoking.

The voice of my education said to me
He must be killed,
For in Sicily the black, black snakes are innocent, the gold
    are venomous.

And voices in me said, If you were a man
You would take a stick and break him now, and finish him
    off.

But must I confess how I liked him,
How glad I was he had come like a guest in quiet, to drink
    at my water-trough
And depart peaceful, pacified, and thankless,
Into the burning bowels of this earth?   30

Was it cowardice, that I dared not kill him?
Was it perversity, that I longed to talk to him?
Was it humility, to feel honoured?
I felt so honoured.

And yet those voices:
If you were not afraid, you would kill him!

And truly I was afraid, I was most afraid,
But even so, honoured still more
That he should seek my hospitality
From out the dark door of the secret earth.   40

He drank enough
And lifted his head, dreamily, as one who has drunken,
And flickered his tongue like a forked night on the air, so
  black,
Seeming to lick his lips,
And looked around like a god, unseeing, into the air,
And slowly turned his head,
And slowly, very slowly, as if thrice adream,
Proceeded to draw his slow length curving round
And climb again the broken bank of my wall-face.

And as he put his head into that dreadful hole,   50
And as he slowly drew up, snake-easing his shoulders, and
  entered farther,
A sort of horror, a sort of protest against his withdrawing
  into that horrid black hole,
Deliberately going into the blackness, and slowly drawing
  himself after,
Overcame me now his back was turned.

I looked round, I put down my pitcher,
I picked up a clumsy log
And threw it at the water-trough with a clatter.

I think it did not hit him,
But suddenly that part of him that was left behind
  convulsed in undignified haste,
Writhed like lightning, and was gone   60
Into the black hole, the earth-lipped fissure in the wall-
  front,
At which, in the intense still noon, I stared with
  fascination.

And immediately I regretted it.
I thought how paltry, how vulgar, what a mean act!
I despised myself and the voices of my accursèd human
    education.

And I thought of the albatross,
And I wished he would come back, my snake.

For he seemed to me again like a king,
Like a king in exile, uncrowned in the underworld,
Now due to be crowned again.   70

And so, I missed my chance with one of the lords
Of life.
And I have something to expiate;
A pettiness.

D. H. LAWRENCE

7
To a Fat Lady Seen from a Train

O why do you walk through the fields in gloves,
    Missing so much and so much?
O fat white woman whom nobody loves,
Why do you walk through the fields in gloves,
When the grass is soft as the breast of doves
    And shivering-sweet to the touch?
O why do you walk through the fields in gloves,
    Missing so much and so much?

FRANCES CORNFORD

8

Baseball

The game of baseball is not a metaphor
and I know it's not really life.
The chalky green diamond, the lovely
dusty brown lanes I see from airplanes
multiplying around the cities
are only neat playing fields.
Their structure is not the frame
of history carved out of forest,
that is not what I see on my ascent.

And down in the stadium,   10
the veteran catcher guiding the young
pitcher through the innings, the line
of concentration between them,
that delicate filament is not
like the way you are helping me,
only it reminds me when I strain
for analogies, the way a rookie strains
for perfection, and the veteran,
in his wisdom, seems to promise it,
it glows from his upheld glove,   20

and the man in front of me
in the grandstand, drinking banana
daiquiris from a thermos,
continuing through a whole dinner
to the aromatic cigar even as our team
is shut out, nearly hitless, he is
not like the farmer that Auden speaks
of in Breughel's Icarus,

or the four inevitable woman-hating
drunkards, yelling hugging   30
each other, and moving up and down
continuously for more beer

and the young wife trying to understand
what a full count could be
to please her husband happy in
his old dreams, or the little boy
in the Yankees cap already nodding
off to sleep against his father,
program and popcorn memories
sliding into the future,   40
and the old woman from Lincoln, Maine
screaming at the Yankee slugger
with wounded knees to break his leg

this is not a microcosm,
not even a slice of life

and the terrible slumps,
when the greatest hitter mysteriously
goes hitless for weeks, or
the pitcher's stuff is all junk
who threw like a magician all last month,   50
or the days when our guys look
like Sennett cops, slipping, bumping
each other, then suddenly, the play
that wasn't humanly possible, the Kid
we know isn't ready for the big leagues,
leaps into the air to catch a ball
that should have gone downtown,

and coming off the field is hugged
and bottom-slapped by the sudden
sorcerers, the winning team   60

the question of what makes a man
slump when his form, his eye,
his power aren't to blame, this isn't
like the bad luck that hounds us,
and his frustration in the games
not like our deep rage
for disappointing ourselves

the ball park is an artifact,
manicured safe, 'scene in an Easter egg,'
and the order of the ball game,   70
the firm structure with the mystery
of accidents always contained,
not the wild field we wander in,
where I'm trying to recite the rules,
to repeat the statistics of the game,
and the wind keeps carrying my words away

GAIL MAZUR

9

Walking Around

It so happens I'm tired of just being a man.
I go to a movie, drop in at the tailor's — it so happens —
feeling wizened and numbed, like a big, wooly swan,
awash on an ocean of clinkers and causes.

A whiff from a barbershop does it: I yell bloody murder.
All I ask is a little vacation from things: from boulders and
    woolens,
from gardens, institutional projects, merchandise,
eyeglasses, elevators — I'd rather not look at them.

It so happens I'm fed up — with my feet and my
    fingernails
and my hair and my shadow.   10
Being a man leaves me cold: that's how it is.

Still — it would be lovely
to wave a cut lily and panic a notary,
or finish a nun with a left to the ear.
It would be nice
just to walk down the street with a green switchblade
    handy,
whooping it up till I die of the shivers.

I won't live like this — like a root in a shadow,
wide-open and wondering, teeth chattering sleepily,
going down to the dripping entrails of the universe   20
absorbing things, taking things in, eating three squares a
    day.

I've had all I'll take from catastrophe.
I won't have it this way, muddling through like a root or a
    grave,
all alone underground, in a morgue of cadavers,
cold as a stiff, dying of misery.

That's why Monday flares up like an oil-slick,
when it sees me up close, with the face of a jailbird,
or squeaks like a broken-down wheel as it goes,
stepping hot-blooded into the night.

Something shoves me toward certain damp houses, into
    certain dark corners,   30
into hospitals, with bones flying out of the windows;
into shoe stores and shoemakers smelling of vinegar,
streets frightful as fissures laid open.

There, trussed to the doors of the houses I loathe
are the sulphurous birds, in a horror of tripes,
dental plates lost in a coffeepot,
mirrors
that must surely have wept with the nightmare and shame
    of it all;
and everywhere, poisons, umbrellas, and belly buttons.

I stroll unabashed, in my eyes and my shoes   40
and my rage and oblivion.
I go on, crossing offices, retail orthopedics,
courtyards with laundry hung out on a wire:
the blouses and towels and the drawers newly washed,
slowly dribbling a slovenly tear.

PABLO NERUDA
Translated by BEN BELITT

10

I Know Where I'm Going

I know where I'm going,
I know who's going with me,
I know who I love,
But the dear knows who I'll marry.

I'll have stockings of silk,
Shoes of fine green leather,
Combs to buckle my hair
And a ring for every finger.

Feather beds are soft,
Painted rooms are bonny;
But I'd leave them all
To go with my love Johnny.

Some say he's dark,
I say he's bonny,
He's the flower of them all
My handsome, coaxing Johnny.

I know where I'm going,
I know who's going with me,
I know who I love,
But the dear knows who I'll marry.

ANONYMOUS

Waterloo Express

The Waterloo Express is big and important with its
glass eye, the eye of a fanatic. Sometimes they are

so important they pass you by, headed for a great
destination and bending the rails into a pure musical
    phrase.

Snatched loose from my baggage and address, goodbyes
    falling
away in flakes of dead skin, you'd say I was a high

pariah, sleepless and nowhere to go. Who do you think
I am? I bet you think I'm running away from home or

a man who never done me wrong. I bet you think
I'm twenty, with the fragile soul of a wild fawn.   10

Well, I used to think so too, but the job didn't pay much
and anyhow I never liked the taste of wages.

I like it here in the middle element where this
express is ripping up the dawn like an old ticket

whose engine is blowing the towns away
and even I am barely holding on.

There they go — a toe, a finger, my coat — honey,
you'd hardly recognize me, pared down to one white eye.

It has the cynical glint of a dynamite salesman.

PAULETTE JILES

The Road Not Taken

Two roads diverged in a yellow wood,
And sorry I could not travel both
And be one traveler, long I stood
And looked down one as far as I could
To where it bent in the undergrowth;

Then took the other, as just as fair,
And having perhaps the better claim,
Because it was grassy and wanted wear;
Though as for that the passing there
Had worn them really about the same,

And both that morning equally lay
In leaves no step had trodden black.
Oh, I kept the first for another day!
Yet knowing how way leads on to way,
I doubted if I should ever come back.

I shall be telling this with a sigh
Somewhere ages and ages hence:
Two roads diverged in a wood, and I —
I took the one less traveled by,
And that has made all the difference.

ROBERT FROST

13

Ulysses

It little profits that an idle king,
By this still hearth, among these barren crags,
Match'd with an aged wife, I mete and dole
Unequal laws unto a savage race,
That hoard, and sleep, and feed, and know not me.
I cannot rest from travel: I will drink
Life to the lees: all times I have enjoy'd
Greatly, have suffer'd greatly, both with those
That loved me, and alone; on shore, and when
Thro' scudding drifts the rainy Hyades   10
Vext the dim sea: I am become a name;
For always roaming with a hungry heart
Much have I seen and known; cities of men
And manners, climates, councils, governments,
Myself not least, but honour'd of them all;
And drunk delight of battle with my peers,
Far on the ringing plains of windy Troy.
I am a part of all that I have met;
Yet all experience is an arch wherethro'
Gleams that untravell'd world, whose margin fades   20
For ever and for ever when I move.
How dull it is to pause, to make an end,
To rust unburnish'd, not to shine in use!
As tho' to breathe were life. Life piled on life
Were all too little, and of one to me
Little remains: but every hour is saved
From that eternal silence, something more,
A bringer of new things; and vile it were
For some three suns to store and hoard myself,

And this grey spirit yearning in desire   30
To follow knowledge, like a sinking star,
Beyond the utmost bound of human thought.
    This is my son, mine own Telemachus,
To whom I leave the sceptre and the isle —
Well-loved of me, discerning to fulfil
This labour, by slow prudence to make mild
A rugged people, and thro' soft degrees
Subdue them to the useful and the good.
Most blameless is he, centred in the sphere
Of common duties, decent not to fail   40
In offices of tenderness, and pay
Meet adoration to my household gods,
When I am gone. He works his work, I mine.
    There lies the port; the vessel puffs her sail:
There gloom the dark broad seas. My mariners,
Souls that have toil'd, and wrought, and thought with me —
That ever with a frolic welcome took
The thunder and the sunshine, and opposed
Free hearts, free foreheads — you and I are old;
Old age hath yet his honour and his toil;   50
Death closes all: but something ere the end,
Some work of noble note, may yet be done,
Not unbecoming men that strove with Gods.
The lights begin to twinkle from the rocks:
The long day wanes: the slow moon climbs: the deep
Moans round with many voices. Come, my friends,
'Tis not too late to seek a newer world.
Push off, and sitting well in order smite
The sounding furrows; for my purpose holds
To sail beyond the sunset, and the baths   60
Of all the western stars, until I die.

It may be that the gulfs will wash us down:
It may be we shall touch the Happy Isles,
And see the great Achilles, whom we knew.
Tho' much is taken, much abides; and tho'
We are not now that strength which in old days
Moved earth and heaven, that which we are, we are;
One equal temper of heroic hearts,
Made weak by time and fate, but strong in will
To strive, to seek, to find, and not to yield.

ALFRED LORD TENNYSON

14

Ozymandias

I met a traveller from an antique land
Who said: Two vast and trunkless legs of stone
Stand in the desert. Near them on the sand,
Half sunk, a shatter'd visage lies, whose frown
And wrinkled lip and sneer of cold command
Tell that its sculptor well those passions read
Which yet survive, stamp'd on these lifeless things,
The hand that mock'd them and the heart that fed;
And on the pedestal these words appear:
'My name is Ozymandias, king of kings:
Look on my works, ye Mighty, and despair!'
Nothing beside remains. Round the decay
Of that colossal wreck, boundless and bare,
The lone and level sands stretch far away.

PERCY BYSSHE SHELLEY

15

A Peasant

Iago Prytherch his name, though, be it allowed,
Just an ordinary man of the bald Welsh hills,
Who pens a few sheep in a gap of cloud.
Docking mangels, chipping the green skin
From the yellow bones with a half-witted grin
Of satisfaction, or churning the crude earth
To a stiff sea of clods that glint in the wind —
So are his days spent, his spittled mirth
Rarer than the sun that cracks the cheeks
Of the gaunt sky perhaps once in a week.   10
And then at night see him fixed in his chair
Motionless, except when he leans to gob in the fire.
There is something frightening in the vacancy of his mind.
His clothes, sour with years of sweat
And animal contact, shock the refined,
But affected, sense with their stark naturalness.
Yet this is your prototype, who, season by season
Against siege of rain and the wind's attrition,
Preserves his stock, an impregnable fortress
Not to be stormed even in death's confusion.   20
Remember him then, for he, too, is a winner of wars,
Enduring like a tree under the curious stars.

R. S. THOMAS

16

The Village Master

FROM *The Deserted Village*

Beside yon straggling fence that skirts the way,
With blossom'd furze unprofitably gay,
There, in his noisy mansion, skill'd to rule,
The village master taught his little school.
A man severe he was, and stern to view;
I knew him well, and every truant knew;
Well had the boding tremblers learn'd to trace
The day's disasters in his morning face;
Full well they laugh'd with counterfeited glee
At all his jokes, for many a joke had he;   10
Full well the busy whisper circling round
Convey'd the dismal tidings when he frown'd.
Yet he was kind, or, if severe in aught,
The love he bore to learning was in fault;
The village all declar'd how much he knew;
'Twas certain he could write and cypher too:
Lands he could measure, terms and tides presage,
And even the story ran that he could gauge:
In arguing, too, the parson own'd his skill,
For, even though vanquish'd, he could argue still;   20
While words of learned length and thundering sound
Amazed the gazing rustics rang'd around;
And still they gaz'd, and still the wonder grew,
That one small head could carry all he knew.
But past is all his fame. The very spot
Where many a time he triumph'd is forgot.

OLIVER GOLDSMITH

17

Sir Penny

FROM *Carmina Burana*

The hand that holds a heavy purse
Makes right of wrong, better of worse.
Sir Penny binds all bargains fast;
Rough is smooth when he has passed.
Who but Sir Penny settles wars?
He is the prince of counselors.
    Sir Penny's law no man can budge
      In courts ecclesiastic;
    Make room for Penny, ye who judge
      With consciences elastic.   10

Where Sir Penny's voice is heard
The sense of right is sadly blurred.
The poor man seldom finds redress
Whose one hope is his righteousness;
But pampered Dives needs no pull
Beyond the name of bountiful;
    Whate'er he asks, the judge concedes,
      And thanks his condescension.
    The man for whom Sir Penny pleads
      Makes good his whole intention.   20

While Penny vaunts, the wise man grieves
For justice fallen among thieves:
For courts that hear, to line their pockets,
The lamest suits that shame their dockets.

Wherever money's power is found
The poor man gets the run-around;
  The best of pleas is brushed aside
    That has no cash to back it,
  And lawful judgments are denied
    By those who own the racket.   30

Here's a case, let none deny it,
Fixed before the court can try it;
But when poor Codrus starts a suit,
Case dismissed — he's destitute;
Greed for money now disgraces
And infects grammatical cases:
  Our 'takers away,' the *ablative*,
    Rogues that deserve suppression,
  Prey on our *datives*, 'those who give,'
    While *genitives* keep possession.   40

The fingers of the great, it's funny,
Are magnets for attracting money;
Whenever profits are in view
They put a price on all they do;
And further, risking retribution,
Assess a tax on absolution:
  Priests there are who think their cure
    Is less of souls than *soldi*;
  May angels ban that flock impure
    Whose holiness is mouldy.   50

'Give, and it shall be given you,'
So runs the precept old and true.
The piety of our wicked livers
Cries fervently for generous givers,

But not to help the poor, nor those
Who sink beneath their weight of woes.
   He whose purse with silver sags
     Laughs at bounds and measures;
   Holy are his money-bags,
     Holy be his pleasures.

ANONYMOUS

Translated by GEORGE F. WHICHER

18

The Unknown Citizen

TO
JS/07/M/378
THIS MARBLE MONUMENT
IS ERECTED BY THE STATE

He was found by the Bureau of Statistics to be
One against whom there was no official complaint,
And all the reports on his conduct agree
That, in the modern sense of an old-fashioned word, he
    was a saint,
For in everything he did he served the Greater
    Community.

Except for the War till the day he retired
He worked in a factory and never got fired,
But satisfied his employers, Fudge Motors Inc.
Yet he wasn't a scab or odd in his views,
For his Union reports that he paid his dues,   10
(Our report on his Union shows it was sound)
And our Social Psychology workers found
That he was popular with his mates and liked a drink.
The Press are convinced that he bought a paper every day
And that his reactions to advertisements were normal in
    every way.
Policies taken out in his name prove that he was fully
    insured,
And his Health-card shows he was once in hospital but left
    it cured.
Both Producers Research and High-Grade Living declare
He was fully sensible to the advantages of the Instalment
    Plan
And had everything necessary to the Modern Man,   20
A phonograph, a radio, a car and a frigidaire.
Our researchers into Public Opinion are content
That he held the proper opinions for the time of year;
When there was peace, he was for peace; when there was
    war, he went.
He was married and added five children to the population,
Which our Eugenist says was the right number for a parent
    of his generation.
And our teachers report that he never interfered with their
    education.
Was he free? Was he happy? The question is absurd:
Had anything been wrong, we should certainly have heard.

W. H. AUDEN

19

Impromptu on Charles II

God bless our good and gracious King,
   Whose promise none relies on;
Who never said a foolish thing,
   Nor ever did a wise one.

JOHN WILMOT, EARL OF ROCHESTER

20

Salutation

O generation of the thoroughly smug
   and thoroughly uncomfortable,
I have seen fishermen picnicking in the sun,
I have seen them with untidy families,
I have seen their smiles full of teeth
   and heard ungainly laughter.
And I am happier than you are,
And they were happier than I am;
And the fish swim in the lake
   and do not even own clothing.

EZRA POUND

You Hear That Fat Frog

You hear that fat frog
In the seat of honor, singing
Bass? . . . that's the boss.

ISSA
Translated by PETER BEILENSON

22

My Grumbling Wife

(*Three versions of a poem by Issa*)

小言いう相手もあらば今日の月

My grumbling wife —
   if only she were here!
      This moon tonight . . .

HAROLD HENDERSON

If my grumbling wife
   Were still alive
I just might
Enjoy tonight's moon.

HARRY BEHN

   If only she were here,
My complaining partner —
    Today's moon.

RICHARD LEWIS

Ko-goto | *iu* | *aite* | *mo* | *araba* | *kyō-no-tsuki*
'Small-words' | saying | companion | also | if-be-here |
today's-moon.

ISSA

[34]

23

An Old Woman's Lamentations

The man I had a love for — a great rascal would kick me in the gutter — is dead thirty years and over it, and it is I am left behind, grey and aged. When I do be minding the good days I had, minding what I was one time, and what it is I'm come to, and when I do look on my own self, poor and dry, and pinched together, it wouldn't be much would set me raging in the streets.

Where is the round forehead I had, and the fine hair, and the two eyebrows, and the eyes with a big gay look out of them would bring folly from a great scholar? Where is my straight shapely nose, and two ears, and my chin with a valley in it, and my lips were red and open?

Where are the pointed shoulders were on me, and the long arms and nice hands to them? Where is my bosom was as white as any, or my straight rounded sides?

It's the way I am this day — my forehead is gone away into furrows, the hair of my head is grey and whitish, my eyebrows are tumbled from me, and my two eyes have died out within my head   those eyes that would be laughing to the men, — my nose has a hook on it, my ears are hanging down, and my lips are sharp and skinny.

That's what's left over from the beauty of a right woman — a bag of bones, and legs the like of two shrivelled sausages going beneath it.

It's of the like of that we old hags do be thinking, of the good times are gone away from us, and we crouching on our hunkers by a little fire of twigs, soon kindled and soon spent, we that were the pick of many.

J. M. SYNGE
after FRANÇOIS VILLON

[35]

24

Penelope's Despair

Not that she didn't recognize him in the dim light of the
    fire;
it wasn't that he was disguised, wearing rags like a beggar.
No. There were clear signs:
the scar on the knee-cap, his strength, the cunning look.
Frightened, leaning against the wall, she sought for some
    excuse,
a delay, to avoid answering so as not to give herself up.
Was it for him she had wasted twenty years waiting and
    dreaming?
Was it for this wretched stranger, soaked in blood, with his
    white beard?
She fell speechless on a chair.
She looked closely at the slaughtered suitors on the floor
as if looking at her own dead desires
and she said 'welcome'
her voice sounding to her as if coming from a distance, as
    if belonging to someone else.
Her loom in the corner cast shadows across the ceiling like
    a cage,
the birds she had woven with bright red threads among
    green leaves
suddenly turned gray and black
flying low on her flat sky.

YANNIS RITSOS
Translated by NIKOS STANGOS

25

Little Green Tree

It looks like to me
My good-time days done past.
Nothin' in this world
Is due to last.

I used to play
And I played so dog-gone hard.
Now old age has
Dealt my bad-luck card.

I look down the road
And I see a little tree.
A little piece down the road.
I see a little tree.

Them cool green leaves
Is waitin' to shelter me.

O, little tree!

LANGSTON HUGHES

26

Lines

FROM 'The Garden of Proserpine'

We are not sure of sorrow,
    And joy was never sure;
To-day will die to-morrow;
    Time stoops to no man's lure;
And love, grown faint and fretful,
With lips but half regretful
Sighs, and with eyes forgetful
    Weeps that no loves endure.

From too much love of living,
    From hope and fear set free,
We thank with brief thanksgiving
    Whatever gods may be
That no life lives for ever;
That dead men rise up never;
That even the weariest river
    Winds somewhere safe to sea.

Then star nor sun shall waken,
    Nor any change of light:
Nor sound of waters shaken,
    Nor any sound or sight:
Nor wintry leaves nor vernal,
Nor days nor things diurnal;
Only the sleep eternal
    In an eternal night.

ALGERNON CHARLES SWINBURNE

27

The Hitherandthithering Waters Of

FROM *Finnegan's Wake*

Can't hear with the waters of. The chittering waters of.
Flittering bats, fieldmice bawk talk. Ho! Are you not gone
ahome? What Thom Malone? Can't hear with bawk of
bats, all thim liffeying waters of. Ho, talk save us! My foos
won't moos. I feel as old as yonder elm. A tale told of
Shaun or Shem? All Livia's daughtersons. Dark hawks hear
us. Night! Night! My ho head halls. I feel as heavy as yonder stone. Tell me of John or Shaun? Who were Shem and
Shaun the living sons or daughters of? Night now! Tell
me, tell me, tell me, elm! Night night! Telmetale of stem
or stone. Beside the rivering waters of, hitherandthithering
waters of. Night!

JAMES JOYCE

The Love Song of J. Alfred Prufrock

S'io credesse che mia risposta fosse
A persona che mai tornasse al mondo,
Questa fiamma staria senza piu scosse.
Ma perciocche giammai di questo fondo
Non torno vivo alcun, s'i'odo il vero,
Senza tema d'infamia ti rispondo.

Let us go then, you and I,
When the evening is spread out against the sky
Like a patient etherised upon a table;
Let us go, through certain half-deserted streets,
The muttering retreats
Of restless nights in one-night cheap hotels
And sawdust restaurants with oyster-shells:
Streets that follow like a tedious argument
Of insidious intent
To lead you to an overwhelming question . . .   10
Oh, do not ask, 'What is it?'
Let us go and make our visit.

In the room the women come and go
Talking of Michelangelo.

The yellow fog that rubs its back upon the window-panes,
The yellow smoke that rubs its muzzle on the window-
        panes
Licked its tongue into the corners of the evening,
Lingered upon the pools that stand in drains,
Let fall upon its back the soot that falls from chimneys,
Slipped by the terrace, made a sudden leap,   20

And seeing that it was a soft October night,
Curled once about the house, and fell asleep.

And indeed there will be time
For the yellow smoke that slides along the street
Rubbing its back upon the window-panes;
There will be time, there will be time
To prepare a face to meet the faces that you meet;
There will be time to murder and create,
And time for all the works and days of hands
That lift and drop a question on your plate;   30
Time for you and time for me,
And time yet for a hundred indecisions,
And for a hundred visions and revisions,
Before the taking of a toast and tea.

In the room the women come and go
Talking of Michelangelo.

And indeed there will be time
To wonder, 'Do I dare?' and, 'Do I dare?'
Time to turn back and descend the stair,
With a bald spot in the middle of my hair —   40
[They will say: 'How his hair is growing thin!']
My morning coat, my collar mounting firmly to the chin,
My necktie rich and modest, but asserted by a simple pin —
[They will say: 'But how his arms and legs are thin!']
Do I dare
Disturb the universe?
In a minute there is time
For decisions and revisions which a minute will reverse.

For I have known them all already, known them all —
Have known the evenings, mornings, afternoons,　　　　　50
I have measured out my life with coffee spoons;
I know the voices dying with a dying fall
Beneath the music from a farther room.
　　So how should I presume?

And I have known the eyes already, known them all —
The eyes that fix you in a formulated phrase,
And when I am formulated, sprawling on a pin,
When I am pinned and wriggling on the wall,
Then how should I begin
To spit out all the butt-ends of my days and ways?　　　60
　　And how should I presume?

And I have known the arms already, known them all —
Arms that are braceleted and white and bare
[But in the lamplight, downed with light brown hair!]
Is it perfume from a dress
That makes me so digress?
Arms that lie along a table, or wrap about a shawl.
　　And should I then presume?
　　And how should I begin?

　　　　　　. . . . . .

Shall I say, I have gone at dusk through narrow streets　　70
And watched the smoke that rises from the pipes
Of lonely men in shirt-sleeves, leaning out of windows?. . .

I should have been a pair of ragged claws
Scuttling across the floors of silent seas.

　　　　　　. . . . . .

And the afternoon, the evening, sleeps so peacefully!
Smoothed by long fingers,
Asleep . . . tired . . . or it malingers,
Stretched on the floor, here beside you and me.
Should I, after tea and cakes and ices,
Have the strength to force the moment to its crisis?   80
But though I have wept and fasted, wept and prayed,
Though I have seen my head [grown slightly bald] brought
    in upon a platter,
I am no prophet — and here's no great matter;
I have seen the moment of my greatness flicker,
And I have seen the eternal Footman hold my coat, and
    snicker,
And in short, I was afraid.

And would it have been worth it, after all,
After the cups, the marmalade, the tea,
Among the porcelain, among some talk of you and me,
Would it have been worth while,   90
To have bitten off the matter with a smile,
To have squeezed the universe into a ball
To roll it toward some overwhelming question,
To say: 'I am Lazarus, come from the dead,
Come back to tell you all, I shall tell you all' —
If one, settling a pillow by her head,
    Should say: 'That is not what I meant at all.
    That is not it, at all.'

And would it have been worth it, after all,
Would it have been worth while,   100
After the sunsets and the dooryards and the sprinkled
    streets,

After the novels, after the teacups, after the skirts that trail
    along the floor —
And this, and so much more? —
It is impossible to say just what I mean!
But as if a magic lantern threw the nerves in patterns on a
    screen:
Would it have been worth while
If one, settling a pillow or throwing off a shawl,
And turning toward the window, should say:
   'That is not it at all,
   That is not what I meant, at all.'   110

. . . . . .

No! I am not Prince Hamlet, nor was meant to be;
Am an attendant lord, one that will do
To swell a progress, start a scene or two,
Advise the prince; no doubt, an easy tool,
Deferential, glad to be of use,
Politic, cautious, and meticulous;
Full of high sentence, but a bit obtuse;
At times, indeed, almost ridiculous —
Almost, at times, the Fool.

I grow old . . . I grow old . . .   120
I shall wear the bottoms of my trousers rolled.

Shall I part my hair behind? Do I dare to eat a peach?
I shall wear white flannel trousers, and walk upon the
    beach.
I have heard the mermaids singing, each to each.

I do not think that they will sing to me.

I have seen them riding seaward on the waves
Combing the white hair of the waves blown back
When the wind blows the water white and black.

We have lingered in the chambers of the sea
By sea-girls wreathed with seaweed red and brown   130
Till human voices wake us, and we drown.

T. S. ELIOT

29

A Kiss

Rose kissed me to-day.
   Will she kiss me to-morrow?
Let it be as it may,
Rose kissed me to-day.
But the pleasure gives way
   To a savour of sorrow; —
Rose kissed me to-day, —
   Will she kiss me to-morrow?

AUSTIN DOBSON

30

Western Wind

Western wind, when wilt thou blow,
   The small rain down can rain?
Christ, if my love were in my arms
   And I in my bed again!

ANONYMOUS

31

Sonnet XVIII

Shall I compare thee to a summer's day?
Thou art more lovely and more temperate.
Rough winds do shake the darling buds of May,
And summer's lease hath all too short a date:
Sometime too hot the eye of heaven shines,
And often is his gold complexion dimm'd;
And every fair from fair some time declines,
By chance, or nature's changing course, untrimm'd;
But thy eternal summer shall not fade
Nor lose possession of that fair thou ow'st;
Nor shall Death brag thou wand'rest in his shade,
When in eternal lines to time thou grow'st.
  So long as men can breathe or eyes can see,
  So long lives this, and this gives life to thee.

WILLIAM SHAKESPEARE

32

Sonnet XXX

When to the sessions of sweet silent thought
I summon up remembrance of things past,
I sigh the lack of many a thing I sought,
And with old woes new wail my dear time's waste.
Then can I drown an eye, unus'd to flow,
For precious friends hid in death's dateless night,
And weep afresh love's long-since-cancell'd woe,
And moan th'expense of many a vanish'd sight.
Then can I grieve at grievances foregone,
And heavily from woe to woe tell o'er
The sad account of fore-bemoaned moan,
Which I new pay as if not paid before.
   But if the while I think on thee, dear friend,
   All losses are restor'd, and sorrows end.

WILLIAM SHAKESPEARE

33

Sonnet: How Do I Love Thee?

How do I love thee? Let me count the ways.
I love thee to the depth and breadth and height
My soul can reach, when feeling out of sight
For the ends of Being and ideal Grace.
I love thee to the level of every day's
Most quiet need, by sun and candlelight.
I love thee freely, as men strive for Right;
I love thee purely, as they turn from Praise.
I love thee with the passion put to use
In my old griefs, and with my childhood's faith;
I love thee with a love I seemed to lose
With my lost saints, — I love thee with the breath,
Smiles, tears, of all my life! — and, if God choose,
I shall but love thee better after death.

ELIZABETH BARRETT BROWNING

34
You Never Touch

You never touch
This soft skin
Surging with hot blood.
Are you not bored,
Expounding the Way?

YOSANO AKIKO
Translated by GEOFFREY BOWNAS
and ANTHONY THWAITE

35

The Ill-Tempered Lover

I wish my tongue were a quiver the size of a huge cask
Packed and crammed with long black venomous rankling
　　darts.
I'd fling you more full of them, and joy in the task,
Than ever Sebastian was, or Caesar, with thirty-three
　　swords in his heart.

I'd make a porcupine out of you, or a pin-cushion, say;
The shafts should stand so thick you'd look like a headless
　　hen
Hung up by the heels, with the long bare red neck
　　stretching, curving, and dripping away
From the soiled floppy ball of ruffled feathers standing on
　　end.

You should bristle like those cylindrical brushes they use to
　　scrub out bottles,
Not even to reach the kindly earth with the soles of your
　　prickled feet.
And I would stand by and watch you wriggle and writhe,
　　gurgling through the barbs in your throttle
Like a woolly caterpillar pinned on its back — man, that
　　would be sweet!

LOUIS MACKAY

36

The Song of the Mad Prince

Who said, 'Peacock Pie'?
The old King to the sparrow:
Who said, 'Crops are ripe'?
Rust to the harrow:
Who said, 'Where sleeps she now?
Where rests she now her head,
Bathed in eve's loveliness'? —
That's what I said.

Who said, 'Ay, mum's the word'?
Sexton to willow:
Who said, 'Green dusk for dreams,
Moss for a pillow'?
Who said, 'All Time's delight
Hath she for narrow bed;
Life's troubled bubble broken'?
That's what I said.

WALTER DE LA MARE

37

Tom O' Bedlam's Song

From the hag and hungry goblin
That into rags would rend ye
And the spirit that stan' by the naked man
In the Book of Moons defend ye!
That of your five sound senses
You never be forsaken
Nor travel from yourselves with Tom
Abroad to beg your bacon.

    Nor never sing 'Any food, any feeding,
    Money, drink or clothing':
    Come dame or maid, be not afraid,
    Poor Tom will injure nothing.

Of thirty bare years have I
Twice twenty been enragèd
And of forty bin three times fifteen
In durance soundly cagèd
In the lordly lofts of Bedlam
On stubble soft and dainty,
Brave bracelets strong, sweet whips ding dong,
With wholesome hunger plenty.

    And now I sing 'Any food, any feeding,
    Money, drink or clothing':
    Come dame or maid, be not afraid,
    Poor Tom will injure nothing.

ANONYMOUS

38

The Mad Gardener's Song

He thought he saw an Elephant,
  That practised on a fife:
He looked again, and found it was
  A letter from his wife.
'At length I realise,' he said,
  'The bitterness of Life!'

He thought he saw a Buffalo
  Upon the chimney-piece:
He looked again, and found it was
  His Sister's Husband's Niece.   10
'Unless you leave this house,' he said,
  I'll send for the Police!'

He thought he saw a Rattlesnake
  That questioned him in Greek:
He looked again, and found it was
  The Middle of Next Week.
'The one thing I regret,' he said,
  'Is that it cannot speak!'

He thought he saw a Banker's Clerk
  Descending from the bus: 20
He looked again, and found it was
  A Hippopotamus:
'If this should stay to dine,' he said,
  'There won't be much for us!'

He thought he saw a Kangaroo
  That worked a coffee-mill:

He looked again, and found it was
   A Vegetable-Pill.
'Were I to swallow this,' he said,
   'I should be very ill!'   30

He thought he saw a Coach-and-Four
   That stood beside his bed:
He looked again, and found it was
   A Bear without a Head.
'Poor thing,' he said, 'poor silly thing!
   It's waiting to be fed!'

He thought he saw an Albatross
   That fluttered round the lamp:
He looked again, and found it was
   A Penny-Postage-Stamp.   40
'You'd best be getting home,' he said:
   'The nights are very damp!'

He thought he saw a Garden-Door
   That opened with a key:
He looked again, and found it was
   A Double Rule of Three:
'And all its mystery,' he said,
   'Is clear as day to me!'

He thought he saw an Argument
   That proved he was the Pope: 50
He looked again, and found it was
   A Bar of Mottled Soap.
'A fact so dread,' he faintly said,
   'Extinguishes all hope!'

LEWIS CARROLL

[55]

39

A Man Hired by John Smith and Co.

A man hired by John Smith and Co.
Loudly declared he would tho
    Man that he saw
    Dumping dirt near his store.
The drivers, therefore, didn't do.

MARK TWAIN

40

The Lines of the Hand

From a letter thrown on the table a line comes which runs across the pine plank and descends by one of the legs. Just watch, you see that the line continues across the parquet floor, climbs the wall and enters a reproduction of a Boucher painting, sketches the shoulder of a woman reclining on a divan, and finally gets out of the room via the roof and climbs down the chain of lightning rods to the street. Here it is difficult to follow it because of the transit system, but by close attention you can catch it climbing the wheel of a bus parked at the corner, which carries it as far 10 as the docks. It gets off there down the seam on the shiny nylon stocking of the blondest passenger, enters the hostile territory of the customs sheds, leaps and squirms and zigzags its way to the largest dock, and there (but it's difficult to see, only the rats follow it to clamber aboard) it climbs onto the ship with the engines rumbling, crosses the planks of the first-class deck, clears the major hatch with difficulty, and in a cabin where an unhappy man is drinking cognac and hears the parting whistle, it climbs the trouser seam, across the knitted vest, slips back to the elbow, and 20 with a final push finds shelter in the palm of the right hand, which is just beginning to close around the butt of a revolver.

JULIO CORTÁZAR
Translated by PAUL BLACKBURN

41

The Twa Corbies

As I was walking all alane,
I heard twa corbies° making a mane:° ravens moan
The tane unto the tither did say,
'Whar sall we gang° and dine the day?' go

' — In behint yon auld fail° dyke   turf
I wot there lies a new-slain knight;
And naebody kens that he lies there
But his hawk, his hound, and his lady fair.

'His hound is to the hunting gane,
His hawk to fetch the wild-fowl hame,
His lady's ta'en anither mate,
So we may mak' our dinner sweet.

'Ye'll sit on his white hause-bane,° neck-bone
And I'll pike out his bonny blue e'en:
Wi' ae lock o' his gowden hair
We'll theek° our nest when it grows bare. thatch

'Mony a one for him maks mane,
But nane sall ken whar he is gane:
O'er his white banes, when they are bare,
The wind sall blaw for evermair.'

ANONYMOUS

42

Sir Patrick Spens

The king sits in Dumferling toune,
   Drinking the blude-reid wine:
'O whar will I get guid sailor,
   To sail this schip of mine?'

Up and spak an eldern knicht,
   Sat at the kings richt kne:
'Sir Patrick Spence is the best sailor
   That sails upon the se.'

The king has written a braid° letter,   commanding
   And signd it wi his hand,
And sent it to Sir Patrick Spence,
   Was walking on the sand.

The first line that Sir Patrick red,
   A loud lauch lauched he;
The next line that Sir Patrick red,   15
   The teir blinded his ee.

'O wha is this has don this deid,
   This ill deid don to me,
To send me out this time o' the yeir,
   To sail upon the se!

'Mak hast, mak hast, my mirry men all,
   Our guid schip sails the morne:'
'O say na sae, my master deir,
   For I feir a deadlie storme.

'Late late yestreen I saw the new moone,   25
  Wi the auld moone in hir arme,
And I feir, I feir, my deir master,
  That we will cum to harme.'

O our Scots nobles wer richt laith°   loath
  To weet their cork-heild schoone;°   cork-heeled shoes
Bot lang owre° a' the play wer playd,   before
  Thair hats they swam aboone.°   above

O lang, lang may their ladies sit,
  Wi thair fans into their hand,
Or eir they se Sir Patrick Spence   35
  Cum sailing to the land.

O lang, lang may the ladies stand,
  Wi thair gold kems in their hair,
Waiting for thair ain deir lords,
  For they'll se thame na mair.

Haf owre, haf owre to Aberdour,
  It's fiftie fadom deip,
And thair lies guid Sir Patrick Spence,
  Wi the Scots lords at his feit.

ANONYMOUS

43

You'd Better Believe Him

A FABLE

Discovered an old rocking-horse in Woolworth's,
He tried to feed it but without much luck
So he stroked it, had a long conversation about
The trees it came from, the attics it had visited.
Tried to take it out then
But the store detective he
Called the store manager who
Called the police who in court next morning said
'He acted strangely when arrested,
His statement read simply "I believe in rocking-horses".
We have reason to believe him mad.'
'Quite so,' said the prosecution,
'Bring in the rocking-horse as evidence.'
'I'm afraid it's escaped sir,' said the store manager,
'Left a hoof-print as evidence
On the skull of the store detective.'
'Quite so,' said the prosecution, fearful of the neighing
Out in the corridor.

BRIAN PATTEN

44
The Artist

Mr. T
       bareheaded
              in a soiled undershirt
his hair standing out
       on all sides
              stood on his toes
heels together
       arms gracefully
              for the moment
curled above his head!   10
       Then he whirled about
              bounded
into the air
       and with an entrechat
              perfectly achieved
completed the figure.
       My mother
              taken by surprise
where she sat
       in her invalid's chair   20
              was left speechless.
'Bravo!' she cried at last
       and clapped her hands.
              The man's wife
came from the kitchen:
       'What goes on here?' she said.
              But the show was over.

                    WILLIAM CARLOS WILLIAMS

45
The Six Strings

The guitar
makes dreams cry.
The crying of lost
souls
escapes from its round
mouth.
And like the tarantula
it weaves a huge star
to catch sighs
that float on its black
wooden tank.

FEDERICO GARCÍA LORCA
Translated by DONALD HALL

46

Song for Saint Cecilia's Day, 1687

From Harmony, from heavenly Harmony
    This universal frame began:
  When Nature underneath a heap
    Of jarring atoms lay
  And could not heave her head,
The tuneful voice was heard from high
    Arise, ye more than dead!
Then cold, and hot, and moist, and dry
In order to their stations leap,
    And Music's power obey.   10
From harmony, from heavenly harmony
    This universal frame began:
    From harmony to harmony
Through all the compass of the notes it ran,
The diapason closing full in Man.

What passion cannot Music raise and quell?
    When Jubal struck the chorded shell
  His listening brethren stood around,
    And, wondering, on their faces fell
  To worship that celestial sound.   20
Less than a god they thought there could not dwell
    Within the hollow of that shell
    That spoke so sweetly and so well.
What passion cannot Music raise and quell?

The trumpet's loud clangor
   Excites us to arms,
With shrill notes of anger
   And mortal alarms.
The double double double beat
   Of the thundering drum   30
   Cries 'Hark! the foes come;
Charge, charge, 'tis too late to retreat!'

The soft complaining flute
   In dying notes discovers
   The woes of hopeless lovers,
Whose dirge is whisper'd by the warbling lute.

   Sharp violins proclaim
Their jealous pangs and desperation,
Fury, frantic indignation,
Depth of pains, and height of passion   40
   For the fair disdainful dame.

But oh! what art can teach,
What human voice can reach
   The sacred organ's praise?
Notes inspiring holy love,
   Notes that wing their heavenly ways
To mend the choirs above.

Orpheus could lead the savage race,
And trees unrooted left their place
   Sequacious of the lyre: 50
But bright Cecilia raised the wonder higher:
When to her Organ vocal breath was given,
An Angel heard, and straight appear'd —
   Mistaking Earth for Heaven!

Grand Chorus

As from the power of sacred lays
   The spheres began to move,
And sung the great Creator's praise
   To all the blest above;
So when the last and dreadful hour
This crumbling pageant shall devour   60
The trumpet shall be heard on high,
That dead shall live, the living die,
And Music shall untune the sky.

JOHN DRYDEN

47

On First Looking into Chapman's Homer

Much have I travelled in the realms of gold,
  And many goodly states and kingdoms seen;
  Round many western islands have I been
Which bards in fealty to Apollo hold.
Oft of one wide expanse had I been told
  That deep-browed Homer ruled as his demesne:
  Yet did I never breathe its pure serene
Till I heard Chapman speak out loud and bold:
Then felt I like some watcher of the skies
  When a new planet swims into his ken;
Or like stout Cortez, when with eagle eyes
  He stared at the Pacific — and all his men
Looked at each other with a wild surmise —
  Silent, upon a peak in Darien.

JOHN KEATS

48

Ode on a Grecian Urn

Thou still unravish'd bride of quietness,
  Thou foster-child of silence and slow time,
Sylvan historian, who canst thus express
  A flowery tale more sweetly than our rhyme:
What leaf-fring'd legend haunts about thy shape
  Of deities or mortals, or of both,
    In Tempe or the dales of Arcady?
What men or gods are these? What maidens loth?
  What mad pursuit? What struggle to escape?
    What pipes and timbrels? What wild ecstasy?   10

Heard melodies are sweet, but those unheard
  Are sweeter; therefore, ye soft pipes, play on;
Not to the sensual ear, but, more endear'd,
  Pipe to the spirit ditties of no tone:
Fair youth, beneath the trees, thou canst not leave
  Thy song, nor ever can those trees be bare;
    Bold Lover, never, never canst thou kiss,
Though winning near the goal — yet, do not grieve;
  She cannot fade, though thou hast not thy bliss,
    For ever wilt thou love, and she be fair!   20

Ah, happy, happy boughs! that cannot shed
  Your leaves, nor ever bid the Spring adieu;
And, happy melodist, unwearied,
  For ever piping songs for ever new;
More happy love! more happy, happy love!

For ever warm and still to be enjoy'd,
　For ever panting, and for ever young;
All breathing human passion far above,
　That leaves a heart high-sorrowful and cloy'd,
　　A burning forehead, and a parching tongue.　　　30

Who are these coming to the sacrifice?
　To what green altar, O mysterious priest,
Lead'st thou that heifer lowing at the skies,
　And all her silken flanks with garlands drest?
What little town by river or sea shore,
　Or mountain-built with peaceful citadel,
　　Is emptied of this folk, this pious morn?
And, little town, thy streets for evermore
　Will silent be; and not a soul to tell
　　Why thou art desolate, can e'er return.　　　40

O Attic shape! Fair attitude! with brede
　Of marble men and maidens overwrought,
With forest branches and the trodden weed;
　Thou, silent form, dost tease us out of thought
As doth eternity: Cold Pastoral!
　When old age shall this generation waste,
　　Thou shalt remain, in midst of other woe
Than ours, a friend to man, to whom thou say'st,
　'Beauty is truth, truth beauty', — that is all
　　Ye know on earth, and all ye need to know.

JOHN KEATS

49

Sonnet: When I Have Fears

When I have fears that I may cease to be
   Before my pen has glean'd my teeming brain,
Before high-pilèd books, in charact'ry,
   Hold like rich garners the full ripen'd grain;
When I behold, upon the night's starr'd face,
   Huge cloudy symbols of a high romance,
And feel that I may never live to trace
   Their shadows, with the magic hand of chance;
And when I feel, fair creature of an hour!
   That I shall never look upon thee more,
Never have relish in the faery power
   Of unreflecting love; — then on the shore
Of the wide world I stand alone, and think,
Till Love and Fame to nothingness do sink.

JOHN KEATS

50

Song of Myself

SELECTIONS

[1]

I celebrate myself, and sing myself,
And what I assume you shall assume,
For every atom belonging to me as good belongs to you.

I loafe and invite my soul,
I lean and loafe at my ease observing a spear of summer
    grass.

My tongue, every atom of my blood, form'd from this soil,
    this air,
Born here of parents born here from parents the same, and
    their parents the same,
I, now thirty-seven years old in perfect health begin,
Hoping to cease not till death.

Creeds and schools in abeyance,
Retiring back a while sufficed at what they are, but never
    forgotten,
I harbor for good or bad, I permit to speak at every hazard,
Nature without check with original energy.

[*From* 6]
. . .

A child said *What is the grass?* fetching it to me with full
    hands;

How could I answer the child? I do not know what it is
    any more than he.

I guess it must be the flag of my disposition, out of hopeful
    green stuff woven.

Or I guess it is the handkerchief of the Lord,
A scented gift and remembrancer designedly dropt,
Bearing the owner's name someway in the corners, that we
    may see and remark, and say *Whose?*

Or I guess the grass is itself a child, the produced babe of
    the vegetation.

Or I guess it is a uniform hieroglyphic,
And it means, Sprouting alike in broad zones and narrow
    zones,
Growing among black folks as among white,
Kanuck, Tuckahoe, Congressman, Cuff, I give them the
    same, I receive them the same.

And now it seems to me the beautiful uncut hair of graves.
. . .

[*From* 33]
. . .

I am the man, I suffer'd, I was there.

The disdain and calmness of martyrs,
The mother of old, condemn'd for a witch, burnt with dry
    wood, her children gazing on,
The hounded slave that flags in the race, leans by the fence,
    blowing, cover'd with sweat,
The twinges that sting like needles his legs and neck, the
    murderous buckshot and the bullets,
All these I feel or am.

[72]

I am the hounded slave, I wince at the bite of the dogs,
Hell and despair are upon me, crack and again crack the
    marksmen,
I clutch the rails of the fence, my gore dribs, thinn'd with
    the ooze of my skin,
I fall on the weeds and stones,   10
The riders spur their unwilling horses, haul close,
Taunt my dizzy ears and beat me violently over the head
    with whip-stocks.

Agonies are one of my changes of garments,
I do not ask the wounded person how he feels, I myself
    become the wounded person,
My hurts turn livid upon me as I lean on a cane and
    observe.

I am the mash'd fireman with breast-bone broken,
Tumbling walls buried me in their debris,
Heat and smoke I inspired, I heard the yelling shouts of
    my comrades,
I heard the distant click of their picks and shovels,
They have clear'd the beams away, they tenderly lift me
    forth.   20

I lie in the night air in my red shirt, the pervading hush is
    for my sake.
Painless after all I lie exhausted but not so unhappy,
White and beautiful are the faces around me, the heads are
    bared of their fire-caps,
The kneeling crowd fades with the light of the torches.

Distant and dead resuscitate,
They show as the dial or move as the hands of me, I am
    the clock myself.
. . .

[52]

The spotted hawk swoops by and accuses me, he complains
    of my gab and my loitering.

I too am not a bit tamed, I too am untranslatable,
I sound my barbaric yawp over the roofs of the world.

The last scud of day holds back for me,
It flings my likeness after the rest and true as any on the
    shadow'd wilds,
It coaxes me to the vapor and the dusk.

I depart as air, I shake my white locks at the runaway sun,
I effuse my flesh in eddies, and drift it in lacy jags.

I bequeath myself to the dirt to grow from the grass I love,
If you want me again look for me under your boot-soles.

You will hardly know who I am or what I mean,
But I shall be good health to you nevertheless,
And filter and fibre your blood.

Failing to fetch me at first keep encouraged,
Missing me one place search another,
I stop somewhere waiting for you.

WALT WHITMAN

51

A Supermarket in California

What thoughts I have of you tonight, Walt Whitman, for I walked down the sidestreets under the trees with a headache self-conscious looking at the full moon.

In my hungry fatigue, and shopping for images, I went into the neon fruit supermarket, dreaming of your enumerations!

What peaches and what penumbras! Whole families shopping at night! Aisles full of husbands! Wives in the avocados, babies in the tomatoes! — and you, Garcia Lorca, what were you doing down by the watermelons?   10

I saw you, Walt Whitman, childless, lonely old grubber, poking among the meats in the refrigerator and eyeing the grocery boys.

I heard you asking questions of each: Who killed the pork chops? What price bananas? Are you my Angel?

I wandered in and out of the brilliant stacks of cans following you, and followed in my imagination by the store detective.

We strode down the open corridors together in our solitary fancy tasting artichokes, possessing every frozen deli- 20
cacy, and never passing the cashier.

Where are we going, Walt Whitman? The doors close in an hour. Which way does your beard point tonight?

(I touch your book and dream of our odyssey in the supermarket and feel absurd.)

Will we walk all night through solitary streets? The trees add shade to shade, lights out in the houses, we'll both be lonely.

Will we stroll dreaming of the lost America of love past
blue automobiles in driveways, home to our silent cottage?   30
    Ah, dear father, graybeard, lonely old courage-teacher,
what America did you have when Charon quit poling his
ferry and you got out on a smoking bank and stood watching the boat disappear on the black waters of Lethe?

ALLEN GINSBERG

52

Sonnet LV

Not marble, nor the gilded monuments
Of princes, shall outlive this powerful rhyme;
But you shall shine more bright in these contents
Than unswept stone, besmeared with sluttish time.
When wasteful war shall statues overturn,
And broils root out the work of masonry,
Nor Mars his sword nor war's quick fire shall burn
The living record of your memory.
'Gainst death and all-oblivious enmity
Shall you pace forth; your praise shall still find room
Even in the eyes of all posterity
That wear this world out to the ending doom.
    So, till the judgment that yourself arise,
    You live in this, and dwell in lovers' eyes.

WILLIAM SHAKESPEARE

53
On His Books

When I am dead, I hope it may be said:
His sins were scarlet, but his books were read.

HILAIRE BELLOC

54
Jim,

WHO RAN AWAY FROM HIS NURSE, AND WAS EATEN
BY A LION.

There was a Boy whose name was Jim;
His Friends were very good to him.
They gave him Tea, and Cakes, and Jam,
And slices of delicious Ham,
And Chocolate with pink inside,
And little Tricycles to ride,
And read him Stories through and through,
And even took him to the Zoo —
But there it was the dreadful Fate
Befell him, which I now relate.   10

You know — at least you *ought* to know,
For I have often told you so —
That Children never are allowed
To leave their Nurses in a Crowd;
Now this was Jim's especial Foible,
He ran away when he was able,
And on this inauspicious day
He slipped his hand and ran away!
He hadn't gone a yard when —

                Bang!

With open Jaws, a Lion sprang,  20
And hungrily began to eat
The Boy: beginning at his feet.

Now just imagine how it feels
When first your toes and then your heels,
And then by gradual degrees,
Your shins and ankles, calves and knees,
Are slowly eaten, bit by bit.
No wonder Jim detested it!
No wonder that he shouted 'Hi!'
The Honest Keeper heard his cry, 30
Though very fat he almost ran
To help the little gentleman.
'Ponto!' he ordered as he came
(For Ponto was the Lion's name),
'Ponto!' he cried, with angry Frown.
'Let go, Sir! Down, Sir! Put it down!'

The Lion made a sudden Stop,
He let the Dainty Morsel drop,
And slunk reluctant to his Cage,
Snarling with Disappointed Rage. 40
But when he bent him over Jim,
The Honest Keeper's Eyes were dim.
The Lion having reached his Head,
The Miserable Boy was dead!

When Nurse informed his Parents, they
Were more Concerned than I can say: —
His Mother, as She dried her eyes,
Said, 'Well — it gives me no surprise,
He would not do as he was told!'
His Father, who was self-controlled, 50
Bade all the children round attend
To James' miserable end,
And always keep a-hold of Nurse
For fear of finding something worse.

HILAIRE BELLOC
Illustrations by B.T.B.

55
Nursery Rhyme of Innocence and Experience

I had a silver penny
   And an apricot tree
And I said to the sailor
   On the white quay

'Sailor O sailor
   Will you bring me
If I give you my penny
   And my apricot tree

'A fez from Algeria
   An Arab drum to beat   10
A little gilt sword
   And a parakeet?'

And he smiled and he kissed me
   As strong as death
And I saw his red tongue
   And I felt his sweet breath

'You may keep your penny
   And your apricot tree
And I'll bring your presents
   Back from sea.'   20

O the ship dipped down
   On the rim of the sky
And I waited while three
   Long summers went by

Then one steel morning
   On the white quay
I saw a grey ship
   Come in from sea

Slowly she came
   Across the bay   30
For her flashing rigging
   Was shot away

All round her wake
   The seabirds cried
And flew in and out
   Of the hole in her side

Slowly she came
   In the path of the sun
And I heard the sound
   Of a distant gun   40

And a stranger came running
   Up to me
From the deck of the ship
   And he said, said he

'O are you the boy
   Who would wait on the quay
With the silver penny
   And the apricot tree?

'I've a plum-coloured fez
   And a drum for thee   50
And a sword and a parakeet
   From over the sea.'

'O where is the sailor
   With bold red hair?
And what is that volley
   On the bright air?

'O where are the other
   Girls and boys?
And why have you brought me
   Children's toys?'

CHARLES CAUSLEY

56

Rite of Passage

As the guests arrive at my son's party
they gather in the living room —
short men, men in first grade
with smooth jaws and chins.
Hands in pockets, they stand around
jostling, jockeying for place, small fights
breaking out and calming. One says to another
How old are you? Six. I'm seven. So?
They eye each other, seeing themselves
tiny in the other's pupils. They clear their   10
throats a lot, a room of small bankers,
they fold their arms and frown. *I could beat you
up*, a seven says to a six,
the dark cake, round and heavy as a
turret, behind them on the table. My son,
freckles like specks of nutmeg on his cheeks,
chest narrow as the balsa keel of a
model boat, long hands
cool and thin as the day they guided him
out of me, speaks up as a host   20
for the sake of the group.
We could easily kill a two-year-old,
he says in his clear voice. The other
men agree, they clear their throats
like Generals, they relax and get down to
playing war, celebrating my son's life.

SHARON OLDS

[83]

57
Backdrop Addresses Cowboy

Starspangled cowboy
sauntering out of the almost-
silly West, on your face
a porcelain grin,
tugging a papier-mâché cactus
on wheels behind you with a string,

you are innocent as a bathtub
full of bullets.

Your righteous eyes, your laconic
trigger-fingers   10
people the streets with villains:
as you move, the air in front of you
blossoms with targets

and you leave behind you a heroic
trail of desolation:
beer bottles
slaughtered by the side
of the road, bird-
skulls bleaching in the sunset.

I ought to be watching   20
from behind a cliff or a cardboard storefront
when the shooting starts, hands clasped
in admiration,

but I am elsewhere.

Then what about me

what about the I
confronting you on that border
you are always trying to cross?

I am the horizon
you ride towards, the thing you can never lasso   30

I am also what surrounds you:
my brain
scattered with your
tincans, bones, empty shells,
the litter of your invasions.

I am the space you desecrate
as you pass through.

                           MARGARET ATWOOD

58

The Death of the Ball Turret Gunner

From my mother's sleep I fell into the State,
And I hunched in its belly till my wet fur froze.
Six miles from earth, loosed from its dream of life,
I woke to black flak and the nightmare fighters.
When I died they washed me out of the turret with a hose.

RANDALL JARRELL

59

APO 96225

A young man once went off to war
in a far country.
When he had time, he wrote home and
said, 'Sure rains here a lot.'

But his mother, reading between the lines,
wrote, 'We're quite concerned. Tell us
what it's really like.'

And the young man responded, 'Wow, you ought
to see the funny monkeys!'

To which the mother replied, 'Don't   10
hold back, how is it?'

And the young man wrote, 'The sunsets here
are spectacular.'

In her next letter the mother
wrote, 'Son we want you to tell us
everything.'

So the next time he wrote,
'Today I killed a man.
Yesterday I helped drop napalm on women and
children. Tomorrow we are going to use   20
gas.'

And the father wrote, 'Please don't
write such depressing letters. You're upsetting
your mother.'

So, after a while, the young man wrote, 'Sure rains a
lot here . . .'

LARRY ROTTMANN

60

Strange Meeting

It seemed that out of the battle I escaped
Down some profound dull tunnel, long since scooped
Through granites which Titanic wars had groined.
Yet also there encumbered sleepers groaned,
Too fast in thought or death to be bestirred.
Then, as I probed them, one sprang up, and stared
With piteous recognition in fixed eyes,
Lifting distressful hands as if to bless.
And by his smile, I knew that sullen hall,
By his dead smile I knew we stood in Hell.   10
With a thousand pains that vision's face was grained;
Yet no blood reached there from the upper ground,
And no guns thumped, or down the flues made moan.
'Strange friend,' I said, 'here is no cause to mourn.'
'None,' said the other, 'save the undone years,
The hopelessness. Whatever hope is yours,
Was my life also; I went hunting wild
After the wildest beauty in the world,
Which lies not calm in eyes, or braided hair,
But mocks the steady running of the hour,   20
And if it grieves, grieves richlier than here.
For by my glee might many men have laughed,
And of my weeping something had been left,
Which must die now. I mean the truth untold,
The pity of war, the pity war distilled.
Now men will go content with what we spoiled.
Or, discontent, boil bloody, and be spilled.
They will be swift with swiftness of the tigress,
None will break ranks, though nations trek from progress.

Courage was mine, and I had mystery,   30
Wisdom was mine, and I had mastery;
To miss the march of this retreating world
Into vain citadels that are not walled.
Then, when much blood had clogged their chariot-wheels
I would go up and wash them from sweet wells,
Even with truths that lie too deep for taint.
I would have poured my spirit without stint
But not through wounds; not on the cess of war.
Foreheads of men have bled where no wounds were.
I am the enemy you killed, my friend.   40
I knew you in this death: for so you frowned
Yesterday through me as you jabbed and killed.
I parried; but my hands were loath and cold.
Let us sleep now.' . . .

WILFRED OWEN

61

Naming of Parts

To-day we have naming of parts. Yesterday,
We had daily cleaning. And to-morrow morning,
We shall have what to do after firing. But to-day,
To-day we have naming of parts. Japonica
Glistens like coral in all of the neighbouring gardens,
    And to-day we have naming of parts.

This is the lower sling swivel. And this
Is the upper sling swivel, whose use you will see,
When you are given your slings. And this is the piling
    swivel,
Which in your case you have not got. The branches   10
Hold in the gardens their silent, eloquent gestures,
   Which in our case we have not got.

This is the safety-catch, which is always released
With an easy flick of the thumb. And please do not let me
See anyone using his finger. You can do it quite easy
If you have any strength in your thumb. The blossoms
Are fragile and motionless, never letting anyone see
   Any of them using their finger.

And this you can see is the bolt. The purpose of this
Is to open the breech, as you see. We can slide it   20
Rapidly backwards and forwards: we call this
Easing the spring. And rapidly backwards and forwards
The early bees are assaulting and fumbling the flowers:
   They call it easing the Spring.

They call it easing the Spring: it is perfectly easy
If you have any strength in your thumb: like the bolt,
And the breech, and the cocking-piece, and the point of
    balance,
Which in our case we have not got; and the almond-
    blossom
Silent in all of the gardens and the bees going backwards
    and forwards,
   For to-day we have naming of parts.

HENRY REED

62

War on the Periphery

Around the battlements go by
Soldier men against the sky,
Violent lovers, husbands, sons,
Guarding my peaceful life with guns.

My pleasures, how discreet they are!
A little booze, a little car,
Two little children and a wife
Living a small suburban life.

My little children eat my heart;
At seven o'clock we kiss and part,
At seven o'clock we meet again;
They eat my heart and grow to men.

I watch their tenderness with fear
While on the battlements I hear
The violent, obedient ones
Guarding my family with guns.

GEORGE JOHNSTON

63

Lullaby

Someone would like to have you for her child
But you are mine.
Someone would like to rear you on a costly mat
But you are mine.
Someone would like to place you on a camel blanket
But you are mine.
I have you to rear on a torn old mat.
Someone would like to have you as her child
But you are mine.

AKAN PEOPLE, AFRICA
Translated by ULLI BEIER

64

To a Sad Daughter

All night long the hockey pictures
gaze down at you
sleeping in your tracksuit.
Belligerent goalies are your ideal.
Threats of being traded
cuts and wounds
— all this pleases you.
O my god! you say at breakfast
reading the sports page over the Alpen
as another player breaks his ankle   10
or assaults the coach.

When I thought of daughters
I wasn't expecting this
but I like this more.
I like all your faults
even your purple moods
when you retreat from everyone
to sit in bed under a quilt.
And when I say 'like'
I mean of course 'love'   20
but that embarrasses you.
You who feel superior to black and white movies
(coaxed for hours to see *Casablanca*)
though you were moved
by *Creature from the Black Lagoon*.

One day I'll come swimming
beside your ship or someone will

and if you hear the siren
listen to it. For if you close your ears
only nothing happens. You will never change.   30

I don't care if you risk
your life to angry goalies
creatures with webbed feet.
You can enter their caves and castles
their glass laboratories. Just
don't be fooled by anyone but yourself.

This is the first lecture I've given you.
You're 'sweet sixteen' you said.
I'd rather be your closest friend
than your father. I'm not good at advice   40
you know that, but ride
the ceremonies
until they grow dark.

Sometimes you are so busy
discovering your friends
I ache with a loss
— but that is greed.
And sometimes I've gone
into *my* purple world
and lost you.   50

One afternoon I stepped
into your room. You were sitting
at the desk where I now write this.
Forsythia outside the window
and sun spilled over you
like a thick yellow miracle

as if another planet
was coaxing you out of the house
— all those possible worlds! —
and you, meanwhile, busy with mathematics.   60

I cannot look at forsythia now
without loss, or joy for you.
You step delicately
into the wild world
and your real prize will be
the frantic search.
Want everything. If you break
break going out not in.
How you live your life I don't care
but I'll sell my arms for you,   70
hold your secrets forever.

If I speak of death
which you fear now, greatly,
it is without answers,
except that each
one we know is
in our blood.
Don't recall graves.
Memory is permanent.
Remember the afternoon's   80
yellow suburban annunciation.
Your goalie
in his frightening mask
dreams perhaps
of gentleness.

MICHAEL ONDAATJE

65
Girl's-Eye View of Relatives

FIRST LESSON

The thing to remember about fathers is, they're men.
A girl has to keep it in mind.
They are dragon-seekers, bent on improbable rescues.
Scratch any father, you find
Someone chock-full of qualms and romantic terrors,
Believing change is a threat —
Like your first shoes with heels on, like your first bicycle
It took such months to get.

Walk in strange woods, they warn you about the snakes
    there.
Climb, and they fear you'll fall.
Books, angular boys, or swimming in deep water —
Fathers mistrust them all.
Men are the worriers. It is difficult for them
To learn what they must learn:
How you have a journey to take and very likely,
For a while, will not return.

TURN OF THE SCREW

Girl cousins condescend. They wear
Earrings, and dress like fashion's sample,
Have speaking eyes and curly hair.
And parents point to their example.
But the boy cousins one's allotted
Are years too young for one. Or spotted.

TRIOLET AGAINST SISTERS

Sisters are always drying their hair.
    Locked into rooms, alone,
They pose at the mirror, shoulders bare,
Trying this way and that their hair,
Or fly importunate down the stair
    To answer a telephone.
Sisters are always drying their hair,
    Locked into rooms, alone.

THE ADVERSARY

A mother's hardest to forgive.
Life is the fruit she longs to hand you,
Ripe on a plate. And while you live,
Relentlessly she understands you.

PHYLLIS MCGINLEY

66

Home After Three Months Away

Gone now the baby's nurse,
a lioness who ruled the roost
and made the Mother cry.
She used to tie
gobbets of porkrind in bowknots of gauze —
three months they hung like soggy toast
on our eight foot magnolia tree,
and helped the English sparrows
weather a Boston winter.

Three months, three months!   10
Is Richard now himself again?
Dimpled with exaltation,
my daughter holds her levee in the tub.
Our noses rub,
each of us pats a stringy lock of hair —
they tell me nothing's gone.
Though I am forty-one,
not forty now, the time I put away
was child's-play. After thirteen weeks
my child still dabs her cheeks   20
to start me shaving. When
we dress her in her sky-blue corduroy,
she changes to a boy,
and floats my shaving brush
and washcloth in the flush. . . .

Dearest, I cannot loiter here
in lather like a polar bear.

Recuperating, I neither spin nor toil.
Three stories down below,
a choreman tends our coffin's length of soil,   30
and seven horizontal tulips blow.
Just twelve months ago,
these flowers were pedigreed
imported Dutchmen; now no one need
distinguish them from weed.
Bushed by the late spring snow,
they cannot meet
another year's snowballing enervation.

I keep no rank nor station.
Cured, I am frizzled, stale and small.

ROBERT LOWELL

67

Once Upon a Time

Once upon a time, son,
they used to laugh with their hearts
and laugh with their eyes;
but now they only laugh with their teeth,
while their ice-block-cold eyes
search behind my shadow.

There was a time indeed
they used to shake hands with their hearts;
but that's gone, son.
Now they shake hands without hearts   10
while their left hands search
my empty pockets.

'Feel at home,' 'Come again,'
they say, and when I come
again and feel
at home, once, twice,
there will be no thrice —
for then I find doors shut on me.

So I have learned many things, son.
I have learned to wear many faces   20
like dresses — homeface,
officeface, streetface, hostface, cock-
tailface, with all their conforming smiles
like a fixed portrait smile.

And I have learned too
to laugh with only my teeth
and shake hands without my heart.

I have also learned to say, 'Goodbye,'
when I mean 'Goodriddance';
to say 'Glad to meet you,'   30
without being glad; and to say 'It's been
nice talking to you,' after being bored.

But believe me, son.
I want to be what I used to be
when I was like you. I want
to unlearn all these muting things.
Most of all, I want to relearn
how to laugh, for my laugh in the mirror
shows only my teeth like a snake's bare fangs!

So show me, son,   40
how to laugh; show me how
I used to laugh and smile
once upon a time when I was like you.

GABRIEL OKARA

Anyone Lived in a Pretty How Town

anyone lived in a pretty how town
(with up so floating many bells down)
spring summer autumn winter
he sang his didn't he danced his did.

Women and men(both little and small)
cared for anyone not at all
they sowed their isn't they reaped their same
sun moon stars rain

children guessed(but only a few
and down they forgot as up they grew   10
autumn winter spring summer)
that noone loved him more by more

when by now and tree by leaf
she laughed his joy she cried his grief
bird by snow and stir by still
anyone's any was all to her

someones married their everyones
laughed their cryings and did their dance
(sleep wake hope and then)they
said their nevers they slept their dream   20

stars rain sun moon
(and only the snow can begin to explain
how children are apt to forget to remember
with up so floating many bells down)

one day anyone died i guess
(and noone stooped to kiss his face)
busy folk buried them side by side
little by little and was by was

all by all and deep by deep
and more by more they dream their sleep   30
noone and anyone earth by april
wish by spirit and if by yes.

Women and men(both dong and ding)
summer autumn winter spring
reaped their sowing and went their came
sun moon stars rain

E. E. CUMMINGS

To Every Thing There Is a Season

To every thing there is a season, and a time to every purpose under the heaven:

A time to be born, and a time to die; a time to plant, and a time to pluck up that which is planted;

A time to kill, and a time to heal; a time to break down, and a time to build up;

A time to weep, and a time to laugh; a time to mourn, and a time to dance;

A time to cast away stones, and a time to gather stones together; a time to embrace, and a time to refrain from embracing;

A time to get, and a time to lose; a time to keep, and a time to cast away;

A time to rend, and a time to sew; a time to keep silence, and a time to speak;

A time to love, and a time to hate; a time of war, and a time of peace.

ECCLESIASTES 3: 1–8
THE BIBLE, KING JAMES VERSION

Robert Frost Pg.

304.

Tiger Tiger Pg 114

Pg. 67
Once upon a time

Oman Khayyam.

Pg 205
The Shepherd to his
Love Pg 175

Pg 69 to Every thing
there is a season

70

Deuteronomy

The bush. Yes. It burned like they said it did,
lit up like an oak in October — except
that there is no October in Egypt. Voices
came at me and told me to take off my shoes
and I did that. That desert is full of men's shoes.
And the flame screamed *I am what I am.*
I am whatever it is that is me,
and nothing can but something needs to be
done about it. If anyone
asks, all you can say is, I sent me.   10

I went, but I brought my brother to do
the talking, and I did the tricks — the Nile
full of fishguts and frogs, the air opaque
and tight as a scab, the white-hot hail,
and boils, and bugs, and when nothing had worked right
we killed them and ran. We robbed them of every
goddamned thing we could get at and carry
and took off, and got through the marsh at low tide
with the wind right, and into the desert. The animals
died, of course, but we kept moving.   20

Abraham came up easy. We took
the unknown road and ate hoarfrost and used
a volcano for a compass. I had no plan.
We went toward the mountains. I wanted, always,
to die in the mountains, not in that delta.
And not in a boat, at night, in swollen water.

We travelled over dead rock and drank dead water,
and the hoarfrost wasn't exactly hoarfrost.
They claimed it tasted like coriander,
but no two men are agreed on the taste   30
of coriander. Anyway,
we ate it, and from time to time we caught quail.

Men and half-men and women, we marched
and plodded into those hills, and they exploded
into labyrinths of slag. The air licked us
like a hot tongue, twisting and flapping and gurgling
through the smoke like men suffocating or drowning,
     saying
An eye for an eye, and on certain occasions
two eyes for one eye. Either way, you model me
in thin air or unwritten words, not in wood,   40
not in metal. I am gone from the metal when the metal
hits the mold. You will not get me into any image
which will not move when I move, and move
with my fluency. Moses! Come up!

I went, but I wore my shoes and took a waterskin.
I climbed all day, with the dust eating holes
in my coat, and choking me, and the rock cooking me.
What I found was a couple of flat stones
marked up as if the mountain had written all over them.
I was up there a week, working to cool them,   50
hungry and sweating and unable to make sense of them,
and I fell coming down and broke both of them.
Topping it all, I found everybody down there drooling
over Aaron's cheap figurines, and Aaron chortling.

I went up again to get new stones
and the voices took after me that time and threw me
up between the rocks and said I could see them.
They were right. I could see them. I was standing right
    behind them
and I saw them. I saw the mask's insides,
and what I saw is what I have always seen.   60
I saw the fire and it flowed and it was moving away
and not up into me. I saw nothing
and it was widening all the way around me.
I collected two flat stones and I cut them
so they said what it seemed to me two stones
should say, and I brought them down without dropping
    them.

The blisters must have doubled my size, and Aaron said
I almost glowed in the dark when I got down.
Even so, it seemed I was pulling my stunts
more often then than in Egypt. I had to,   70
to hold them. They had to be led to new land,
and all of them full of crackpot proverbs and cockeyed
ideas about directions. Aaron and I
outbellowed them day after day and in spite of it
they died. Some of weakness, certainly, but so many of
    them
died of being strong. The children stood up to it
best, out of knowing no different — but with no
idea what to do with a ploughshare, no
idea what a river is. What could they do
if they got there? What can they even know how to wish
    for?   80

I promised them pasture, apple trees, cedar,
waterfalls, snow in the hills, sweetwater
wells instead of these arroyos, wild grapes. . . .
Words. And whatever way I say them, words only.
I no longer know why I say them, even though
the children like hearing them. They come when I call
     them
and their eyes are bright, but the light in them is empty.
It is too clear. It contains . . . the clarity only.
But they come when I call to them. Once I used to sing
     them
a song about an eagle and a stone, and each time   90
I sang it, somehow the song seemed changed
and the words drifted into the sunlight. I do not
remember the song now, but I remember
that I sang it, and the song was the law and the law
was the song. The law is a song, I am certain. . . .
And I climbed to the head of this canyon. They said
I could look down at the new land
if I sat here, and I think it is so, but my eyes
are no longer strong, and I am tired now of looking.

ROBERT BRINGHURST

71

Lines

Whan that° Aprillè with his shourès soote°   When   sweet showers
The droghte of March hath percèd to the roote,
And bathèd every veyne in swich licour°   such liquid, sap
Of which vertu° engendred is the flour;   By power of which
Whan Zephirus° eek° with his swetè breeth   west wind   moreover
Inspirèd hath in every holt° and heeth°   grove   heath
The tendre croppès,° and the yongè sonne   shoots
Hath in the Ram his halfè cours y-ronne,
And smalè foweles maken melodye,
That slepen al the nyght with open eye, —
So priketh hem° Nature in hir corages,° —   stirs them   their hearts
Thanne longen° folk to goon° on pilgrimages,   long   go
And palmeres for to seken° straungè strondes,°   seek   foreign shores
To fernè halwes kowthe° in sondry londes;   distant shrines known
And specially, from every shirès ende
Of Engèlond, to Caunturbury they wende,
The hooly blisful martir for to seke,
That hem hath holpen° whan that they were   helped
    seeke.

GEOFFREY CHAUCER

72

St Yves' Poor

Jeffik was there, and Matthieu, and brown Bran,
Warped in old wars and babbling of the sword,
And Jannedik, a white rose pinched and paled
With the world's frosts, and many more beside,
Lamed, rheumed and palsied, aged, impotent
Of all but hunger and blind lifted hands.
I set the doors wide at the given hour,
Took the great basket piled with bread, the fish
Yet silvered of the sea, the curds of milk,
And called them Brethren, brake, and blest, and gave.　　10

For O, my Lord, the house dove knows her nest
Above my window builded from the rain;
In the brown mere the heron finds her rest,
But these shall seek in vain.
And O, my Lord, the thrush may fold her wing,
The curlew seek the long lift of the seas,
The wild swan sleep amid his journeying, —
There is no rest for these.

Thy dead are sheltered; housed and warmed they wait
Under the golden fern, the falling foam;　　　　　　20
But these, Thy living, wander desolate
And have not any home.

I called them Brethren, brake, and blest, and gave.
Old Jeffik had her withered hand to show,
Young Jannedik had dreamed of death, and Bran
Would tell me wonders wrought on fields of war,

When Michael and his warriors rode the storm,
And all the heavens were thrilled with clanging spears, —
Ah, God, my poor, my poor. — Till there came one
Wrapped in foul rags, who caught me by the robe,   30
And pleaded, 'Bread, my father.'

                                In his hand
I laid the last loaf of the daily dole,
Saw on the palm a red wound like a star,
And bade him, 'Let me bind it.'
                            'These my wounds,'
He answered softly, 'Daily dost thou bind.'
And I, 'My son, I have not seen thy face.
But thy bruised feet have trodden on my heart.
I will get water for thee.'
                        'These my hurts,'
Again he answered, 'daily dost thou wash.'
And I once more, 'My son, I know thee not.   40
But the bleak wind blows bitter from the sea,
And even the gorse is perished. Rest thee here.'
And he again, 'My rest is in thy heart.
I take from thee as I have given to thee.
Dost thou not know Me, Breton?'
                        I, — 'My Lord!' —

A scent of lilies on the cold sea-wind,
A thin, white blaze of wings, a face of flame
Over the gateway, and the vision passed,
And there were only Matthieu and brown Bran,
And the young girl, the foam-white Jannedik,   50
Wondering to see their father rapt from them,
And Jeffik weeping o'er her withered hand.

MARJORIE PICKTHALL

73

Heaven and Hell

And when we die at last,
we really know very little about what happens then.
But people who dream
have often seen the dead appear to them
just as they were in life.
Therefore we believe life does not end here on earth.

We have heard of three places where men go after death:
There is the Land of the Sky, a good place
where there is no sorrow and fear.
There have been angatoks who went there   10
and came back to tell us about it:
They saw people playing ball, happy people
who did nothing but laugh and amuse themselves.
What we see from down here in the form of stars
are the lighted windows of the villages of the dead
in the Land of the Sky.

Then there are two other worlds of the dead underground:
Way deep down is a place just like here on earth
except on earth you starve
and down there they live in plenty.   20
The caribou graze in great herds
and there are endless plains
with juicy berries that are nice to eat.
Down there too, everything
is happiness and fun for the dead.

But there is another place, the Land of the Miserable,
right under the surface of the earth we walk on.
There go all the lazy men who were poor hunters,
and all women who refused to be tattooed,
not caring to suffer a little to become beautiful.   30
They had no life in them when they lived
so now after death they must squat on their haunches
with hanging heads, bad-tempered and silent,
and live in hunger and idleness
because they wasted their lives.
Only when a butterfly comes flying by
do they lift their heads
(as young birds open pink mouths uselessly after a gnat)
and when thcy snap at it, a puff of dust
comes out of their dry throats.   40

Of course it may be
that all I have been telling you is wrong
for you cannot be certain about what you cannot see.
But these are the stories that our people tell.

NETSILIK ORIGIN (INUIT)
Translated by EDWARD FIELD

74
The Tyger

(An Early Draft)

1 Tyger Tyger burning bright
   In the forests of the night
   What immortal hand & eye
                      or
   Could frame thy fearful symmetry
   Dare

2 In what distant deeps or skies
   Burnt in
   Burnt the fire of thine eyes
   The cruel
   On what wings dare he aspire
   What the hand dare sieze the fire

3 And what shoulder & what art
   Could twist the sinews of thy heart
   And when thy heart began to beat
   What dread hand & what dread feet

   Could fetch it from the furnace deep
   And in thy horrid ribs dare steep
   In the well of sanguine woe
   In what clay & in what mould
   Were thy eyes of fury rolld

4 What the hammer   what the chain
  Where   where
  In what furnace was thy brain
  What the anvil   what the arm
                         arm
                         grasp
                         clasp
               dread grasp
  Could its deadly terrors clasp
  Dare   grasp
                         clasp

6 Tyger Tyger burning bright
  In the forests of the night
  What immortal hand & eye
  Dare form thy fearful symmetry
        frame

2 Burnt in distant deeps or skies
  The cruel fire of thine eyes
  Could heart descend or wings aspire
  What the hand dare sieze the fire

5 And did he laugh his work to see
       dare he smile
             laugh
  What the shoulder   what the knee
          ankle
  Did he who made the lamb make thee
  Dare
  When the stars threw down their spears
  And waterd heaven with their tears

WILLIAM BLAKE

[115]

The Tyger

(The Final Version)

Tyger! Tyger! burning bright
In the forests of the night,
What immortal hand or eye
Could frame thy fearful symmetry?

In what distant deeps or skies
Burnt the fire of thine eyes?
On what wings dare he aspire?
What the hand dare seize the fire?

And what shoulder, and what art,
Could twist the sinews of thy heart?
And when thy heart began to beat,
What dread hand? and what dread feet?

What the hammer? what the chain?
In what furnace was thy brain?
What the anvil? what dread grasp
Dare its deadly terrors clasp?

When the stars threw down their spears,
And water'd heaven with their tears,
Did he smile his work to see?
Did he who made the Lamb make thee?

Tyger! Tyger! burning bright
In the forests of the night,
What immortal hand or eye
Dare frame thy fearful symmetry?

WILLIAM BLAKE

75

Then the Lord Answered Job
Out of the Whirlwind

Then the Lord answered Job out of the whirlwind and
said,

Who is this that darkeneth counsel by words without
knowledge?

Gird up now thy loins like a man; for I will demand of
thee, and answer thou me.

Where wast thou when I laid the foundations of the
earth? declare, if thou hast understanding.

Who hath laid the measures thereof, if thou knowest? or
who hath stretched the line upon it?   10

Whereupon are the foundations thereof fastened? or who
laid the corner-stone thereof;

When the morning stars sang together, and all the sons
of God shouted for joy?

Or who shut up the sea with doors, when it brake forth,
as if it had issued out of the womb?

When I made the cloud the garment thereof, and thick
darkness a swaddling band for it,

And brake up for it my decreed place, and set bars and
doors,   20

And said, Hitherto shalt thou come, but no further: and
here shall thy proud waves be stayed?

Canst thou bind the sweet influences of Pleiades, or
loose the bands of Orion?

Canst thou bring forth Mazzaroth in his season? or canst thou guide Arcturus with his sons?

Knowest thou the ordinances of heaven? canst thou set the dominion thereof in the earth?

Canst thou lift up thy voice to the clouds, that abundance of waters may cover thee?   30

Canst thou send lightnings, that they may go, and say unto thee, Here we are?

JOB 38: 1-11, 31-35

THE BIBLE, KING JAMES VERSION

76
Apparently With No Surprise

Apparently with no surprise
To any happy Flower
The Frost beheads it at its play —
In accidental power —
The blonde Assassin passes on —
The Sun proceeds unmoved
To measure off another Day
For an Approving God.

EMILY DICKINSON

77
The Last Night That She Lived

The last Night that She lived
It was a Common Night
Except the Dying — this to Us
Made Nature different.

We noticed smallest things —
Things overlooked before
By this great light upon our Minds
Italicized — as 'twere.

As We went out and in
Between Her final Room   10
And Rooms where Those to be alive
Tomorrow were, a Blame

That Others could exist
While She must finish quite
A Jealousy for Her arose
So nearly infinite —

We waited while She passed —
It was a narrow time —
Too jostled were Our Souls to speak
At length the notice came.   20

She mentioned, and forgot —
Then lightly as a Reed
Bent to the Water, struggled scarce —
Consented, and was dead —

And We — We placed the Hair —
And drew the Head erect —
And then an awful leisure was
Belief to regulate —

EMILY DICKINSON

78

Within My Garden, Rides a Bird

Within my Garden, rides a Bird
Upon a single Wheel —
Whose spokes a dizzy Music make
As 'twere a travelling Mill —

He never stops, but slackens
Above the Ripest Rose —
Partakes without alighting
And praises as he goes,

Till every spice is tasted —
And then his Fairy Gig
Reels in remoter atmospheres —
And I rejoin my Dog,

And He and I, perplex us
If positive, 'twere we —
Or bore the Garden in the Brain
This Curiosity —

But He, the best Logician,
Refers my clumsy eye —
To just vibrating Blossoms!
An Exquisite Reply!

EMILY DICKINSON

79
Mushrooms

Overnight, very
Whitely, discreetly,
Very quietly

Our toes, our noses
Take hold on the loam,
Acquire the air.

Nobody sees us,
Stops us, betrays us;
The small grains make room.

Soft fists insist on   10
Heaving the needles,
The leafy bedding,

Even the paving.
Our hammers, our rams,
Earless and eyeless,

Perfectly voiceless,
Widen the crannies,
Shoulder through holes. We

Diet on water,
On crumbs of shadow,   20
Bland-mannered, asking

Little or nothing.
So many of us!
So many of us!

We are shelves, we are
Tables, we are meek,
We are edible,

Nudgers and shovers
In spite of ourselves.
Our kind multiplies: 30

We shall by morning
Inherit the earth.
Our foot's in the door.

                                   SYLVIA PLATH

80

Natural Prayer

POEM FOR SEVERAL VOICES

ooooooooooooooooooooooooooooooooooooooooooooooo,   th' bees
bring home th' groceries, th' groceries, th' groceries, hummm
                                                         m
                                                         m
                                                         m
                                                         m
                                                         m
                                                         m
                                                         m   10
                                                         m
                                                         m
                                                         m
                                                         m
                                                         m
                                                         m
                                                         m
                                                         m
                                                         m
mmmmmmmmmmmmmmmmmmmmmmmmmmmmmmmmmmmmmmmmmmmmm   20
o
o
o
o
o
o
o
o
o
o
o, th' bees bring home th' dust
   th' bees bring home th' protein
               o
               o
               o
               o
               o
               o   40
               o
ooooooooooooooooooooooooooooooo
th' bees bring home th' powder
plantation fields forever
th' bees bring home magnolia bread
th' bees bring home th' dust

th' bees bring home th' bread, oooo
                        o
                         o   50
                         o
                         o
oooooooooooooooooooooooooooooo
I love to watch them pack, th' powder, in their
        baskets
I love to watch them pack, th' powder, in their baskets
I love to watch them pack, th' powder, in their baskets
                        elbow baskets
                        elbow baskets
                        O
                        O   60
                        O
                        O
OOOOOOOOOOOOOOOOOOOOOOOOOOOO
th' lovely bees bring home magnolia dust
th' lovely bees bring home th' bread, de,dum
                    de,dum
                    de,dum
                    de,dum
                      o
                      o   70
                      o
            ooooooooooooo
            hummmmmm

                    JOE ROSENBLATT

Forsythia

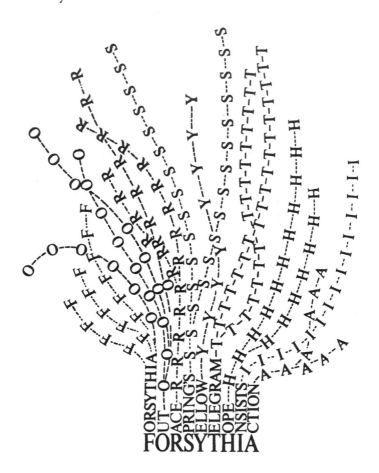

MARY ELLEN SOLT

& So the Little Fieldmouse Said

The Swimmer's Moment

For everyone
The swimmer's moment at the whirlpool comes,
But many at that moment will not say
'This is the whirlpool, then.'
By their refusal they are saved
From the black pit, and also from contesting
The deadly rapids, and emerging in
The mysterious, and more ample, further waters.
And so their bland-blank faces turn and turn
Pale and forever on the rim of suction   10
They will not recognize.
Of those who dare the knowledge
Many are whirled into the ominous centre
That, gaping vertical, seals up
For them an eternal boon of privacy,
So that we turn away from their defeat
With a despair, not for their deaths, but for
Ourselves, who cannot penetrate their secret
Nor even guess at the anonymous breadth
Where one or two have won: 20
(The silver reaches of the estuary).

MARGARET AVISON

Not Waving But Drowning

Nobody heard him, the dead man,
But still he lay moaning:
I was much further out than you thought
And not waving but drowning.

Poor chap, he always loved larking
And now he's dead
It must have been too cold for him his heart gave way,
They said.

Oh, no no no, it was too cold always
(Still the dead one lay moaning)
I was much too far out all my life
And not waving but drowning.

STEVIE SMITH

85

Dover Beach

The sea is calm to-night.
The tide is full, the moon lies fair
Upon the straits; — on the French coast the light
Gleams and is gone; the cliffs of England stand,
Glimmering and vast, out in the tranquil bay.
Come to the window, sweet is the night-air!
Only, from the long line of spray
Where the sea meets the moon-blanch'd land,

Listen! you hear the grating roar
Of pebbles which the waves draw back, and fling,   10
At their return, up the high strand,
Begin, and cease, and then again begin,
With tremulous cadence slow, and bring
The eternal note of sadness in.

Sophocles long ago
Heard it on the Aegaean, and it brought
Into his mind the turbid ebb and flow
Of human misery; we
Find also in the sound a thought,
Hearing it by this distant northern sea.   20

The Sea of Faith
Was once, too, at the full, and round earth's shore
Lay like the folds of a bright girdle furl'd.
But now I only hear
Its melancholy, long, withdrawing roar,
Retreating, to the breath
Of the night-wind, down the vast edges drear
And naked shingles of the world.

Ah, love, let us be true
To one another! for the world, which seems   30
To lie before us like a land of dreams,
So various, so beautiful, so new,
Hath really neither joy, nor love, nor light,
Nor certitude, nor peace, nor help for pain;
And we are here as on a darkling plain
Swept with confused alarms of struggle and flight,
Where ignorant armies clash by night.

MATTHEW ARNOLD

86

Lines

COMPOSED A FEW MILES ABOVE TINTERN ABBEY, ON REVISITING
THE BANKS OF THE WYE DURING A TOUR. JULY 13, 1798

Five years have past; five summers, with the length
Of five long winters! and again I hear
These waters, rolling from their mountain-springs
With a soft inland murmur. — Once again
Do I behold these steep and lofty cliffs,
That on a wild secluded scene impress
Thoughts of more deep seclusion; and connect
The landscape with the quiet of the sky.
The day is come when I again repose
Here, under this dark sycamore, and view   10
These plots of cottage-ground, these orchard-tufts,
Which at this season, with their unripe fruits,
Are clad in one green hue, and lose themselves
'Mid groves and copses. Once again I see
These hedge-rows, hardly hedge-rows, little lines
Of sportive wood run wild: these pastoral farms,
Green to the very door; and wreaths of smoke
Sent up, in silence, from among the trees!
With some uncertain notice, as might seem
Of vagrant dwellers in the houseless woods,   20
Or of some Hermit's cave, where by his fire
The Hermit sits alone.
                              These beauteous forms,
Through a long absence, have not been to me
As is a landscape to a blind man's eye:

But oft, in lonely rooms, and 'mid the din
Of towns and cities, I have owed to them,
In hours of weariness, sensations sweet,
Felt in the blood, and felt along the heart;
And passing even into my purer mind,
With tranquil restoration: — feelings too   30
Of unremembered pleasure: such, perhaps,
As have no slight or trivial influence
On that best portion of a good man's life,
His little, nameless, unremembered acts
Of kindness and of love. Nor less, I trust,
To them I may have owed another gift,
Of aspect more sublime; that blessed mood,
In which the burthen of the mystery,
In which the heavy and the weary weight
Of all this unintelligible world,   40
Is lightened: — that serene and blessed mood,
In which the affections gently lead us on, —
Until, the breath of this corporeal frame
And even the motion of our human blood
Almost suspended, we are laid asleep
In body, and become a living soul:
While with an eye made quiet by the power
Of harmony, and the deep power of joy,
We see into the life of things.
                              If this
Be but a vain belief, yet, oh! how oft —   50
In darkness and amid the many shapes
Of joyless daylight; when the fretful stir
Unprofitable, and the fever of the world,
Have hung upon the beatings of my heart —
How oft, in spirit, have I turned to thee,
O sylvan Wye! thou wanderer thro' the woods,

How often has my spirit turned to thee!

   And now, with gleams of half-extinguished thought,
With many recognitions dim and faint,
And somewhat of a sad perplexity,   60
The picture of the mind revives again:
While here I stand, not only with the sense
Of present pleasure, but with pleasing thoughts
That in this moment there is life and food
For future years. And so I dare to hope,
Though changed, no doubt, from what I was when first
I came among these hills; when like a roe
I bounded o'er the mountains, by the sides
Of the deep rivers, and the lonely streams,
Wherever nature led: more like a man   70
Flying from something that he dreads than one
Who sought the thing he loved. For nature then
(The coarser pleasures of my boyish days,
And their glad animal movements all gone by)
To me was all in all. — I cannot paint
What then I was. The sounding cataract
Haunted me like a passion: the tall rock,
The mountain, and the deep and gloomy wood,
Their colours and their forms, were then to me
An appetite; a feeling and a love,   80
That had no need of a remoter charm,
By thought supplied, nor any interest
Unborrowed from the eye. — That time is past,
And all its aching joys are now no more,
And all its dizzy raptures. Not for this
Faint I, nor mourn nor murmur; other gifts
Have followed; for such loss, I would believe,
Abundant recompense. For I have learned

To look on nature, not as in the hour
Of thoughtless youth; but hearing oftentimes   90
The still, sad music of humanity,
Nor harsh nor grating, though of ample power
To chasten and subdue. And I have felt
A presence that disturbs me with the joy
Of elevated thoughts; a sense sublime
Of something far more deeply interfused,
Whose dwelling is the light of setting suns,
And the round ocean and the living air,
And the blue sky, and in the mind of man:
A motion and a spirit, that impels   100
All thinking things, all objects of all thought,
And rolls through all things. Therefore am I still
A lover of the meadows and the woods,
And mountains; and of all that we behold
From this green earth; of all the mighty world
Of eye, and ear, — both what they half create,
And what perceive; well pleased to recognise
In nature and the language of the sense
The anchor of my purest thoughts, the nurse,
The guide, the guardian of my heart, and soul   110
Of all my moral being.
                        Nor perchance,
If I were not thus taught, should I the more
Suffer my genial spirits to decay:
For thou art with me here upon the banks
Of this fair river; thou my dearest Friend,
My dear, dear Friend; and in thy voice I catch
The language of my former heart, and read
My former pleasures in the shooting lights
Of thy wild eyes. Oh! yet a little while
May I behold in thee what I was once,   120

My dear, dear Sister! and this prayer I make,
Knowing that Nature never did betray
The heart that loved her; 'tis her privilege,
Through all the years of this our life, to lead
From joy to joy: for she can so inform
The mind that is within us, so impress
With quietness and beauty, and so feed
With lofty thoughts, that neither evil tongues,
Rash judgments, nor the sneers of selfish men,
Nor greetings where no kindness is, nor all   130
The dreary intercourse of daily life,
Shall e'er prevail against us, or disturb
Our cheerful faith, that all which we behold
Is full of blessings. Therefore let the moon
Shine on thee in thy solitary walk;
And let the misty mountain-winds be free
To blow against thee: and, in after years,
When these wild ecstasies shall be matured
Into a sober pleasure; when thy mind
Shall be a mansion for all lovely forms,   140
Thy memory be as a dwelling-place
For all sweet sounds and harmonies; oh! then,
If solitude, or fear, or pain, or grief,
Should be thy portion, with what healing thoughts
Of tender joy wilt thou remember me,
And these my exhortations! Nor, perchance —
If I should be where I no more can hear
Thy voice, nor catch from thy wild eyes these gleams
Of past existence — wilt thou then forget
That on the banks of this delightful stream   150
We stood together; and that I, so long
A worshipper of Nature, hither came
Unwearied in that service: rather say

[136]

With warmer love — oh! with far deeper zeal
Of holier love. Nor wilt thou then forget
That after many wanderings, many years
Of absence, these steep woods and lofty cliffs,
And this green pastoral landscape, were to me
More dear, both for themselves and for thy sake!

WILLIAM WORDSWORTH

87

The Shepheardes Lament

FROM *The Shepheardes Calender*

DECEMBER

Thus is my sommer worne away and wasted,
Thus is my haruest hastened all to rathe:°   too soo[n]
The eare° that budded faire, is burnt and blasted,   ear of c[orn]
And all my hoped gaine is turned to scathe.°   loss
  Of all the seede, that in my youth was sowne,
  Was nought but brakes° and brambles to be mowne.   bracken

And thus of all my haruest hope I haue
Nought reaped but a weedye crop of care:
Which, when I thought haue thresht in swelling sheaue,
Cockel° for corne, and chaffe for barley bare.   a weed
  Soone as the chaffe should in the fan be fynd,°   found
  All was blowne away of the wauering wynd.

So now my yeare drawes to his latter terme,
My spring is spent, my sommer burnt vp quite:
My haruest hasts to stirre vp winter sterne,   15
And bids him clayme with rigorous rage hys right.
  So nowe he stormes with many a sturdy stoure,°   turmoil
  So now his blustring blast eche coste° doth scoure.   directio[n]

The carefull cold hath nypt my rugged rynde,°   skin
And in my face deepe furrowes eld° hath pight:°   old age   set
My head besprent° with hoary frost I fynd,   besprinkled
And by myne eie the Crow his clawe dooth wright.
   Delight is layd abedde, and pleasure past,
   No sonne now shines, cloudes han all ouercast.

Now leaue ye shepheards boyes your merry glee,   25
My Muse is hoarse and weary of thys stounde:°   noise
Here will I hang my pype vpon this tree,
Was neuer pype of reede did better sounde.
   Winter is come, that blowes the bitter blaste,
   And after Winter dreerie death does hast.

Gather ye together my little flocke,
My little flock, that was to me so liefe:°   dear
Let me, ah lette me in your folds ye lock,
Ere the breme° Winter breede you greater griefe.   bitter
   Winter is come, that blowes the balefull breath,   35
   And after Winter commeth timely death.

EDMUND SPENSER

88

Branwell's Lament

FROM *A Suit of Nettles*

JUNE

    I am like a hollow tree
Where the owl & weasel hide
    I am like a hollow tree
Dead in the forest of his brothers.

    My feet are sensitive as brains
Put hats upon them
    My feet are sensitive as brains
All the ground is grassed with knives.

    These fingers that once played
Nimbly the harp   10
    These fingers that once played
Are soft & suck as leeches.

    My throat where once a song
Flew out like a golden bird
    My throat where once a song
Is a woodpecker's bitten door.

    My eyes are the entrances
To the kingfishers' nests
    My eyes are the entrances
Tunnels of clay lined with fish bones.   20

    I see the red sun sink
For the last time this far north.
The full moon rises: my thoughts fly forth.
Leap forth, oh bird of prey & turncoat ermine,
    Nebula out of my mind
        That swampy fair
Where the bittern pumps from its cistern of despair.

JAMES REANEY

89

The Country North of Belleville

Bush land scrub land —
> Cashel Township and Wollaston
Elzevir McClure and Dungannon
green lands of Weslemkoon Lake
where a man might have some
> opinion of what beauty
is and none deny him
> > for miles —

Yet this is the country of defeat
where Sisyphus rolls a big stone   10
year after year up the ancient hills
picnicking glaciers have left strewn
with centuries' rubble
> > backbreaking days
> > in the sun and rain
when realization seeps slow in the mind
without grandeur or self-deception in
> > noble struggle
of being a fool —

A country of quiescence and still distance   20
a lean land
> not like the fat south
with inches of black soil on
> earth's round belly —
And where the farms are
> it's as if a man stuck
both thumbs in the stony earth and pulled

                    it apart
                    to make room
enough between the trees   30
for a wife
            and maybe some cows and
            room for some
of the more easily kept illusions —
And where the farms have gone back
to forest
            are only soft outlines
            shadowy differences —

Old fences drift vaguely among the trees
            a pile of moss-covered stones   40
gathered for some ghost purpose
has lost meaning under the meaningless sky
            — they are like cities under water
and the undulating green waves of time
            are laid on them —

This is the country of our defeat
            and yet
during the fall plowing a man
might stop and stand in a brown valley of the furrows
            and shade his eyes to watch for the same   50
            red patch mixed with gold
            that appears on the same
            spot in the hills
            year after year
            and grow old
plowing and plowing a ten-acre field until
the convolutions run parallel with his own brain —

And this is a country where the young
                    leave quickly
unwilling to know what their fathers know   60
or think the words their mothers do not say —

Herschel Monteagle and Faraday
lakeland rockland and hill country
a little adjacent to where the world is
a little north of where the cities are and
sometime
we may go back there
                    to the country of our defeat
Woolaston Elzevir and Dungannon
and Weslemkoon lake land   70
where the high townships of Cashel
                    McClure and Marmora once were —
But it's been a long time since
and we must enquire the way
          of strangers —

AL PURDY

90

My '48 Pontiac

All winter long it wouldn't start
standing in the yard covered with snow
I'd go out at 10 below zero and coax
and say
       'Where's your pride?'
and kick it disgustedly
Finally snow covered everything
but television aerials and the world was
a place nobody came to
so white it couldn't be looked at   10
before nothing was something
But the old Pontiac lay there
affirming its identity
like some prehistoric vegetarian
stupidly unaware of snow
waiting for Tyrannosaurus Rex
to come along and bite off its fenders
'You no good American Pontiac you
(I'd say)
you're a disgrace to General Motors'   20
then go out and hitch up the dog team
When June hurried by it still wouldn't start
only stop
and the wreckers hauled it away

Now and then I go to visit my old friend
at Bud's Auto Wreckers
being sentimental about rubber and metal
I think it's glad to see me
and wags both tail lights
a true heart thumping eagerly   30

under the torn seat covers
I sit behind the wheel
on a parched August afternoon
and we drive thru a glitter of broken glass
among suicides and automotive murders
mangled chryslers and volkswagens
metal twisted into a look
of fierce helplessness
reversed violence in hunchback shapes
and containing it still   40
waiting to explode outward

We drive between dismantled buicks and
studebakers and one stuckup old cadillac
driven to Bud's by a doddering chauffeur
who used to play poker with Roman chariot drivers
and a silent crumpled grey plymouth
with bloodstains on the instrument panel
where a girl died
a '41 de soto with all the chrome gone
still excited from drag races   50
and quivering blondes whose bottoms it liked

My last visit was by moonlight and flashlight
to Bud's Auto Wreckers
where the old Pontiac waited
I turned the speedometer back to 5,000 miles
changed the oil
polished the headlights to look at death
adjusted the rear view mirror to look at life
gave it back its ownership card
and went away   60
puzzled by things

AL PURDY

[146]

91

The Dancing Cabman

Alone on the lawn
  The cabman dances;
In the dew of dawn
  He kicks and prances.
His bowler is set
  On his bullet head,
For his boots are wet,
  And his aunt is dead.
There on the lawn
  As the light advances,   10
On the tide of the dawn,
  The cabman dances.

Swift and strong
  As a garden roller,
He dances along
  In his little bowler,
Skimming the lawn
  With royal grace,
The dew of the dawn
  On his great red face.   20
To fairy flutes,
  As the light advances,
In square black boots
  The cabman dances.

J. B. MORTON

92

Cheerio My Deario

(*By* ARCHY THE COCKROACH)

well boss i met
mehitabel the cat
trying to dig a
frozen lamb chop
out of a snow
drift the other day

a helluva comedown
that is for me archy
she says a few
brief centuries   10
ago one of old
king
tut
ankh
amens favourite
queens and today
the village scavenger
but wotthehell
archy wotthehell
its cheerio   20
my deario that
pulls a lady through

see here mehitabel
i said i thought
you told me that
it was cleopatra
you used to be
before you
transmigrated into
the carcase of a cat   30
where do you get
this tut
ankh
amen stuff
question mark

i was several
ladies my little
insect says she
being cleopatra was
only an incident   40
in my career
and i was always getting
the rough end of it
always being
misunderstood by some
strait laced
prune faced bunch
of prissy mouthed
sisters of uncharity
the things that   50
have been said
about me archy
exclamation point

and all simply
because i was a
live dame
the palaces i have
been kicked out of
in my time
exclamation point   60

but wotthehell
little archy wot
thehell
its cheerio
my deario
that pulls a
lady through
exclamation point

framed archy always
framed that is the   70
story of all my lives
no chance for a dame
with the anvil chorus
if she shows a little
motion it seems to
me only yesterday
that the luxor local
number one of
the ladies axe
association got me in   80
dutch with king tut and
he slipped me the
sarcophagus always my
luck yesterday an empress
and today too

emaciated to interest
a vivisectionist but
toujours gai archy
toujours gai and always
a lady in spite of hell   90
and transmigration
once a queen
always a queen
archy
period

one of her
feet was frozen
but on the other three
she began to caper and
dance singing its   100
cheerio my deario
that pulls a lady
through her morals may
have been mislaid somewhere
in the centuries boss but
i admire her spirit
                    archy

DON MARQUIS

93
Indian Summer

In youth, it was a way I had
    To do my best to please,
And change, with every passing lad,
    To suit his theories.

But now I know the things I know,
    And do the things I do;
And if you do not like me so,
    To hell, my love, with you!

DOROTHY PARKER

94
The Constant Lover

Out upon it, I have lov'd
  Three whole days together;
And am like to love three more,
  If it prove fair weather.

Time shall molt away his wings
  Ere he shall discover
In the whole wide world again
  Such a constant lover.

But the spite on't is, no praise
  Is due at all to me:
Love with me had made no stays
  Had it any been but she.

Had it any been but she
  And that very face,
There had been at least ere this
  A dozen dozen in her place.

SIR JOHN SUCKLING

95
The Braw Wooer

Last May a braw° wooer cam doun the lang glen,   °handsome
    And sair° wi' his love he did deave° me;   °greatly °deafe[n]
I said there was naething I hated like men —
    The deuce° gae wi'm, to believe me, believe me;   °devil
    The deuce gae wi'm to believe me.

He spake o' the darts in my bonie black een,°   °eyes
    And vow'd for my love he was diein',
I said he might die when he liket — for Jean —
    The Lord forgie me for liein', for liein';
    The Lord forgie me for liein'!   10

A weel-stocket mailen,° himself for the laird,   °farm
    And marriage aff-hand, were his proffers;
I never loot° on that I keen'd° it, or car'd,   °let °longed fo[r]
    But thought I might have waur° offers, waur   °worse
      offers;
    But thought I might hae waur offers.

But what wad ye think? — in a fortnight or less —
    The deil tak his taste to gae near her!
He up the *Gate-slack*° to my black cousin, Bess —   °road through a g[len]
    Guess ye how, the jad!° I could bear her, could   °hussy
      bear her;
    Guess ye how, the jad! I could bear her.   20

But a' the neist week, as I petted° wi' care,   *felt ill-humoured*
   I gaed to the tryst° o' Dalgarnock;   *meeting place*
And wha but my fine fickle wooer was there,
   I glowr'd as I'd seen a warlock,° a warlock,   *demon, sorcerer*
   I glowr'd as I'd seen a warlock.

But owre my left shouther I gae him a blink,
   Lest neibours might say I was saucy;
My wooer he caper'd as he'd been in drink,
   And vow'd I was his dear lassie, dear lassie,
   And vow'd I was his dear lassie.   30

I spier'd for° my cousin fu' couthy° and sweet, *asked after   pleasant*
   Gin° she had recover'd her hearin',   *If, whether*
And how her new shoon fit her auld shachl't° feet, *shambling*
   But heavens! how he fell a swearin', a swearin',
   But heavens! how he fell a swearin'.

He begged, for gudesake, I wad be his wife,
   Or else I wad kill him wi' sorrow;
So e'en to preserve the poor body in life,
   I think I maun° wed him to-morrow,   *must*
      to-morrow;
   I think I maun wed him to-morrow.

ROBERT BURNS

96

As I Walked Out One Evening

As I walked out one evening,
　Walking down Bristol Street,
The crowds upon the pavement
　Were fields of harvest wheat.

And down by the brimming river
　I heard a lover sing
Under an arch of the railway:
　'Love has no ending.

I'll love you, dear, I'll love you
　Till China and Africa meet,   10
And the river jumps over the mountain
　And the salmon sing in the street.

I'll love you till the ocean
　Is folded and hung up to dry,
And the seven stars go squawking
　Like geese about the sky.

The years shall run like rabbits,
　For in my arms I hold
The Flower of the Ages,
　And the first love of the world'.   20

But all the clocks in the city
　Began to whirr and chime:
'O let not Time deceive you,
　You cannot conquer Time.

In the burrows of the Nightmare
  Where Justice naked is,
Time watches from the shadow
  And coughs when you would kiss.

In headaches and in worry
  Vaguely life leaks away,
And Time will have his fancy
  Tomorrow or today.

Into many a green valley
  Drifts the appalling snow;
Time breaks the threaded dances
  And the diver's brilliant bow.

O plunge your hands in water,
  Plunge them in up to the wrist;
Stare, stare in the basin
  And wonder what you've missed.

The glacier knocks in the cupboard,
  The desert sighs in the bed,
And the crack in the tea-cup opens
  A lane to the land of the dead.

Where the beggars raffle the banknotes
  And the Giant is enchanting to Jack,
And the Lily-white Boy is a Roarer,
  And Jill goes down on her back.

O look, look in the mirror,
  O look in your distress;
Life remains a blessing
  Although you cannot bless.

30

40

50

O stand, stand at the window
   As the tears scald and start;
You shall love your crooked neighbor
   With your crooked heart.'

It was late, late in the evening,
   The lovers they were gone;
The clocks had ceased their chiming,
   And the deep river ran on.

W. H. AUDEN

97

The Sick Rose

O Rose, thou art sick!
The invisible worm,
That flies in the night,
In the howling storm,

Has found out thy bed
Of crimson joy;
And his dark secret love
Does thy life destroy.

WILLIAM BLAKE

98

Tears, Idle Tears

Tears, idle tears, I know not what they mean,
Tears from the depth of some divine despair
Rise in the heart, and gather to the eyes,
In looking on the happy Autumn-fields,
And thinking of the days that are no more.

Fresh as the first beam glittering on a sail,
That brings our friends up from the underworld,
Sad as the last which reddens over one
That sinks with all we love below the verge;
So sad, so fresh, the days that are no more.

Ah, sad and strange as in dark summer dawns
The earliest pipe of half-awaken'd birds
To dying ears, when unto dying eyes
The casement slowly grows a glimmering square;
So sad, so strange, the days that are no more.

Dear as remember'd kisses after death,
And sweet as those by hopeless fancy feign'd
On lips that are for others; deep as love,
Deep as first love, and wild with all regret;
O Death in Life, the days that are no more.

ALFRED LORD TENNYSON

99
In Memoriam

VII

Dark house, by which once more I stand
   Here in the long unlovely street,
   Doors, where my heart was used to beat
So quickly, waiting for a hand,

A hand that can be clasp'd no more —
   Behold me, for I cannot sleep,
   And like a guilty thing I creep
At earliest morning to the door.

He is not here; but far away
   The noise of life begins again,
   And ghastly thro' the drizzling rain
On the bald street breaks the blank day.

LIV

Oh yet we trust that somehow good
   Will be the final goal of ill,
   To pangs of nature, sins of will,
Defects of doubt, and taints of blood;

That nothing walks with aimless feet;
   That not one life shall be destroy'd,
   Or cast as rubbish to the void,
When God hath made the pile complete;

That not a worm is cloven in vain;
    That not a moth with vain desire
    Is shrivell'd in a fruitless fire,
Or but subserves another's gain.

Behold, we know not anything;
    I can but trust that good shall fall
    At last — far off — at last, to all,
And every winter change to spring.

So runs my dream: but what am I?
    An infant crying in the night:
    An infant crying for the light:
And with no language but a cry.

CXV

Now fades the last long streak of snow,
    Now burgeons every maze of quick
    About the flowering squares, and thick
By ashen roots the violets blow.

Now rings the woodland loud and long,
    The distance takes a lovelier hue,
    And drown'd in yonder living blue
The lark becomes a sightless song.

Now dance the lights on lawn and lea,
    The flocks are whiter down the vale,
    And milkier every milky sail
On winding stream or distant sea;

Where now the seamew pipes, or dives
    In yonder greening gleam, and fly

The happy birds, that change their sky
To build and brood; that live their lives

From land to land; and in my breast
   Spring wakens too; and my regret
   Becomes an April violet,
And buds and blossoms like the rest.

CXVIII

Contemplate all this work of Time,
   The giant labouring in his youth;
   Nor dream of human love and truth,
As dying Nature's earth and lime;

But trust that those we call the dead
   Are breathers of an ampler day
   For ever nobler ends. They say
The solid earth whereon we tread

In tracts of fluent heat began,
   And grew to seeming-random forms,   10
   The seeming prey of cyclic storms,
Till at the last arose the man;

Who throve and branch'd from clime to clime,
   The herald of a higher race,
   And of himself in higher place,
If so he type this work of time

Within himself, from more to more;
   Or, crown'd with attributes of woe
   Like glories, move his course, and show
That life is not as idle ore,   20

But iron dug from central gloom,
    And heated hot with burning fears,
    And dipt in baths of hissing tears,
And batter'd with the shocks of doom

To shape and use. Arise and fly
    The reeling Faun, the sensual feast;
    Move upward, working out the beast,
And let the ape and tiger die.

CXXIII

There rolls the deep where grew the tree.
    O earth, what changes hast thou seen!
    There where the long street roars, hath been
The stillness of the central sea.

The hills are shadows, and they flow
    From form to form, and nothing stands;
    They melt like mist, the solid lands,
Like clouds they shape themselves and go.

But in my spirit will I dwell,
    And dream my dream, and hold it true;
    For tho' my lips may breathe adieu,
I cannot think the thing farewell.

ALFRED LORD TENNYSON

100

A Valediction: Forbidding Mourning

As virtuous men pass mildly away
   And whisper to their souls to go,
Whilst some of their sad friends do say,
   'The breath goes now,' and some say, 'No:'

So let us melt, and make no noise,
   No tear-floods, nor sigh-tempests move;
'Twere profanation of our joys
   To tell the laity our love.

Moving of th'earth brings harms and fears;
   Men reckon what it did, and meant.   10
But trepidation of the spheres,
   Though greater far, is innocent.

Dull sublunary lovers' love —
   Whose soul is sense — cannot admit
Absence, because it doth remove
   Those things which elemented it.

But we by a love so much refined
   That ourselves know not what it is,
Inter-assured of the mind,
   Care less eyes, lips, and hands to miss.   20

Our two souls, therefore, which are one,
   Though I must go, endure not yet
A breach, but an expansion,
   Like gold to airy thinness beat.

If they be two, they are two so
   As stiff twin compasses are two;
Thy soul, the fixed foot, makes no show
   To move, but doth, if th'other do.

And though it in the centre sit,
   Yet, when the other far doth roam,   30
It leans and harkens after it,
   And grows erect, as that comes home.

Such wilt thou be to me, who must,
   Like th'other foot, obliquely run;
Thy firmness makes my circle just,
   And makes me end where I begun.

JOHN DONNE

101

Death

Death, be not proud, though some have called thee
Mighty and dreadful, for thou art not so:
For those whom thou think'st thou dost overthrow
Die not, poor Death; nor yet canst thou kill me.
From Rest and Sleep, which but thy picture be,
Much pleasure, then from thee much more must flow;
And soonest our best men with thee do go —
Rest of their bones and souls' delivery!
Thou'rt slave to fate, chance, kings, and desperate men,
And dost with poison, war, and sickness dwell;
And poppy or charms can make us sleep as well
And better than thy stroke. Why swell'st thou then?
    One short sleep past, we wake eternally,
    And death shall be no more: Death, thou shalt die!

JOHN DONNE

102

The Last Hour of Faustus

FROM *The Tragical History of Dr Faustus*

Faustus speaks

Ah, Faustus,
Now hast thou but one bare hour to live,
And then thou must be damned perpetually!
Stand still, you ever-moving spheres of Heaven,
That time may cease, and midnight never come.
Fair Nature's eye, rise, rise again and make
Perpetual day; or let this hour be but
A year, a month, a week, a natural day,
That Faustus may repent and save his soul!
O lente, lente, currite noctis equi!   10
The stars move still, time runs, the clock will strike,
The Devil will come, and Faustus must be damned.
O, I'll leap up to my God! Who pulls me down?
See, see where Christ's blood streams in the firmament!
One drop would save my soul — half a drop: ah, my
    Christ!
Ah, rend not my heart for naming of my Christ!
Yet will I call on him: O spare me, Lucifer! —
Where is it now? 'tis gone; and see where God
Stretcheth out his arm, and bends his ireful brows!
Mountain and hills come, come and fall on me,   20
And hide me from the heavy wrath of God!
No! no!
Then will I headlong run into the earth;
Earth gape! O no, it will not harbour me!

You stars that reigned at my nativity,
Whose influence hath allotted death and hell,
Now draw up Faustus like a foggy mist
Into the entrails of yon labouring clouds,
That when they vomit forth into the air,
My limbs may issue from their smoky mouths,   30
So that my soul may but ascend to Heaven.

(The clock strikes the half hour)

Ah, half the hour is past! 'twill all be past anon!
O God!
If thou wilt not have mercy on my soul,
Yet for Christ's sake whose blood hath ransomed me,
Impose some end to my incessant pain;
Let Faustus live in hell a thousand years —
A hundred thousand, and — at last — be saved!
O, no end is limited to damned souls!
Why wert thou not a creature wanting soul?   40
Or why is this immortal that thou hast?
Ah, Pythagoras' metempsychosis! were that true,
This soul should fly from me, and I be changed
Unto some brutish beast! all beasts are happy,
For, when they die,
Their souls are soon dissolved in elements;
But mine must live, still to be plagued in hell.
Curst be the parents that engendered me!
No, Faustus: curse, thyself: curse Lucifer
That hath deprived thee of the joys of Heaven.   50

(The clock strikes twelve)

O, it strikes, it strikes! Now, body, turn to air,
Or Lucifer will bear thee quick to hell.
O soul, be changed into little water-drops,
And fall into the ocean — ne'er be found.

(Devils enter)

My God! my God! look not so fierce on me!
Adders and serpents, let me breathe awhile!
Ugly hell, gape not! come not, Lucifer!
I'll burn my books — Ah Mephistophilis!

CHRISTOPHER MARLOWE

103

Welsh Night

FROM *Under Milk Wood*

FIRST VOICE *(very softly)*

To begin at the beginning:

It is spring, moonless night in the small town, starless and bible-black, the cobblestreets silent and the hunched, courters'-and-rabbits' wood limping invisible down to the sloeblack, slow, black, crowblack, fishingboat-bobbing sea. The houses are blind as moles (though moles see fine to-night in the snouting, velvet dingles) or blind as Captain Cat there in the muffled middle by the pump and the town clock, the shops in mourning, the Welfare Hall in widows' weeds. And all the people of the lulled and dumbfound town are sleeping now.

Listen. It is night moving in the streets, the processional salt slow musical wind in Coronation Street and Cockle Row, it is the grass growing on Llaregyb Hill, dewfall, starfall, the sleep of birds in Milk Wood.

Listen. It is night in the chill, squat chapel, hymning in bonnet and brooch and bombazine black, butterfly choker and bootlace bow, coughing like nannygoats, sucking mintoes, fortywinking hallelujah; night in the four-ale, quiet as a domino; in Ocky Milkman's lofts like a mouse with gloves; in Dai Bread's bakery flying like black flour. It is to-night in Donkey Street, trotting silent, with seaweed on its hooves, along the cockled cobbles, past curtained fernpot, text and trinket, harmonium, holy dresser, watercolours done by hand, china dog and rosy tin teacaddy. It is night neddying among the snuggeries of babies.

Look. It is night, dumbly, royally winding through the Coronation cherry trees; going through the graveyard of Bethesda with winds gloved and folded, and dew doffed; tumbling by the Sailors Arms.

DYLAN THOMAS

104

Reason Has Moons

Reason has moons, but moons not hers
  Lie mirror'd on her sea,
Confounding her astronomers,
  But oh, delighting me.

RALPH HODGSON

105

Hymn to Diana

Queen and huntress, chaste and fair,
  Now the sun is laid to sleep,
Seated in thy silver chair,
    State in wonted manner keep:
      Hesperus entreats thy light,
      Goddess excellently bright.

Earth, let not thy envious shade
  Dare itself to interpose;
Cynthia's shining orb was made
    Heaven to clear when day did close:
      Bless us then with wishèd sight,
      Goddess excellently bright.

Lay thy bow of pearl apart,
  And thy crystal-shining quiver;
Give unto the flying hart
    Space to breathe, how short soever:
      Thou that mak'st a day of night,
      Goddess excellently bright.

BEN JONSON

106

Golden Slumbers

Golden slumbers kiss your eyes,
Smiles awake you when you rise.
Sleep, pretty wantons, do not cry,
And I will sing a lullaby.
Rock them, rock them, lullaby.

Care is heavy, therefore sleep you;
You are care, and care must keep you;
Sleep, pretty wantons, do not cry,
And I will sing a lullaby:
Rock them, rock them, lullaby.

THOMAS DEKKER

107

Night Bells

Two bells   six bells   two bells   six bells
On a blue pavilion
Out across a smooth blue pavilion
And between each bell
One clear cry of a woman
'Lord God you made the night too long too long.'

CARL SANDBURG

108

Snail

Little snail,
Dreaming you go.
Weather and rose
Is all you know.

Weather and rose
Is all you see,
Drinking
The dewdrop's
Mystery.

LANGSTON HUGHES

109

Climbing Mount Fuji

Snail, my little friend,
    Slowly, oh very slowly
        Climb up Mount Fuji.

ISSA
From a version by R.H. BLYTH

110

David

I

David and I that summer cut trails on the Survey,
All week in the valley for wages, in air that was steeped
In the wail of mosquitoes, but over the sunalive week-ends
We climbed, to get from the ruck of the camp, the surly

Poker, the wrangling, the snoring under the fetid
Tents, and because we had joy in our lengthening coltish
Muscles, and mountains for David were made to see over,
Stairs from the valleys and steps to the sun's retreats.

II

Our first was Mount Gleam. We hiked in the long
    afternoon
To a curling lake and lost the lure of the faceted   10
Cone in the swell of its sprawling shoulders. Past
The inlet we grilled our bacon, the strips festooned

On a poplar prong, in the hurrying slant of the sunset.
Then the two of us rolled in the blanket while round us
    the cold
Pines thrust at the stars. The dawn was a floating
Of mists till we reached to the slopes above timber, and
    won

To snow like fire in the sunlight. The peak was upthrust
Like a fist in a frozen ocean of rock that swirled
Into valleys the moon could be rolled in. Remotely
    unfurling
Eastward the alien prairie glittered. Down through the
    dusty   20

Skree on the west we descended, and David showed me
How to use the give of shale for giant incredible
Strides. I remember, before the larches' edge,
That I jumped a long green surf of juniper flowing

Away from the wind, and landed in gentian and saxifrage
Spilled on the moss. Then the darkening firs
And the sudden whirring of water that knifed down a fern-
    hidden
Cliff and splashed unseen into mist in the shadows.

III

One Sunday on Rampart's arête a rainsquall caught us,
And passed, and we clung by our blueing fingers and
    bootnails   30
An endless hour in the sun, not daring to move
Till the ice had steamed from the slate. And David taught
    me

How time on a knife-edge can pass with the guessing of
    fragments
Remembered from poets, the naming of strata beside one,
And matching of stories from schooldays. . . . We crawled
    astride
The peak to feast on the marching ranges flagged

[176]

By the fading shreds of the shattered stormcloud. Lingering
There it was David who spied to the south, remote,
And unmapped, a sunlit spire on Sawback, an overhang
Crooked like a talon. David named it the Finger.   40

That day we chanced on the skull and the splayed white
     ribs
Of a mountain goat underneath a cliff-face, caught
On a rock. Around were the silken feathers of hawks.
And that was the first I knew that a goat could slip.

IV

And then Inglismaldie. Now I remember only
The long ascent of the lonely valley, the live
Pine spirally scarred by lightning, the slicing pipe
Of invisible pika, and great prints, by the lowest

Snow, of a grizzly. There it was too that David
Taught me to read the scroll of coral in limestone   50
And the beetle-seal in the shale of ghostly trilobites,
Letters delivered to man from the Cambrian waves.

V

On Sundance we tried from the col and the going was
     hard.
The air howled from our feet to the smudged rocks
And the papery lake below. At an outthrust we baulked
Till David clung with his left to a dint in the scarp,

Lobbed the iceaxe over the rocky lip,
Slipped from his holds and hung by the quivering pick,
Twisted his long legs up into space and kicked
To the crest. Then grinning, he reached with his freckled
     wrist   60

And drew me up after. We set a new time for that climb.
That day returning we found a robin gyrating
In grass, wing-broken. I caught it to tame but David
Took and killed it, and said, 'Could you teach it to fly?'

VI

In August, the second attempt, we ascended The Fortress.
By the forks of the Spray we caught five trout and fried
    them
Over a balsam fire. The woods were alive
With the vaulting of mule-deer and drenched with clouds
    all the morning,

Till we burst at noon to the flashing and floating round
Of the peaks. Coming down we picked in our hats the
    bright   70
And sunhot raspberries, eating them under a mighty
Spruce, while a marten moving like quicksilver scouted us.

VII

But always we talked of the Finger on Sawback, unknown
And hooked, till the first afternoon in September we
    slogged
Through the musky woods, past a swamp that quivered
    with frog-song,
And camped by a bottle-green lake. But under the cold

Breath of the glacier sleep would not come, the moon-light
Etching the Finger. We rose and trod past the feathery
Larch, while the stars went out, and the quiet heather
Flushed, and the skyline pulsed with the surging bloom   80

Of incredible dawn in the Rockies. David spotted
Bighorns across the moraine and sent them leaping
With yodels the ramparts redoubled and rolled to the peaks,
And the peaks to the sun. The ice in the morning thaw

Was a gurgling world of crystal and cold blue chasms,
And seracs that shone like frozen saltgreen waves.
At the base of the Finger we tried once and failed. Then
    David
Edged to the west and discovered the chimney; the last

Hundred feet we fought the rock and shouldered and
    kneed
Our way for an hour and made it. Unroping we formed   90
A cairn on the rotting tip. Then I turned to look north
At the glistening wedge of giant Assiniboine, heedless

Of handhold. And one foot gave. I swayed and shouted.
David turned sharp and reached out his arm and steadied
    me,
Turning again with a grin and his lips ready
To jest. But the strain crumbled his foothold. Without

A gasp he was gone. I froze to the sound of grating
Edge-nails and fingers, the slither of stones, the lone
Second of silence, the nightmare thud. Then only
The wind and the muted beat of unknowing cascades.   100

VIII

Somehow I worked down the fifty impossible feet
To the ledge, calling and getting no answer but echoes
Released in the cirque, and trying not to reflect
What an answer would mean. He lay still, with his lean

Young face upturned and strangely unmarred, but his legs
Splayed beneath him, beside the final drop,
Six hundred feet sheer to the ice. My throat stopped
When I reached him, for he was alive. He opened his gray

Straight eyes and brokenly murmured 'over . . . over'.
And I, feeling beneath him a cruel fang   110
Of the ledge thrust in his back, but not understanding,
Mumbled stupidly, 'Best not to move,' and spoke

Of his pain. But he said, 'I can't move. . . . If only I felt
Some pain.' Then my shame stung the tears to my eyes
As I crouched, and I cursed myself, but he cried,
Louder, 'No, Bobbie! Don't ever blame yourself.

I didn't test my foothold.' He shut the lids
Of his eyes to the stare of the sky, while I moistened his
     lips
From our water flask and tearing my shirt into strips
I swabbed the shredded hands. But the blood slid   120

From his side and stained the stone and the thirsting
     lichens,
And yet I dared not lift him up from the gore
Of the rock. Then he whispered, 'Bob, I want to go over!'
This time I knew what he meant and I grasped for a lie

And said, 'I'll be back here by midnight with ropes
And men from the camp and we'll cradle you out.' But I
     knew
That the day and the night must pass and the cold dews
Of another morning before such men unknowing

The ways of mountains could win to the chimney's top.
And then, how long? And he knew . . . and the hell of
   hours   130
After that, if he lived till we came, roping him out.
But I curled beside him and whispered, 'The bleeding will
   stop.

You can last.' He said only, 'Perhaps. . . . For what? A
   wheelchair,
Bob?' His eyes brightening with fever upbraided me.
I could not look at him more and said, 'Then I'll stay
With you.' But he did not speak, for the clouding fever.

I lay dazed and stared at the long valley,
The glistening hair of a creek on the rug stretched
By the firs, while the sun leaned round and flooded the
   ledge,
The moss, and David still as a broken doll.   140

I hunched to my knees to leave, but he called and his voice
Now was sharpened with fear. 'For Christ's sake push me
   over!
If I could move. . . . Or die. . . .' The sweat ran from his
   forehead.
But only his eyes moved. A hawk was buoying

Blackly its wings over the wrinkled ice.
The purr of a waterfall rose and sank with the wind.
Above us climbed the last joint of the Finger
Beckoning bleakly the wide indifferent sky.

Even then in the sun it grew cold lying there. . . . And I
   knew
He had tested his holds. It was I who had not. . . . I
   looked   150

At the blood on the ledge, and the far valley. I looked
At last in his eyes. He breathed, 'I'd do it for you, Bob.'

IX

I will not remember how nor why I could twist
Up the wind-devilled peak, and down through the
    chimney's empty
Horror, and over the traverse alone. I remember
Only the pounding fear I would stumble on It

When I came to the grave-cold maw of the bergschrund
    . . . reeling
Over the sun-cankered snowbridge, shying the caves
In the névé . . . the fear, and the need to make sure It was
    there
On the ice, the running and falling and running, leaping   160

Of gaping greenthroated crevasses, alone and pursued
By the Finger's lengthening shadow. At last through the
    fanged
And blinding seracs I slid to the milky wrangling
Falls at the glacier's snout, through the rocks piled huge

On the humped moraine, and into the spectral larches,
Alone. By the glooming lake I sank and chilled
My mouth but I could not rest and stumbled still
To the valley, losing my way in the ragged marsh.

I was glad of the mire that covered the stains, on my ripped
Boots, of his blood, but panic was on me, the reek   170
Of the bog, the purple glimmer of toadstools obscene
In the twilight. I staggered clear to a firewaste, tripped

And fell with a shriek on my shoulder. It somehow eased
My heart to know I was hurt, but I did not faint
And I could not stop while over me hung the range
Of the Sawback. In blackness I searched for the trail by the
    creek

And found it . . . My feet squelched a slug and horror
Rose again in my nostrils. I hurled myself
Down the path. In the woods behind some animal yelped.
Then I saw the glimmer of tents and babbled my story.   180

I said that he fell straight to the ice where they found him,
And none but the sun and incurious clouds have lingered
Around the marks of that day on the ledge of the Finger,
That day, the last of my youth, on the last of our
    mountains.

EARLE BIRNEY

On His Blindness

When I consider how my light is spent
Ere half my days, in this dark world and wide,
And that one talent which is death to hide
Lodged with me useless, though my soul more bent
To serve therewith my Maker, and present
My true account, lest He returning chide, —
'Doth God exact day-labour, light denied?'
I fondly ask: — But Patience, to prevent
That murmur, soon replies, 'God doth not need
Either man's work, or His own gifts; who best
Bear His mild yoke, they serve Him best. His state
Is kingly; thousands at His bidding speed
And post o'er land and ocean without rest;
They also serve who only stand and wait.'

JOHN MILTON

112

Hail, Holy Light

FROM *Paradise Lost*, Book III

Hail, holy Light, offspring of Heaven first-born!
Or of th' Eternal coeternal beam
May I express thee unblamed? since God is light,
And never but in unapproached light
Dwelt from eternity, dwelt then in thee,
Bright effluence of bright essence increate!
Or hear'st thou rather pure ethereal stream,
Whose fountain who shall tell? before the Sun,
Before the Heavens, thou wert, and at the voice
Of God, as with a mantle, didst invest   10
The rising world of waters dark and deep,
Won from the void and formless Infinite!
Thee I revisit now with bolder wing,
Escaped the Stygian Pool, though long detained
In that obscure sojourn, while in my flight,
Through utter and through middle darkness borne,
With other notes than to th' Orphean lyre
I sung of Chaos and eternal Night,
Taught by the Heavenly Muse to venture down
The dark descent, and up to reascend,   20
Though hard and rare: thee I revisit safe,
And feel thy sovran vital lamp; but thou
Revisit'st not these eyes, that roll in vain
To find thy piercing ray, and find no dawn;
So thick a drop serene hath quenched their orbs,
Or dim diffusion veiled. Yet not the more
Cease I to wander where the Muses haunt

Clear spring, or shady grove, or sunny hill,
Smit with the love of sacred song: but chief
Thee, Sion, and the flowery brooks beneath,   30
That wash thy hallowed feet, and warbling flow,
Nightly I visit: nor sometimes forget
Those other two equalled with me in fate,
So were I equalled with them in renown,
Blind Thamyris and blind Maeonides,
And Tiresias and Phineus, prophets old:
Then feed on thoughts that voluntary move
Harmonious numbers; as the wakeful bird
Sings darkling, and, in shadiest covert hid,
Tunes her nocturnal note. Thus with the year   40
Seasons return; but not to me returns
Day, or the sweet approach of even or morn,
Or sight of vernal bloom, or summer's rose,
Or flocks, or herds, or human face divine;
But cloud instead and ever-during dark
Surrounds me, from the cheerful ways of men
Cut off, and for the book of knowledge fair,
Presented with a universal blank
Of Nature's works, to me expunged and rased,
And wisdom at one entrance quite shut out.   50
So much the rather thou, Celestial Light,
Shine inward, and the mind through all her powers
Irradiate; there plant eyes; all mist from thence
Purge and disperse, that I may see and tell
Of things invisible to mortal sight.

JOHN MILTON

113
God's Grandeur

The world is charged with the grandeur of God.
It will flame out, like shining from shook foil;
It gathers to a greatness, like the ooze of oil
Crushed. Why do men then now not reck his rod?
Generations have trod, have trod, have trod;
And all is seared with trade; bleared, smeared with toil;
And wears man's smudge and shares man's smell: the soil
Is bare now, nor can foot feel, being shod.
And for all this, nature is never spent;
There lives the dearest freshness deep down things;
And though the last lights off the black West went
Oh, morning, at the brown brink eastward, springs —
Because the Holy Ghost over the bent
World broods with warm breast and with ah! bright wings.

GERARD MANLEY HOPKINS

Hurrahing in Harvest

Summer ends now; now, barbarous in beauty, the stooks
    arise
  Around: up above, what wind-walks! what lovely
  behaviour
  Of silk-sack clouds! has wilder, wilful-wavier
Meal-drift moulded ever and melted across skies?

I walk, I lift up, I lift up heart, eyes,
  Down all that glory in the heavens to glean our Saviour;
  And éyes, heárt, what looks, what lips yet gave you a
Rapturous love's greeting of realer, of rounder replies?

And the azurous hung hills are his world-wielding
    shoulder
  Majestic — as a stallion stalwart, very-violet-sweet! —
These things, these things were here and but the beholder
  Wanting; which two when they once meet,
The heart rears wings bold and bolder
  And hurls for him, O half hurls earth for him off under
  his feet.

GERARD MANLEY HOPKINS

115

Snow

The room was suddenly rich and the great bay-window
    was
Spawning snow and pink roses against it
Soundlessly collateral and incompatible:
World is suddener than we fancy it.

World is crazier and more of it than we think,
Incorrigibly plural. I peel and portion
A tangerine and spit the pips and feel
The drunkenness of things being various.

And the fire flames with a bubbling sound for world
Is more spiteful and gay than one supposes —
On the tongue on the eyes on the ears in the palms of
    one's hands —
There is more than glass between the snow and the huge
    roses.

LOUIS MACNEICE

The Lonely Land

Cedar and jagged fir
uplift sharp barbs
against the gray
and cloud-piled sky;
and in the bay
blown spume and windrift
and thin, bitter spray
snap
at the whirling sky;
and the pine trees   10
lean one way.
A wild duck calls
to her mate,
and the ragged
and passionate tones
stagger and fall,
and recover,
and stagger and fall,
on these stones —
are lost   20
in the lapping of water
on smooth, flat stones.

This is a beauty
of dissonance,
this resonance
of stony strand,
this smoky cry
curled over a black pine
like a broken
and wind-battered branch   30

when the wind
bends the tops of the pines
and curdles the sky
from the north.

This is the beauty
of strength
broken by strength
and still strong.

A. J. M. SMITH

Thoughts from Underground

FROM *The Journals of Susanna Moodie*

When I first reached this country
I hated it
and I hated it more each year:

in summer the light a
violent blur, the heat
thick as a swamp,
the green things fiercely
shoving themselves upwards, the
eyelids bitten by insects.

In winter our teeth were brittle   10
with cold. We fed on squirrels.
At night the house cracked.
In the mornings, we thawed
the bad bread over the stove.

Then we were made successful
and I felt I ought to love
this country.
            I said I loved it
and my mind saw double.

I began to forget myself   20
in the middle
of sentences. Events
were split apart.

I fought. I constructed
desperate paragraphs of praise, everyone
ought to love it because
and set them up at intervals

    due to natural resources, native industry, superior
    penitentiaries
    we will all be rich and powerful   30

flat as highway billboards

    who can doubt it, look how
    fast Belleville is growing

(though it is still no place for an english gentleman)

MARGARET ATWOOD

The Immigrants

FROM *The Journals of Susanna Moodie*

They are allowed to inherit
the sidewalks involved as palmlines, bricks
exhausted and soft, the deep
lawnsmells, orchards whorled
to the land's contours, the inflected weather

only to be told they are too poor
to keep it up, or someone
has noticed and wants to kill them; or the towns
pass laws which declare them obsolete.

I see them coming   10
up from the hold smelling of vomit,
infested, emaciated, their skins grey
with travel; as they step on shore

the old countries recede, become
perfect, thumbnail castles preserved
like gallstones in a glass bottle, the
towns dwindle upon the hillsides
in a light paperweight-clear.

They carry their carpetbags and trunks
with clothes, dishes, the family pictures;   20
they think they will make an order
like the old one, sow miniature orchards,
carve children and flocks out of wood

but always they are too poor, the sky
is flat, the green fruit shrivels
in the prairie sun, wood is for burning;
and if they go back, the towns

in time have crumbled, their tongues
stumble among awkward teeth, their ears
are filled with the sound of breaking glass.   30
I wish I could forget them
and so forget myself:

my mind is a wide pink map
across which move year after year
arrows and dotted lines, further and further,
people in railway cars

their heads stuck out of the windows
at stations, drinking milk or singing,
their features hidden with beards or shawls
day and night riding across an ocean of unknown   40
land to an unknown land.

MARGARET ATWOOD

Autobiographical

Out of the ghetto streets where a Jewboy
Dreamed pavement into pleasant Bible-land,
Out of the Yiddish slums where childhood met
The friendly beard, the loutish Sabbath-goy,
Or followed, proud, the Torah-escorting band,
Out of the jargoning city I regret,
Rise memories, like sparrows rising from
The gutter-scattered oats,
Like sadness sweet of synagogal hum,
Like Hebrew violins   10
Sobbing delight upon their Eastern notes.

Again they ring their little bells, those doors
Deemed by the tender-year'd, magnificent:
Old Ashkenazi's cellar, sharp with spice;
The widows' double-parloured candy-stores
And nuggets sweet bought for one sweaty cent;
The warm fresh-smelling bakery, its pies,
Its cakes, its navel'd bellies of black bread;
The lintels candy-poled
Of barber-shop, bright-bottled, green, blue, red;   20
And fruit-stall piled, exotic,
And the big synagogue door, with letters of gold.

Again my kindergarten home is full —
Saturday night — with kin and compatriot:
My brothers playing Russian card-games; my
Mirroring sisters looking beautiful,
Humming the evening's imminent fox-trot;
My uncle Mayer, of blessed memory,

[196]

Still murmuring maariv, counting holy words;
And the two strangers, come   30
Fiery from Volhynia's murderous hordes —
The cards and humming stop.
And I too swear revenge for that pogrom.

Occasions dear: the four-legged aleph named
And angel pennies dropping on my book;
The rabbi patting a coming scholar-head;
My mother, blessing candles, Sabbath-flamed,
Queenly in her Warsovian perruque;
My father pickabacking me to bed
To tell tall tales about the Baal Shem Tov —   40
Letting me curl his beard.
Oh memory of unsurpassing love,
Love leading a brave child
Through childhood's ogred corridors, unfear'd!

The week in the country at my brother's — (May
He own fat cattle in the fields of heaven!)
Its picking of strawberries from grassy ditch,
Its odour of dogrose and of yellowing hay —
Dusty, adventurous, sunny days, all seven! —
Still follow me, still warm me, still are rich   50
With the cow-tinkling peace of pastureland.
The meadow'd memory
Is sodded with its clover, and is spanned
By that same pillow'd sky
A boy on his back one day watched enviously.

And paved again the street: the shouting boys,
Oblivious of mothers on the stoops,
Playing the robust robbers and police,
The corncob battle — all high-spirited noise

Competitive among the lot-drawn groups. 60
Another day, of shaken apple trees
In the rich suburbs, and a furious dog,
And guilty boys in flight;
Hazlenut games, and games in the synagogue —
The burrs, the Haman rattle,
The Torah dance on Simchas Torah night.

Immortal days of the picture calendar
Dear to me always with the virgin joy
Of the first flowering of senses five,
Discovering birds, or textures, or a star, 70
Or tastes sweet, sour, acid, those that cloy;
And perfumes. Never was I more alive.
All days thereafter are a dying off,
A wandering away
From home and the familiar. The years doff
Their innocence.
No other day is ever like that day.

I am no old man fatuously intent
On memoirs, but in memory I seek
The strength and vividness of nonage days, 80
Not tranquil recollection of event.
It is a fabled city that I seek;
It stands in Space's vapours and Time's haze;
Thence comes my sadness in remembered joy
Constrictive of the throat;
Thence do I hear, as heard by a Jewboy,
The Hebrew violins,
Delighting in the sobbed Oriental note.

ABRAHAM KLEIN

This Landscape, These People

I

My eighth spring in England I walk among
   the silver birches of Putney Heath,
    stepping over twigs and stones: being stranger,
    I see but do not touch: only the earth
    permits an attachment. I do not wish
to be seen, and move, eyes at my sides, like a fish.

And do they notice me, I wonder, these
   Englishmen strolling with stiff country strides?
    I lean against a tree, my eyes are knots
    in its bark, my skin the wrinkles in its sides.   10
    I leap hedges, duck under chestnut boughs,
and through the black clay let my swift heels trail like
    ploughs.

A child at a museum, England for me
   is an exhibit within a glass case.
    The country, like an antique chair, has a rope
    across it. I may not sit, only pace
    its frontiers. I slip through ponds, jump ditches,
through galleries of ferns see England in pictures.

II

My seventeen years in India I swam
   along the silver beaches of Bombay,   20
    pulled coconuts from the sky, and tramped
    red horizons with the swagger and sway
    of Romantic youth; with the impudence
of a native tongue, I cried for independence.

A troupe came to town, marched through villages;
   began with two tight-rope walkers, eyes gay
   and bamboos and rope on their bare shoulders;
   a snake charmer joined them, beard long and grey,
   baskets of cobras on his turbaned head;
through villages marched: children, beating on drums, led   30

them from village to village, and jugglers
   joined them and swallowers of swords, eaters
   of fire brandishing flames through the thick air,
   jesters with tongues obscene as crows', creatures
   of the earth: stray dogs, lean jackals, a cow;
stamping, shouting, entertaining, make a row

from village to village they marched to town:
   conjurers to bake bread out of earth, poets
   to recite epics at night. The troupe, grown
   into a nation, halted, squirmed: the sets   40
   for its act, though improvised, were re-cast
from the frames of an antique, slow-moving, dead past.

India halted: as suddenly as a dog,
   barking, hangs out his tongue, stifles his cry.
   An epic turned into a monologue
   of death. The rope lay stiff across the country;
   all fires were eaten, swallowed were all the swords;
the horizons paled, then thickened, blackened with crows.

Born to this continent, all was mine
   to pluck and taste: pomegranates to purple   50
   my tongue and chillies to burn my mouth. Stones
   were there to kick. This landscape, these people —
   bound by the rope, consumed by their fire.
Born here, among these people, I was a stranger.

III

This landscape, these people! Silver birches
    with polished trunks chalked around a chestnut.
    All is fall-of-night still. No thrush reaches
    into the earth for worms, nor pulls at the root
    of a crocus. Dogs have led their masters home.
I stroll, head bowed, hearing only the sound of loam   60

at my heel's touch. Now I am intimate
    with England; we meet, secret as lovers.
    I pluck leaves and speak into the air's mouth;
    as a woman's hair, I deck with flowers
    the willow's branches; I sit by the pond,
my eyes are stars in its stillness; as with a wand,

I stir the water with a finger until
    it tosses waves, until countries appear
    from its dark bed: the road from Putney Hill
    runs across oceans into the harbour   70
    of Bombay. To this country I have come.
Stranger or an inhabitant, this is my home.

ZULFIKAR GHOSE

Bans O' Killing

So yuh a de man, me hear bout!
Ah yuh dem sey dah-teck
Whole heap o' English oat sey dat
Yuh gwine kill dialect!

Meck me get it straight Mass Charlie
For me noh quite undastan,
Yuh gwine kill all English dialect
Or jus Jamaica one?

Ef yuh dah-equal up wid English
Language, den wha meck   10
Yuh gwine go feel inferior, wen
It come to dialect?

Ef yuh kean sing 'Linstead Market'
An 'Wata come a me y'eye',
Yuh wi haffi tap sing 'Auld lang syne'
An 'Comin thru de rye'.

Dah language weh yuh proud o',
Weh yuh honour and respeck,
Po' Mass Charlie! Yuh noh know sey
Dat it spring from dialect!   20

Dat dem start fe try tun language,
From de fourteen century,
Five hundred years gawn an dem got
More dialect dan we!

Yuh wi haffe kill de Lancashire
De Yorkshire, de Cockney
De broad Scotch an de Irish brogue
Before yuh start kill me!

Yuh wi haffe get de Oxford book   30
O'English verse, an tear
Out Chaucer, Burns, Lady Grizelle
An plenty o' Shakespeare!

Wen yuh done kill 'wit' an 'humour'
Wen yuh kill 'Variety'
Yuh wi haffe fine a way fe kill
Originality!

An mine how yuh dah-read dem English
Book deh pon yuh shelf
For ef yuh drop a 'h' yuh mighta
Haffe kill yuhself.

LOUISE BENNETT

What Do I Remember of the Evacuation?

What do I remember of the evacuation?
I remember my father telling Tim and me
About the mountains and the train
And the excitement of going on a trip.
What do I remember of the evacuation?
I remember my mother wrapping
A blanket around me and my
Pretending to fall asleep so she would be happy
Though I was so excited I couldn't sleep
(I hear there were people herded   10
Into the Hastings Park like cattle.
Families were made to move in two hours
Abandoning everything, leaving pets
And possessions at gun point.
I hear families were broken up
Men were forced to work. I heard
It whispered late at night
That there was suffering) and
I missed my dolls.
What do I remember of the evacuation?   20
I remember Miss Foster and Miss Tucker
Who still live in Vancouver
And who did what they could
And loved the children and who gave me
A puzzle to play with on the train.
And I remember the mountains and I was
Six years old and I swear I saw a giant
Gulliver of Gulliver's Travels scanning the horizon
And when I told my mother she believed it too

And I remember how careful my parents were 30
Not to bruise us with bitterness
And I remember the puzzle of Lorraine Life
Who said 'Don't insult me' when I
Proudly wrote my name in Japanese
And Tim flew the Union Jack
When the war was over but Lorraine
And her friends spat on us anyway
And I prayed to the God who loves
All the children in his sight
That I might be white.

JOY KOGAWA

123

Going to Norway

I asked my parents,
'Have you ever thought
of going to Norway?
You are Andersons
and deserve to know
Norway, where we all began.
Do you not wonder
how things are in Norway?
I know that I wonder.'
And my parents said,   10
                              'Yes,
we shall go to Norway,
we are Andersons
and want to see where
our people began.
We are growing old:
we must go now.'
                         Yet they stayed
on the dock, staring
at the water   20
as ship after ship
sailed toward the north,
toward Norway.
                    So I said
to my parents, 'Now,
you must leave now.
These are the boats
that are leaving for Norway.

It is not long
or far.'   30
        Then my parents said,
'Yes, we want to see
Norway: we are Andersons.
But it is so far.'
                They stayed
where they were, watching
the boats leave for Norway
and trying to picture it,
even testing a few words
of that dear language   40
on their tongues
                — but standing
still, never moving,
never climbing aboard,
though I kept pleading,
'Please, now, you must leave now
if you want to see Norway.'
'Norway?' they murmured,
'Norway? Ah, where is that?'
They stood very still,   50
grayness crept through their hair;
it frightened me to see them
growing so old,
for I had not thought
such a thing possible.
At last I said,
                'I must go
to Norway. I am
an Anderson
and want to know   60
where all of us began.

I must go now.'
                    They stood
on the dock, waving
out at the water, and I
waved back over the water
which darkened between us
with distance and tears.

JACK ANDERSON

124

The Lake Isle of Innisfree

I will arise and go now, and go to Innisfree,
And a small cabin build there, of clay and wattles made:
Nine bean-rows will I have there, a hive for the honeybee,
And live alone in the bee-loud glade.

And I shall have some peace there, for peace comes
        dropping slow,
Dropping from the veils of the morning to where the
        cricket sings;
There midnight's all a glimmer, and noon a purple glow,
And evening full of the linnet's wings.

I will arise and go now, for always night and day
I hear lake water lapping with low sounds by the shore;
While I stand on the roadway, or on the pavements grey,
I hear it in the deep heart's core.

WILLIAM BUTLER YEATS

Home Thoughts from Abroad

Oh, to be in England
Now that April's there,
And whoever wakes in England
Sees, some morning, unaware,
That the lowest boughs and the brushwood sheaf
Round the elm-tree bole are in tiny leaf,
While the chaffinch sings on the orchard bough
In England — now!
And after April, when May follows,
And the whitethroat builds, and all the swallows!
Hark, where my blossomed pear-tree in the hedge
Leans to the field and scatters on the clover
Blossoms and dewdrops — at the bent spray's edge —
That's the wise thrush; he sings each song twice over,
Lest you should think he never could recapture
The first fine careless rapture!
And though the fields look rough with hoary dew,
All will be gay when noontide wakes anew
The buttercups, the little children's dower
— Far brighter than this gaudy melon-flower.

ROBERT BROWNING

126

The Farm

Tips of celery,
clouds of

grass — one
day I'll go away.

ROBERT CREELEY

The Railway Children

When we climbed the slopes of the cutting
We were eye-level with the white cups
Of the telegraph poles and the sizzling wires.

Like lovely freehand they curved for miles
East and miles west beyond us, sagging
Under their burden of swallows.

We were small and thought we knew nothing
Worth knowing. We thought words travelled the wires
In the shiny pouches of raindrops,

Each one seeded full with the light
Of the sky, the gleam of the lines, and ourselves
So infinitesimally scaled

We could stream through the eye of a needle.

SEAMUS HEANEY

128

The White Horse

The youth walks up to the white horse, to put its halter on
and the horse looks at him in silence.
They are so silent they are in another world.

D. H. LAWRENCE

129

The Flower-Fed Buffaloes

The flower-fed buffaloes of the spring
In the days of long ago,
Ranged where the locomotives sing
And the prairie flowers lie low: —
The tossing, blooming, perfumed grass
Is swept away by the wheat,
Wheels and wheels and wheels spin by
In the spring that still is sweet.
But the flower-fed buffaloes of the spring
Left us, long ago.
They gore no more, they bellow no more,
They trundle around the hills no more: —
With the Blackfeet, lying low,
With the Pawnees, lying low,
Lying low.

VACHEL LINDSAY

Hawk Roosting

I sit in the top of the wood, my eyes closed.
Inaction, no falsifying dream
Between my hooked head and hooked feet:
Or in sleep rehearse perfect kills and eat.

The convenience of the high trees!
The air's buoyancy and the sun's ray
Are of advantage to me;
And the earth's face upward for my inspection.

My feet are locked upon the rough bark.
It took the whole of Creation
To produce my foot, my each feather:
Now I hold Creation in my foot

Or fly up, and revolve it all slowly —
I kill where I please because it is all mine.
There is no sophistry in my body:
My manners are tearing off heads —

The allotment of death.
For the one path of my flight is direct
Through the bones of the living.
No arguments assert my right:

The sun is behind me.
Nothing has changed since I began.
My eye has permitted no change.
I am going to keep things like this.

TED HUGHES

Cats

Cats, no less liquid than their shadows,
Offer no angles to the wind,
They slip, diminished, neat, through loopholes
Less than themselves; will not be pinned

To rules or routes for journeys; counter-
Attack with non-resistance; twist
Enticing through the curving fingers
And leave an angered, empty fist.

They wait, obsequious as darkness,
Quick to retire, quick to return;
Admit no aims or ethics; flatter
With reservations; will not learn

To answer to their names; are seldom
Truly owned till shot and skinned.
Cats, no less liquid than their shadows,
Offer no angles to the wind.

A. S. J. TESSIMOND

The Prize Cat

Pure blood domestic, guaranteed,
Soft-mannered, musical in purr,
The ribbon had declared the breed,
Gentility was in the fur.

Such feline culture in the gads,
No anger ever arched her back —
What distance since those velvet pads
Departed from the leopard's track!

And when I mused how Time had thinned
The jungle strains within the cells,
How human hands had disciplined
Those prowling optic parallels;

I saw the generations pass
Along the reflex of a spring,
A bird had rustled in the grass,
The tab had caught it on the wing;

Behind the leap so furtive-wild
Was such ignition in the gleam,
I thought an Abyssinian child
Had cried out in the whitethroat's scream.

E. J. PRATT

133
Birds, Bags, Bears, and Buns

The common cormorant or shag
Lays eggs inside a paper bag.
The reason you will see, no doubt,
It is to keep the lightning out,
But what these unobservant birds
Have never noticed is that herds
Of wandering bears may come with buns
And steal the bags to hold the crumbs.

ANONYMOUS

134
Epigram

*(Engraved on the Collar of a dog which
I gave to His Royal Highness)*

I am His Highness' dog at Kew;
Pray tell me, sir, whose dog are you?

ALEXANDER POPE

135

The Proper Study

FROM *An Essay on Man*

Know then thyself, presume not God to scan,
The proper study of Mankind is Man.
Plac'd on this isthmus of a middle state,
A Being darkly wise, and rudely great:
With too much knowledge for the Sceptic side,
With too much weakness for the Stoic's pride,
He hangs between; in doubt to act, or rest;
In doubt to deem himself a God, or Beast;
In doubt his Mind or Body to prefer;
Born but to die, and reas'ning but to err;   10
Alike in ignorance, his reason such,
Whether he thinks too little, or too much:
Chaos of Thought and Passion, all confus'd;
Still by himself abus'd, or disabus'd;
Created half to rise, and half to fall;
Great Lord of all things, yet a prey to all;
Sole judge of Truth, in endless Error hurl'd:
The glory, jest, and riddle of the world!
    Go, wond'rous creature! mount where Science guides,
Go, measure earth, weigh air, and state the tides;   20
Instruct the planets in what orbs to run,
Correct old Time, and regulate the Sun;
Go, soar with Plato to th' empyreal sphere,
To the first good, first perfect, and first fair;
Or tread the mazy round his follow'rs trod,
And quitting sense call imitating God;

As Eastern priests in giddy circles run,
And turn their heads to imitate the Sun.
Go, teach Eternal Wisdom how to rule —
Then drop into thyself, and be a fool!

ALEXANDER POPE

136

Zimri

FROM *Absalom and Achitophel*

In the first rank of these did Zimri stand,
A man so various that he seemed to be
Not one, but all mankind's epitome:
Stiff in opinions, always in the wrong,
Was everything by starts and nothing long;
But in the course of one revolving moon
Was chymist, fiddler, statesman, and buffoon;
Then all for women, painting, rhyming, drinking,
Besides ten thousand freaks that died in thinking.
Blest madman, who could every hour employ
With something new to wish or to enjoy!
Railing and praising were his usual themes,
And both, to show his judgment, in extremes:
So over violent or over civil
That every man with him was God or Devil.
In squandering wealth was his peculiar art;
Nothing went unrewarded but desert.
Beggared by fools whom still he found too late,
He had his jest, and they had his estate.

JOHN DRYDEN

137

The Wif of Bathe

A good wif° was ther of bisidè Bathe,   woman
But she was som-del° deef, and that was scathe.°   somewhat   a p
Of clooth-makyng she haddè swich an haunt°   such a skill
She passèd hem° of Ypres and of Gaunt.   surpassed them
In al the parisshe wif ne was ther noon
That to the offrynge bifore hire sholde goon;°   go
And if ther dide, certeyn so wrooth was she,
That she was out of allè charitee.
Hircoverchiefs° ful fyne weren of ground,° —   head-coverings / texture
I dorstè° swere they weyèden ten pound, —   would dare
That on a Sonday weren upon hir heed.
Hirhosen° weren of fyn scarlet° reed,   leggings   rich cl
Ful streite y-teyd,° and shoes ful moyste and   tightly tied
    newe.
Boold was hir face, and fair, and reed of hewe.
She was a worthy womman al hir lyve.   15
Housbondes at chirchè dore she haddè fyve,
Withouten° oother compaignye in youthe, —   Not to mention
But ther-of nedeth nat to speke as nowthe.°   now
And thries hadde she been at Jerusalem;
She haddè passèd many a straungè° strem;   foreign
At Rome she haddè been, and at Boloigne,
In Galice at Seint Jame, and at Coloigne,
She koude° muchel of wandrynge by the weye.   knew
Gat-tothèd was she, soothly° for to seye.   truly

Upon an amblere esily she sat,   25
Y-wympled wel, and on hir heed an hat
As brood as is a bokeler° or a targe;°   buckler   shield
A foot-mantel° aboute hir hipès large,   outer skirt
And on hire feet a paire of sporès° sharpe.   spurs
In felaweshipe wel koude she laughe and carpe;°   talk
Of remedies of love she knew perchaunce,
For she koude° of that art the oldè daunce!   knew

GEOFFREY CHAUCER

138

Mrs Reece Laughs

Laughter, with us, is no great undertaking,
A sudden wave that breaks and dies in breaking.
Laughter with Mrs Reece is much less simple:
It germinates, it spreads, dimple by dimple,
From small beginnings, things of easy girth,
To formidable redundancies of mirth.

Clusters of subterranean chuckles rise
And presently the circles of her eyes
Close into slits and all the woman heaves
As a great elm with all its mounds of leaves
Wallows before the storm. From hidden sources
A mustering of blind volcanic forces
Takes her and shakes her till she sobs and gapes.
Then all that load of bottled mirth escapes
In one wild crow, a lifting of huge hands,
And creaking stays, a visage that expands
In scarlet ridge and furrow. Thence collapse,
A hanging head, a feeble hand that flaps
An apron-end to stir an air and waft
A steaming face. And Mrs Reece has laughed.

MARTIN ARMSTRONG

139
Silence

My father used to say,
'Superior people never make long visits,
have to be shown Longfellow's grave
or the glass flowers at Harvard.
Self-reliant like the cat —
that takes its prey to privacy,
the mouse's limp tail hanging like a shoelace from its
    mouth —
they sometimes enjoy solitude,
and can be robbed of speech
by speech which has delighted them.
The deepest feeling always shows itself in silence;
not in silence, but restraint.'
Nor was he insincere in saying, 'Make my house your inn.'
Inns are not residences.

MARIANNE MOORE

Talk

The shops, the streets are full of old men
who can't think of a thing to say anymore.
Sometimes, looking at a girl, it
almost occurs to them, but they can't make it out,
they go pawing toward it through the fog.

The young men are still jostling shoulders
as they walk along, tussling at one another with words.
They're excited by talk, they can still see the danger.

The old women, thrifty with words,
haggling for oranges, their mouths   10
take bites out of the air. They know the value of oranges.
They had to learn everything
on their own.

The young women are the worst off, no one has bothered
to show them things.
You can see their minds on their faces,
they are like little lakes before a storm.
They don't know it's confusion that makes them sad.
It's lucky in a way though, because the young men take
a look of confusion for inscrutability, and this   20
excites them and makes them want to own
this face they don't understand,
something to be tinkered with at their leisure.

ROO BORSON

1958

was a fabulous year
when you parked in the lot at the lakeshore
next to the Palais Royale
and necked for hours in those souped up cars,
you
savages of the Fifties, your terrible perfect
bodies
looped around the gearshift, the wheel, along the
dashboard, and the smell, the smell
of his black leather jacket, and the smell,   10
the smell
of the lake and the fish and the United States —

O,
those guys spoke in crazy cryptic monosyllables, and
those girls said nothing and were mean and cracked gum
and looked you up and down like you were *nowhere*,
them in their
black batwing sweaters and skirts with slits
and little black low-heeled shoes and smoking
Black Cat corktips because the package   20
looked mysterious, and
some girls wore crinolines and socks
folded over at least three times
and Peter Pan collars with plastic roses
holding them together —

Someone was always the Queen of the School and
she taught you how to use a lipstick *brush*, not
a messy old tube; she
was Xenobia, she
was Cat Woman, she   30
was so tough she made you faint, who went
like you
to Western Technical High School where
the boys learned shop and the girls
sewed shaky seams in dresses they would never wear,
where
everyone had ducktails and smelled of Vitalis
and you cracked your gum, cracked your gum
and died inside
and looked the whole world up and down.

GWENDOLYN MACEWEN

We Shall Not Escape Hell

We shall not escape Hell, my passionate
sisters, we shall drink black resins —
we who sang our praises to the Lord
with every one of our sinews, even the finest,

we did not lean over cradles or
spinning wheels at night, and now we are
carried off by an unsteady boat
under the skirts of a sleeveless cloak,

we dressed every morning in
fine Chinese silk, and we would
sing our paradisal songs at
the fire of the robbers' camp,

slovenly needlewomen (all
our sewing came apart), dancers,
players upon pipes: we have been
the queens of the whole world!

first scarcely covered by rags,
then with constellations in our hair, in
gaol and at feasts we have
bartered away heaven,

in starry nights, in the apple
orchards of Paradise.
— Gentle girls, my beloved sisters,
we shall certainly find ourselves in Hell!

MARINA TSVETAYEVA
Translated by ELAINE FEINSTEIN

143

Suzanne Takes You Down

Suzanne takes you down
to her place near the river,
you can hear the boats go by
you can stay the night beside her.
And you know that she's half crazy
but that's why you want to be there
and she feeds you tea and oranges
that come all the way from China.
Just when you mean to tell her
that you have no gifts to give her,   10
she gets you on her wave-length
and she lets the river answer
that you've always been her lover.
   And you want to travel with her,
   you want to travel blind
   and you know that she can trust you
   because you've touched her perfect body
   with your mind.

Jesus was a sailor
when he walked upon the water   20
and he spent a long time watching
from a lonely wooden tower
and when he knew for certain
only drowning men could see him
he said All men will be sailors then
until the sea shall free them,
but he himself was broken
long before the sky would open,

forsaken, almost human,
he sank beneath your wisdom like a stone.   30
   And you want to travel with him,
   you want to travel blind
   and you think maybe you'll trust him
   because he touched your perfect body
   with his mind.

Suzanne takes your hand
and she leads you to the river,
she is wearing rags and feathers
from Salvation Army counters.
The sun pours down like honey   40
on our lady of the harbor
as she shows you where to look
among the garbage and the flowers,
there are heroes in the seaweed
there are children in the morning,
they are leaning out for love
they will lean that way forever
while Suzanne she holds the mirror.
   And you want to travel with her
   and you want to travel blind   50
   and you're sure that she can find you
   because she's touched her perfect body
   with her mind.

LEONARD COHEN

144
Passing By

There is a Lady sweet and kind,
Was never face so pleased my mind;
I did but see her passing by,
And yet I love her till I die.

Her gesture, motion, and her smiles,
Her wit, her voice, my heart beguiles,
Beguiles my heart, I know not why,
And yet I love her till I die.

Cupid is wingèd and doth range,
Her country so my love doth change:
But change she earth, or change she sky,
Yet will I love her till I die.

ANONYMOUS

145

A Sweet Disorder

A sweet disorder in the dress
Kindles in clothes a wantonness: —
A lawn about the shoulders thrown
Into a fine distraction:
An erring lace, which here and there
Enthrals the crimson stomacher:
A cuff neglectful, and thereby
Ribbands to flow confusedly:
A winning wave, deserving note,
In the tempestuous petticoat:
A careless shoe-string, in whose tie
I see a wild civility:
Do more bewitch me, than when art
Is too precise in every part.

ROBERT HERRICK

146

Go, Lovely Rose

Go, lovely Rose —
Tell her that wastes her time and me,
That now she knows,
When I resemble her to thee,
How sweet and fair she seems to be.

Tell her that's young,
And shuns to have her graces spied,
That hadst thou sprung
In deserts where no men abide,
Thou must have uncommended died.

Small is the worth
Of beauty from the light retired:
Bid her come forth,
Suffer herself to be desired,
And not blush so to be admired.

Then die — that she
The common fate of all things rare
May read in thee;
How small a part of time they share
That are so wondrous sweet and fair!

EDMUND WALLER

147

To His Coy Mistress

Had we but world enough, and time,
This coyness, Lady, were no crime.
We would sit down, and think which way
To walk, and pass our long love's day.
Thou by the Indian Ganges' side
Shouldst rubies find; I by the tide
Of Humber would complain. I would
Love you ten years before the Flood;
And you should, if you please, refuse
Till the conversion of the Jews.   10
My vegetable love should grow
Vaster than empires, and more slow.
An hundred years should go to praise
Thine eyes, and on thy forehead gaze;
Two hundred to adore each breast;
But thirty thousand to the rest:
An age, at least, to every part,
And the last age should show your heart.
For, Lady, you deserve this state;
Nor would I love at lower rate.   20
   But, at my back, I always hear
Time's winged chariot hurrying near:
And yonder, all before us lie
Deserts of vast eternity.
Thy beauty shall no more be found;
Nor, in the marble vault, shall sound
My echoing song. Then worms shall try
That long preserved virginity:

And your quaint honour turn to dust;
And into ashes all my lust.   30
The grave's a fine and private place,
But none, I think, do there embrace.

  Now, therefore, while the youthful hue
Sits on thy skin like morning dew,
And while thy willing soul transpires
At every pore with instant fires,
Now let us sport us while we may;
And now, like amorous birds of prey,
Rather at once our time devour,
Than languish in his slow-chapt power.   40
Let us roll all our strength, and all
Our sweetness, up into one ball;
And tear our pleasures, with rough strife,
Thorough the iron gates of life.

  Thus, though we cannot make our sun
Stand still, yet we will make him run.

ANDREW MARVELL

148
She Walks in Beauty

She walks in beauty, like the night
  Of cloudless climes and starry skies;
And all that's best of dark and bright
  Meet in her aspect and her eyes:
Thus mellow'd to that tender light
  Which heaven to gaudy day denies.

One shade the more, one ray the less,
  Had half impair'd the nameless grace
Which waves in every raven tress,
  Or softly lightens o'er her face;
Where thoughts serenely sweet express
  How pure, how dear their dwelling-place.

And on that cheek and o'er that brow
  So soft, so calm, yet eloquent,
The smiles that win, the tints that glow
  But tell of days in goodness spent,
A mind at peace with all below,
  A heart whose love is innocent.

LORD BYRON

149

Somewhere I Have Never Travelled, Gladly Beyond

somewhere i have never travelled, gladly beyond
any experience, your eyes have their silence:
in your most frail gesture are things which enclose me,
or which i cannot touch because they are too near

your slightest look easily will unclose me
though i have closed myself as fingers,
you open always petal by petal myself as Spring opens
(touching skilfully, mysteriously) her first rose

or if your wish be to close me, i and
my life will shut very beautifully, suddenly,
as when the heart of this flower imagines
the snow carefully everywhere descending;

nothing which we are to perceive in this world equals
the power of your intense fragility: whose texture
compels me with the colour of its countries,
rendering death and forever with each breathing

(i do not know what it is about you that closes
and opens; only something in me understands
the voice of your eyes is deeper than all roses)
nobody, not even the rain, has such small hands

E. E. CUMMINGS

150

Kubla Khan

In Xanadu did Kubla Khan
A stately pleasure-dome decree:
Where Alph, the sacred river, ran
Through caverns measureless to man
   Down to a sunless sea.
So twice five miles of fertile ground
With walls and towers were girdled round:
And there were gardens bright with sinuous rills
Where blossomed many an incense-bearing tree;
And here were forests ancient as the hills,   10
Enfolding sunny spots of greenery.

But oh! that deep romantic chasm which slanted
Down the green hill athwart a cedarn cover!
A savage place! as holy and enchanted
As e'er beneath a waning moon was haunted
By woman wailing for her demon-lover!
And from this chasm, with ceaseless turmoil seething,
As if this earth in fast thick pants were breathing,
A mighty fountain momently was forced:
Amid whose swift half-intermitted burst   20
Huge fragments vaulted like rebounding hail,
Or chaffy grain beneath the thresher's flail:

And 'mid these dancing rocks at once and ever
It flung up momently the sacred river.
Five miles meandering with a mazy motion
Through wood and dale the sacred river ran,
Then reached the caverns measureless to man,

And sank in tumult to a lifeless ocean:
And 'mid this tumult Kubla heard from far
Ancestral voices prophesying war!   30

    The shadow of the dome of pleasure
    Floated midway on the waves;
    Where was heard the mingled measure
    From the fountain and the caves.
It was a miracle of rare device,
A sunny pleasure-dome with caves of ice!

    A damsel with a dulcimer
    In a vision once I saw:
    It was an Abyssinian maid,
    And on her dulcimer she played,   40
    Singing of Mount Abora.
    Could I revive within me
    Her symphony and song,
    To such a deep delight 'twould win me,
That with music loud and long,
I would build that dome in air,
That sunny dome! those caves of ice!
And all who heard should see them there,
And all should cry, Beware! Beware!
His flashing eyes, his floating hair!   50
Weave a circle round him thrice,
And close your eyes with holy dread,
For he on honey-dew hath fed,
And drunk the milk of Paradise.

                              SAMUEL TAYLOR COLERIDGE

151

The Inferno

FROM *The Divine Comedy*
CANTO THIRD

I AM THE WAY INTO THE CITY OF WOE.
I AM THE WAY TO A FORSAKEN PEOPLE.
I AM THE WAY INTO ETERNAL SORROW.

SACRED JUSTICE MOVED MY ARCHITECT.
I WAS RAISED HERE BY DIVINE OMNIPOTENCE,
PRIMORDIAL LOVE AND ULTIMATE INTELLECT.

ONLY THOSE ELEMENTS TIME CANNOT WEAR
WERE MADE BEFORE ME, AND BEYOND TIME I STAND.
ABANDON ALL HOPE YE WHO ENTER HERE.

These mysteries I read cut into stone   10
   above a gate. And turning I said: 'Master,
   what is the meaning of this harsh inscription?'

And he then as initiate to novice·
   'Here must you put by all division of spirit
   and gather your soul against all cowardice.

This is the place I told you to expect.
   Here you shall pass among the fallen people,
   souls who have lost the good of intellect.'

So saying, he put forth his hand to me,
   and with a gentle and encouraging smile   20
   he led me through the gate of mystery.

Here sighs and cries and wails coiled and recoiled
  on the starless air, spilling my soul to tears.
  A confusion of tongues and monstrous accents toiled

in pain and anger. Voices hoarse and shrill
  and sounds of blows, all intermingled, raised
  tumult and pandemonium that still

whirls on the air forever dirty with it
  as if a whirlwind sucked at sand. And I,
  holding my head in horror, cried: 'Sweet Spirit,   30

what souls are these who run through this black haze?'
  And he to me: 'These are the nearly soulless
  whose lives concluded neither blame nor praise.

They are mixed here with that despicable corps
  of angels who were neither for God nor Satan,
  but only for themselves. The High Creator

scourged them from Heaven for its perfect beauty,
  and Hell will not receive them since the wicked
  might feel some glory over them.' And I:

'Master, what gnaws at them so hideously   40
  their lamentation stuns the very air?'
  'They have no hope of death,' he answered me,

'and in their blind and unattaining state
  their miserable lives have sunk so low
  that they must envy every other fate.

No word of them survives their living season.
  Mercy and Justice deny them even a name.
  Let us not speak of them: look, and pass on.'

I saw a banner there upon the mist.
Circling and circling, it seemed to scorn all pause.   50
So it ran on, and still behind it pressed

a never-ending rout of souls in pain.
I had not thought death had undone so many
as passed before me in that mournful train.

And some I knew among them; last of all
I recognized the shadow of that soul
who, in his cowardice, made the Great Denial.

At once I understood for certain: these
were of that retrograde and faithless crew
hateful to God and to His enemies.   60

These wretches never born and never dead
ran naked in a swarm of wasps and hornets
that goaded them the more the more they fled,

and made their faces stream with bloody gouts
of pus and tears that dribbled to their feet
to be swallowed there by loathsome worms and maggots.

Then looking onward I made out a throng
assembled on the beach of a wide river,
whereupon I turned to him: 'Master, I long

to know what souls these are, and what strange usage   70
makes them as eager to cross as they seem to be
in this infected light.' At which the Sage:

[241]

'All this shall be made known to you when we stand
   on the joyless beach of Acheron.' And I
   cast down my eyes, sensing a reprimand

in what he said, and so walked at his side
   in silence and ashamed until we came
   through the dead cavern to that sunless tide.

There, steering toward us in an ancient ferry
   came an old man with a white bush of hair,   80
   bellowing: 'Woe to you depraved souls! Bury

here and forever all hope of Paradise:
   I come to lead you to the other shore,
   into eternal dark, into fire and ice.

And you who are living yet, I say begone
   from these who are dead.' But when he saw me stand
   against his violence he began again:

'By other windings and by other steerage
   shall you cross to that other shore. Not here! Not here!
   A lighter craft than mine must give you passage.'   90

And my Guide to him: 'Charon, bite back your spleen:
   this has been willed where what is willed must be,
   and is not yours to ask what it may mean.'

The steersman of that marsh of ruined souls,
   who wore a wheel of flame around each eye,
   stifled the rage that shook his woolly jowls.

But those unmanned and naked spirits there
   turned pale with fear and their teeth began to chatter
   at the sound of his crude bellow. In despair

they blasphemed God, their parents, their time on earth,   100
   the race of Adam, and the day and the hour
   and the place and the seed and the womb that gave them
      birth.

But all together they drew to that grim shore
   where all must come who lose the fear of God.
   Weeping and cursing they come for evermore,

and demon Charon with eyes like burning coals
   herds them in, and with a whistling oar
   flails on the stragglers to his wake of souls.

As leaves in autumn loosen and stream down
   until the branch stands bare above its tatters   110
   spread on the rustling ground, so one by one

the evil seed of Adam in its Fall
   cast themselves, at his signal, from the shore
   and streamed away like birds who hear their call.

So they are gone over that shadowy water,
   and always before they reach the other shore
   a new noise stirs on this, and new throngs gather.

'My son,' the courteous Master said to me,
   'all who die in the shadow of God's wrath
   converge to this from every clime and country.   120

And all pass over eagerly, for here
   Divine Justice transforms and spurs them so
   their dread turns wish: they yearn for what they fear.

No soul in Grace comes ever to this crossing;
   therefore if Charon rages at your presence
   you will understand the reason for his cursing.'

When he had spoken, all the twilight country
   shook so violently, the terror of it
   bathes me with sweat even in memory:

the tear-soaked ground gave out a sigh of wind   130
   that spewed itself in flame on a red sky,
   and all my shattered senses left me. Blind,

like one whom sleep comes over in a swoon,
I stumbled into darkness and went down.

DANTE
Translated by JOHN CIARDI

152

The Hollow Men

Mistah Kurtz — he dead.
A penny for the Old Guy.

I

We are the hollow men
We are the stuffed men
Leaning together
Headpiece filled with straw. Alas!
Our dried voices, when
We whisper together
Are quiet and meaningless
As wind in dried grass
Or rats' feet over broken glass
In our dry cellar.   10

Shape without form, shade without colour,
Paralysed force, gesture without motion;
Those who have crossed
With direct eyes, to death's other Kingdom
Remember us — if at all — not as lost
Violent souls, but only
As the hollow men
The stuffed men.

II

Eyes I dare not meet in dreams
In death's dream kingdom   20
These do not appear:
There, the eyes are

[245]

Sunlight on a broken column
There, is a tree swinging
And voices are
In the wind's singing
More distant and more solemn
Than a fading star.
Let me be no nearer
In death's dream kingdom
Let me also wear
Such deliberate disguises
Rat's coat, crowskin, crossed staves
In a field
Behaving as the wind behaves
No nearer —

Not that final meeting
In the twilight kingdom.

III

This is the dead land
This is cactus land
Here the stone images
Are raised, here they receive
The supplication of a dead man's hand
Under the twinkle of a fading star.

Is it like this
In death's other kingdom
Waking alone
At the hour when we are
Trembling with tenderness
Lips that would kiss
Form prayers to broken stone.

[246]

IV

The eyes are not here
There are no eyes here
In this valley of dying stars
In this hollow valley
This broken jaw of our lost kingdoms.

In this last of meeting places
We grope together
And avoid speech

DARKNESS

Gathered on this beach of the tumid river.   60

Sightless, unless
The eyes reappear
And the perpetual star
Multifoliate rose
Of death's twilight kingdom
The hope only
Of empty men.

V

Here we go round the prickly pear
Prickly pear prickly pear
Here we go round the prickly pear   70
At five o'clock in the morning.

Between the idea
And the reality
Between the emotion
And the act
Falls the Shadow

                    For Thine is the Kingdom

Between the conception
And the creation
Between the emotion   80
And the response
Falls the Shadow

                                        Life is very long

Between the desire
And the spasm
Between the potency
And the existence
Between the essence
And the descent
Falls the Shadow   90

                          For Thine is the Kingdom

For Thine is
Life is
For Thine is the

This is the way the world ends
This is the way the world ends
This is the way the world ends
Not with a bang but a whimper.

                                        T. S. ELIOT

153

I Think Continually of Those Who Were Truly Great

I think continually of those who were truly great.
Who, from the womb, remembered the soul's history
Through corridors of light where the hours are suns,
Endless and singing. Whose lovely ambition
Was that their lips, still touched with fire,
Should tell of the Spirit clothed from head to foot in song.
And who hoarded from the Spring branches
The desires falling across their bodies like blossoms.

What is precious is never to forget
The essential delight of the blood drawn from ageless
    springs   10
Breaking through rocks in worlds before our earth;
Never to deny its pleasure in the simple morning light,
Nor its grave evening demand for love;
Never to allow gradually the traffic to smother
With noise and fog the flowering of the spirit.

Near the snow, near the sun, in the highest fields
See how these names are feted by the wavering grass,
And by the streamers of white cloud,
And whispers of wind in the listening sky;
The names of those who in their lives fought for life,   20
Who wore at their hearts the fire's centre.
Born of the sun they travelled a short while towards the
    sun,
And left the vivid air signed with their honour.

STEPHEN SPENDER

154

Great Things

Sweet cyder is a great thing,
    A great thing to me,
Spinning down to Weymouth town
    By Ridgway thirstily,
And maid and mistress summoning
    Who tend the hostelry:
O cyder is a great thing,
    A great thing to me!

The dance is a great thing,
    A great thing to me,   10
With candles lit and partners fit
    For night-long revelry;
And going home when day-dawning
    Peeps pale upon the lea:
O dancing is a great thing,
    A great thing to me!

Love is, yea, a great thing,
    A great thing to me,
When, having drawn across the lawn
    In darkness silently,
A figure flits like one a-wing
    Out from the nearest tree:
O love is, yes, a great thing,
    A great thing to me!

Will these be always great things,
    Great things to me? . . . .
Let it befall that One will call,
    'Soul, I have need of thee';
What then? Joy-jaunts, impassioned flings,
    Love, and its ecstasy,
Will always have been great things,
    Great things to me!

THOMAS HARDY

20

30

155

The Choice

FROM 'A Dialogue of Self and Soul'

A living man is blind and drinks his drop.
What matter if the ditches are impure?
What matter if I live it all once more?
Endure that toil of growing up;
The ignominy of boyhood; the distress
Of boyhood changing into man;
The unfinished man and his pain
Brought face to face with his own clumsiness;

The finished man among his enemies? —
How in the name of Heaven can he escape   10
That defiling and disfigured shape
The mirror of malicious eyes
Casts upon his eyes until at last
He thinks that shape must be his shape?
And what's the good of an escape
If honour find him in the wintry blast?

I am content to live it all again
And yet again, if it be life to pitch
Into the frog-spawn of a blind man's ditch,
A blind man battering blind men;   20
Or into the most fecund ditch of all,
The folly that man does
Or must suffer, if he woos
A proud woman not kindred of his soul.

I am content to follow to its source
Every event in action or in thought;
Measure the lot; forgive myself the lot!
When such as I cast out remorse
So great a sweetness flows into the breast
We must laugh and we must sing,   30
We are blest by everything,
Everything we look upon is blest.

WILLIAM BUTLER YEATS

[253]

156

Virtue

Sweet day! so cool, so calm, so bright!
  The bridal of the earth and sky —
The dew shall weep thy fall to-night;
  For thou must die.

Sweet rose, whose hue angry and brave
  Bids the rash gazer wipe his eye,
Thy root is ever in the grave,
  And thou must die.

Sweet Spring, full of sweet days and roses,
  A box where sweets compacted lie,
My music shows ye have your closes,
  And all must die.

Only a sweet and virtuous soul,
  Like seasoned timber, never gives,
But, though the whole world turn to coal,
  Then chiefly lives.

GEORGE HERBERT

157

Though I Speak With the Tongues of Men and of Angels

Though I speak with the tongues of men and of angels, and have not charity, I am become as sounding brass, or a tinkling cymbal.

And though I have the gift of prophecy, and understand all mysteries, and all knowledge; and though I have all faith, so that I could remove mountains, and have not charity, I am nothing.

And though I bestow all my goods to feed the poor, and though I give my body to be burned, and have not charity, it profiteth me nothing.   10

Charity suffereth long, and is kind; charity envieth not; charity vaunteth not itself, is not puffed up,

Doth not behave itself unseemly, seeketh not her own, is not easily provoked, thinketh no evil;

Rejoiceth not in iniquity, but rejoiceth in the truth;

Beareth all things, believeth all things, hopeth all things, endureth all things.

Charity never faileth: but whether there be prophecies, they shall fail; whether there be tongues, they shall cease; whether there be knowledge, it shall vanish away.   20

For we know in part, and we prophesy in part.

But when that which is perfect is come, then that which is in part shall be done away.

When I was a child, I spake as a child, I understood as a child, I thought as a child: but when I became a man I put away childish things.

For now we see through a glass, darkly; but then face to face: now I know in part; but then shall I know even as also I am known.

And now abideth faith, hope, charity, these three; but the greatest of these is charity.

I CORINTHIANS 13: 1-13
THE BIBLE, KING JAMES VERSION

158

Prayer

teach me song. i
would sing. teach me
love. i would
i were open
to it. teach me
to pray
privately, praise
quietly
those things
i should. show me   10
the grace
of movement
& touch — that much
i would offer
to her. teach me
more — a way
for me
to reach her
who beckons
hesitantly. teach me   20
to be sure

bpNICHOL

159

Plaint Against the Fog

Don't you ever,
You up in the sky,
Don't you ever get tired
Of having the clouds between you and us?

NOOTKA PEOPLE (NATIVE CANADIAN)
Translated by FRANCES DENSMORE

160

Song to Bring Fair Weather

You, whose day it is, make it beautiful.
Get out your rainbow colors,
So it will be beautiful.

NOOTKA PEOPLE (NATIVE CANADIAN)
Translated by FRANCES DENSMORE

An Absolutely Ordinary Rainbow

The word goes round Repins,
the murmur goes round Lorenzinis,
at Tattersalls, men look up from sheets of numbers,
the Stock Exchange scribblers forget the chalk in their
    hands
and men with bread in their pockets leave the Greek Club:
There's a fellow crying in Martin Place. They can't stop
    him.

The traffic in George Street is banked up for half a mile
and drained of motion. The crowds are edgy with talk
and more crowds come hurrying. Many run in the back
    streets
which minutes ago were busy main streets, pointing: 10
There's a fellow weeping down there. No one can stop
    him.

The man we surround, the man no one approaches
simply weeps, and does not cover it, weeps
not like a child, not like the wind, like a man
and does not declaim it, nor beat his breast, nor even
sob very loudly — yet the dignity of his weeping

holds us back from his space, the hollow he makes about
    him
in the midday light, in his pentagram of sorrow,
and uniforms back in the crowd who tried to seize him
stare out at him, and feel, with amazement, their minds   20
longing for tears as children for a rainbow.

Some will say, in the years to come, a halo
or force stood around him. There is no such thing.
Some will say they were shocked and would have stopped
        him
but they will not have been there. The fiercest manhood,
the toughest reserve, the slickest wit amongst us

trembles with silence, and burns with unexpected
judgements of peace. Some in the concourse scream
who thought themselves happy. Only the smallest children
and such as look out of Paradise come near him   30
and sit at his feet, with dogs and dusty pigeons.

Ridiculous, says a man near me, and stops
his mouth with his hands, as if it uttered vomit —
and I see a woman, shining, stretch her hand
and shake as she receives the gift of weeping;
as many as follow her also receive it

and many weep for sheer acceptance, and more
refuse to weep for fear of all acceptance,
but the weeping man, like the earth, requires nothing,
the man who weeps ignores us, and cries out   40
of his writhen face and ordinary body

not words, but grief, not messages, but sorrow
hard as the earth, sheer, present as the sea —
and when he stops, he simply walks between us
mopping his face with the dignity of one
man who has wept, and now has finished weeping.

Evading believers, he hurries off down Pitt Street.

LES MURRAY

Common Magic

Your best friend falls in love
and her brain turns to water.
You can watch her lips move,
making the customary sounds,
but you can see they're merely
words, flimsy as bubbles rising
from some golden sea where she
swims sleek and exotic as a mermaid.

It's always like that.
You stop for lunch in a crowded   10
restaurant and the waitress floats
toward you. You can tell she doesn't care
whether you have the baked or french-fried
and you wonder if your voice comes
in bubbles too.

It's not just women either. Or love
for that matter. The old man
across from you on the bus holds
a young child on his knee; he is singing
to her and his voice is a small boy   20
turning somersaults in the green
country of his blood.
It's only when the driver calls his stop
that he emerges into this puzzle
of brick and tiny hedges. Only then
you notice his shaking hands, his need
of the child to guide him home.

All over the city
you move in your own seasons
through the seasons of others: old women, faces   30
clawed by weather you can't feel
clack dry tongues at passersby
while adolescents seethe
in their glassy atmospheres of anger.

In parks, the children
are alien life-forms, rooted
in the galaxies they've grown through
to get here. Their games weave
the interface and their laughter
tickles that part of your brain where smells   40
are hidden and the nuzzling textures of things.

It's a wonder that anything gets done
at all: a mechanic flails
at the muffler of your car
through whatever storm he's trapped inside
and the mailman stares at numbers
from the haze of a distant summer.

Yet somehow letters arrive and buses
remember their routes. Banks balance.
Mangoes ripen on the supermarket shelves.   50
Everyone manages. You gulp the thin air
of this planet as if it were the only
one you knew. Even the earth you're
standing on seems solid enough.
It's always the chance word, unthinking
gesture that unlocks the face before you.
Reveals the intricate countries
deep within the eyes. The hidden
lives, like sudden miracles,
that breathe there.

BRONWEN WALLACE

163
Richard Cory

Whenever Richard Cory went down town,
   We people on the pavement looked at him:
He was a gentleman from sole to crown,
   Clean favoured, and imperially slim.

And he was always quietly arrayed,
   And he was always human when he talked;
But still he fluttered pulses when he said,
   'Good-morning,' and he glittered when he walked.

And he was rich — yes, richer than a king —
   And admirably schooled in every grace:
In fine, we thought that he was everything
   To make us wish that we were in his place.

So on we worked, and waited for the light,
   And went without the meat, and cursed the bread;
And Richard Cory, one calm summer night,
   Went home and put a bullet through his head.

EDWIN ARLINGTON ROBINSON

164

My Last Duchess

FERRARA

That's my last Duchess painted on the wall,
Looking as if she were alive. I call
That piece a wonder now: Frà Pandolf's hands
Worked busily a day, and there she stands.
Will't please you sit and look at her? I said
'Frà Pandolf' by design, for never read
Strangers like you that pictured countenance,
The depth and passion of its earnest glance,
But to myself they turned (since none puts by
The curtain I have drawn for you, but I)   10
And seemed as they would ask me, if they durst,
How such a glance came there; so, not the first
Are you to turn and ask thus. Sir, 'twas not
Her husband's presence only, called that spot
Of joy into the Duchess' cheek: perhaps
Frà Pandolf chanced to say 'Her mantle laps
Over my lady's wrist too much,' or 'Paint
Must never hope to reproduce the faint
Half-flush that dies along her throat:' such stuff
Was courtesy, she thought, and cause enough   20
For calling up that spot of joy. She had
A heart — how shall I say? — too soon made glad,
Too easily impressed; she liked whate'er
She looked on, and her looks went everywhere.
Sir, 'twas all one! My favour at her breast,
The dropping of the daylight in the West,
The bough of cherries some officious fool
Broke in the orchard for her, the white mule

She rode with round the terrace — all and each
Would draw from her alike the approving speech,   30
Or blush, at least. She thanked men, — good! but thanked
Somehow — I know not how — as if she ranked
My gift of a nine-hundred-years-old name
With anybody's gift. Who'd stoop to blame
This sort of trifling? Even had you skill
In speech — (which I have not) — to make your will
Quite clear to such an one, and say, 'Just this
Or that in you disgusts me; here you miss,
Or there exceed the mark' — and if she let
Herself be lessoned so, nor plainly set   40
Her wits to yours, forsooth, and made excuse,
— E'en then would be some stooping; and I choose
Never to stoop. Oh sir, she smiled, no doubt,
Whene'er I passed her; but who passed without
Much the same smile? This grew; I gave commands;
Then all smiles stopped together. There she stands
As if alive. Will't please you rise? We'll meet
The company below, then. I repeat,
The Count your master's known munificence
Is ample warrant that no just pretence   50
Of mine for dowry will be disallowed;
Though his fair daughter's self, as I avowed
At starting, is my object. Nay, we'll go
Together down, sir. Notice Neptune, though,
Taming a sea-horse, thought a rarity,
Which Claus of Innsbruck cast in bronze for me!

ROBERT BROWNING

The Child Who Walks Backwards

My next-door neighbour tells me
her child runs into things.
Cupboard corners and doorknobs
have pounded their shapes
into his face. She says
he is bothered by dreams,
rises in sleep from his bed
to steal through the halls
and plummet like a wounded bird
down the flight of stairs.   10

This child who climbed my maple
with the sureness of a cat
trips in his room, cracks
his skull on the bedpost,
smacks his cheeks on the floor.
When I ask about the burns
on the back of his knee,
his mother tells me
he walks backwards
into fireplace grates   20
or sits and stares at flames
while sparks burn stars in his skin.

Other children write their names
on the casts that hold
his small bones.
His mother tells me
he runs into things,
walks backwards,
breaks his leg
while she lies   30
sleeping.

LORNA CROZIER

It's Good to Be Here

I'm in trouble, she said
to him. That was the first
time in history that anyone
had ever spoken of me.

It was 1932 when she
was just fourteen years old
and men like him
worked all day for
one stinking dollar.

There's quinine, she said.   10
That's bullshit, he told her.

Then she cried and then
for a long time neither of them
said anything at all and then
their voices kept rising until
they were screaming at each other
and then there was another long silence and then
they began to talk very quietly and at last he said,
well, I guess we'll just have to make the best of it.

While I lay curled up,   20
my heart beating,
in the darkness inside her.

ALDEN NOWLAN

167

Weakness

Old mare whose eyes
are like cracked marbles,
drools blood in her mash,
shivers in her jute blanket.

My father hates weakness worse than hail;
in the morning
    without haste
he will shoot her in the ear, once,
shovel her under in the north pasture.

Tonight
    leaving the stables,
he stands his lantern on an over-turned water pail,
turns,
    cursing her for a bad bargain,
and spreads his coat
carefully over her sick shoulders.

ALDEN NOWLAN

Coyote Pup Meets the Crazy People in Kootenay National Park

Brian brought him in
dumped in the back of his warden's truck and we watched
    him
die, a gasp at a time
spaced so far apart we knew he was
gone but suggested this or that anyway,
his breath hooked on a bone in his lungs,
his brown sides heaving for the sky
and we all felt for him in our different ways
which are the differences between men.
And twice Larry said, 'Poor little fellow.'   10
And Brian: 'I could give him a shot of 'nectine
or a bullet but all I've got
is the .270 and that's
too big.' So we hung on
till Ian pushed down on his ribs:
'Not much there.' And still we
wanted him to run like the wind for the bush.
'Is that it?' I asked, hearing his
last lunge at the air, which it was, anyone
could tell he was gone,   20
off in a new direction
heading out somewhere else and leaving all
or nothing behind in those damn yellow eyes
staring out at me, out into a darkening world
where four men shuffled and laughed,
went in for coffee.

Inside with the rest of the crazy people
sitting down for coffee,
making words do all the work, talking shop, talking
park in the jargon of the civil servant man,   30
we know what chairs to sit in
we listen to the whirl of tongues
and the talk goes wildlife and telex and
choppers   it goes numbers and man-years and
stats it goes nuts for
fifteen minutes
and behind the words sometimes we hear
the anger and sometimes we hear the pettiness
and then the hurt. And someone tries to tell me
what this park really needs   40
what this park is really like, but I know already
it's like a dead coyote pup
lying out in the back of a warden's truck
waiting for the plastic bag we're
going to stuff him in and then we're going to
shove him in the freezer along with
the lamb that got it from the logging truck
along with a half dozen favourite
birds wiped out by cars, specimens now
and we'll save you that way, fella,   50
we'll cut off your head and throw it
up on the roof and wait till the bugs
clean you up and someday your skull will be
passed around
hand to human hand

and not one of them will be
afraid of you   not one of them will let himself know
how the last gasp was also like a sigh
how it was the wrong way to die   in the back of
a warden's truck   looking at steel   60
watched by humans   handled and pitied and
down on your side in the muck
a pup   seven months out of the den.

Coffee's over   we turn from our chairs
notice the blue sky outside
the cold sweet air that comes from the breath
of the animals and we hurry to our places
the crazy people and me, we gotta get back to our
paper work.

DALE ZIEROTH

169

I've Tasted My Blood

If this brain's over-tempered
consider that the fire was want
and the hammers were fists.
I've tasted my blood too much
to love what I was born to.

But my mother's look
was a field of brown oats, soft-bearded;
her voice rain and air rich with lilacs:
and I loved her too much to like
how she dragged her days like a sled over gravel.   10

Playmates? I remember where their skulls roll!
One died hungry, gnawing grey perch-planks;
one fell, and landed so hard he splashed;
and many and many
come up atom by atom
in the worm-casts of Europe.

My deep prayer a curse.
My deep prayer the promise that this won't be.
My deep prayer my cunning,
my love, my anger,   20
and often even my forgiveness
that this won't be and be.
I've tasted my blood too much
to abide what I was born to.

MILTON ACORN

170

SOS

Calling black people
Calling all black people, man woman child
Wherever you are, calling you, urgent, come in
Black People, come in, wherever you are, urgent, calling
you, calling all black people
calling all black people, come in, black people, come
on in.

IMAMU AMIRI BARAKA

171

John Henry

John Henry was a lil baby,
Sittin' on his mama's knee,
Said: 'De Big Bend Tunnel on de C. & O. road
Gonna cause de death of me,
Lawd, Lawd, gonna cause de death of me.'

Cap'n says to John Henry,
'Gonna bring me a steam drill 'round,
Gonna take dat steam drill out on de job,
Gonna whop dat steel on down,
Lawd, Lawd, gonna whop dat steel on down.'   10

John Henry tol' his cap'n,
Lightnin' was in his eye:
'Cap'n, bet yo' las' red cent on me,
Fo' I'll beat it to de bottom or I'll die,
Lawd, Lawd, I'll beat it to de bottom or I'll die.'

Sun shine hot an' burnin',
Wer'n't no breeze a-tall,
Sweat ran down like water down a hill,
Dat day John Henry let his hammer fall,
Lawd, Lawd, dat day John Henry let his hammer fall.   20

John Henry went to de tunnel,
An' dey put him in de lead to drive,
De rock so tall an' John Henry so small,
Dat he lied down his hammer an' he cried,
Lawd, Lawd, dat he lied down his hammer an' he cried.

John Henry started on de right hand,
De steam drill started on de lef' —
'Before I'd let dis steam drill beat me down,
I'd hammer my fool self to death,
Lawd, Lawd, I'd hammer my fool self to death.'   30

White man tol' John Henry,
'Nigger, damn yo' soul,
You might beat dis steam an' drill of mine,
When de rocks in dis mountain turn to gol',
Lawd, Lawd, when de rocks in dis mountain turn to gol'.'

John Henry said to his shaker,
'Nigger, why don' you sing?
I'm throwin' twelve poun's from my hips on down,
Jes' listen to de col' steel ring,
Lawd, Lawd, jes' listen to de col' steel ring.'   40

Oh, de captain said to John Henry,
'I b'lieve this mountain's sinkin' in.'
John Henry said to his captain, oh my!
'Ain' nothin' but my hammer suckin' win',
Lawd, Lawd, ain' nothin' but my hammer suckin' win'.'

John Henry tol' his shaker,
'Shaker, you better pray,
For, if I miss dis six-foot steel,
Tomorrow'll be yo' buryin' day,
Lawd, Lawd, tomorrow'll be yo' buryin' day.'   50

John Henry tol' his captain,
'Look yonder what I see —
Yo' drill's done broke an' yo' hole's done choke,

An' you cain' drive steel like me,
Lawd, Lawd, an' you cain' drive steel like me.'

De man dat invented de steam drill,
Thought he was mighty fine.
John Henry drove his fifteen feet,
An' de steam drill only made nine,
Lawd, Lawd, an' de steam drill only made nine.   60

De hammer dat John Henry swung,
It weighed over nine pound;
He broke a rib in his lef '-han' side,
An' his intrels fell on de groun',
Lawd, Lawd, an' his intrels fell on de groun'.

All de womens in de Wes',
When dey heared of John Henry's death,
Stood in de rain, flagged de eas'-boun' train,
Goin' where John Henry fell dead,
Lawd, Lawd, goin' where John Henry fell dead.   70

John Henry's lil mother,
She was all dressed in red,
She jumped in bed, covered up her head,
Said she didn't know her son was dead,
Lawd, Lawd, didn' know her son was dead.

Dey took John Henry to de graveyard,
An' dey buried him in de san',
An' every locomotive come roarin' by,
Says, 'Dere lays a steel-drivin' man,
Lawd, Lawd, dere lays a steel-drivin' man.'

ANONYMOUS

172

Questions from a Worker Who Reads

Who built Thebes of the seven gates?
In the books you will find the names of kings.
Did the kings haul up the lumps of rock?
And Babylon, many times demolished
Who raised it up so many times? In what houses
Of gold-glittering Lima did the builders live?
Where, the evening that the Wall of China was finished
Did the masons go? Great Rome
Is full of triumphal arches. Who erected them? Over whom
Did the Caesars triumph? Had Byzantium, much praised
    in song   10
Only palaces for its inhabitants? Even in fabled Atlantis
The night the ocean engulfed it
The drowning still bawled for their slaves.

The young Alexander conquered India.
Was he alone?
Caesar beat the Gauls.
Did he not have even a cook with him?

Philip of Spain wept when his armada
Went down. Was he the only one to weep?
Frederick the Second won the Seven Years' War. Who   20
Else won it?

[279]

Every page a victory.
Who cooked the feast for the victors?
Every ten years a great man.
Who paid the bill?

So many reports.
So many questions.

BERTOLT BRECHT
Translated by MICHAEL HAMBURGER

173

London

I wander through each chartered street,
Near where the chartered Thames does flow,
And mark in every face I meet
Marks of weakness, marks of woe.

In every cry of every man,
In every Infant's cry of fear,
In every voice, in every ban,
The mind-forged manacles I hear.

How the Chimney-sweeper's cry
Every black'ning Church appalls;
And the hapless Soldier's sigh
Runs in blood down Palace walls.

But most through midnight streets I hear
How the youthful Harlot's curse
Blasts the new-born Infant's tear,
And blights with plagues the Marriage hearse.

WILLIAM BLAKE

174

The Peace of Wild Things

When despair for the world grows in me
and I wake in the night at the least sound
in fear of what my life and my children's lives may be,
I go and lie down where the wood drake
rests in his beauty on the water, and the great heron feeds.
I come into the peace of wild things
who do not tax their lives with forethought
of grief. I come into the presence of still water.
And I feel above me the day-blind stars
waiting with their light. For a time
I rest in the grace of the world and am free.

WENDELL BERRY

The Shepherd to His Love

Come live with me and be my Love,
And we will all the pleasures prove
That hills and valleys, dale and field,
And all the craggy mountains yield.

There will we sit upon the rocks
And see the shepherds feed their flocks,
By shallow rivers, to whose falls
Melodious birds sing madrigals.

There will I make thee beds of roses
And a thousand fragrant posies,   10
A cap of flowers, and a kirtle
Embroidered all with leaves of myrtle.

A gown made of the finest wool,
Which from our pretty lambs we pull,
Fair lined slippers for the cold,
With buckles of the purest gold.

A belt of straw and ivy buds
With coral clasps and amber studs:
And if these pleasures may thee move,
Come live with me and be my Love.   20

Thy silver dishes for thy meat
As precious as the gods do eat
Shall on an ivory table be
Prepared each day for thee and me.

The shepherd swains shall dance and sing
For thy delight each May-morning:
If these delights thy mind may move,
Then live with me and be my Love.

CHRISTOPHER MARLOWE

The Nymph's Reply

If all the world and love were young,
And truth in every shepherd's tongue,
These pretty pleasures might me move
To live with thee, and be thy Love.

But Time drives flocks from field to fold,
When rivers rage and rocks grow cold;
And Philomel becometh dumb;
The rest complain of cares to come.

The flowers do fade, and wanton fields
To wayward Winter reckoning yields:
A honey tongue, a heart of gall,
Is fancy's spring, but sorrow's fall.

Thy gowns, thy shoes, thy beds of roses,
Thy cap, thy kirtle, and thy posies,
Soon break, soon wither, — soon forgotten,
In folly ripe, in reason rotten.

Thy belt of straw and ivy-buds,
Thy coral clasps and amber studs, —
All these in me no means can move
To come to thee and be thy Love.

But could youth last, and love still breed,
Had joys no date, nor age no need,
Then these delights my mind might move
To live with thee and be thy Love.

SIR WALTER RALEGH

177

Raleigh Was Right

We cannot go to the country
for the country will bring us no peace.
What can the small violets tell us
that grow on furry stems in
the long grass among lance shaped leaves?

Though you praise us
and call to mind the poets
who sung of our loveliness
it was long ago!
long ago! when country people
would plough and sow with
flowering minds and pockets at ease —
if ever this were true.

Not now. Love itself a flower
with roots in a parched ground.
Empty pockets make empty heads.
Cure it if you can but
do not believe that we can live
today in the country
for the country will bring us no peace.

WILLIAM CARLOS WILLIAMS

178

The Term

A rumpled sheet
of brown paper
about the length

and apparent bulk
of a man was
rolling with the

wind slowly over
and over in
the street as

a car drove down
upon it and
crushed it to

the ground. Unlike
a man it rose
again rolling

with the wind over
and over to be as
it was before.

WILLIAM CARLOS WILLIAMS

179
This Is Just to Say

I have eaten
the plums
that were in
the icebox

and which
you were probably
saving
for breakfast

Forgive me
they were delicious
so sweet
and so cold

WILLIAM CARLOS WILLIAMS

Variations on a Theme by William Carlos Williams

1

I chopped down the house that you had been saving to live
    in next summer.
I am sorry, but it was morning, and I had nothing to do
and its wooden beams were so inviting.

2

We laughed at the hollyhocks together
and then I sprayed them with lye.
Forgive me. I simply do not know what I am doing.

3

I gave away the money that you had been saving to live on
    for the next ten years.
The man who asked for it was shabby
and the firm March wind on the porch was so juicy and
    cold.

4

Last evening we went dancing and I broke your leg.
Forgive me. I was clumsy, and
I wanted you here in the wards, where I am the doctor!

KENNETH KOCH

181

In Time of 'The Breaking of Nations'

JEREMIAH 51: 20

I

Only a man harrowing clods
   In a slow silent walk
With an old horse that stumbles and nods
   Half asleep as they stalk.

II

Only thin smoke without flame
   From the heaps of couch-grass;
Yet this will go onward the same
   Though Dynasties pass.

III

Yonder a maid and her wight
   Come whispering by:
War's annals will cloud into night
   Ere their story die.

THOMAS HARDY

182

Sonnet CXVI

Let me not to the marriage of true minds
Admit impediments. Love is not love
Which alters when it alteration finds,
Or bends with the remover to remove:
O no! it is an ever-fixèd mark
That looks on tempests, and is never shaken;
It is the star to every wandering bark,
Whose worth's unknown, although his height be taken.
Love's not Time's fool, though rosy lips and cheeks
Within his bending sickle's compass come;
Love alters not with his brief hours and weeks,
But bears it out ev'n to the edge of doom.
    If this be error, and upon me proved,
    I never writ, nor no man ever loved.

WILLIAM SHAKESPEARE

An Arundel Tomb

Side by side, their faces blurred,
The earl and countess lie in stone,
Their proper habits vaguely shown
As jointed armour, stiffened pleat,
And that faint hint of the absurd —
The little dogs under their feet.

Such plainness of the pre-baroque
Hardly involves the eye, until
It meets his left-hand gauntlet, still
Clasped empty in the other; and   10
One sees, with a sharp tender shock,
His hand withdrawn, holding her hand.

They would not think to lie so long.
Such faithfulness in effigy
Was just a detail friends would see:
A sculptor's sweet commissioned grace
Thrown off in helping to prolong
The Latin names around the base.

They would not guess how early in
Their supine stationary voyage   20
The air would change to soundless damage,
Turn the old tenantry away;
How soon succeeding eyes begin
To look, not read. Rigidly they

Persisted, linked, through lengths and breadths
Of time. Snow fell, undated. Light
Each summer thronged the glass. A bright
Litter of birdcalls strewed the same
Bone-riddled ground. And up the paths
The endless altered people came,   30

Washing at their identity.
Now, helpless in the hollow of
An unarmorial age, a trough
Of smoke in slow suspended skeins
Above their scrap of history,
Only an attitude remains:

Time has transfigured them into
Untruth. The stone fidelity
They hardly meant has come to be
Their final blazon, and to prove   40
Our almost-instinct almost true:
What will survive of us is love.

PHILIP LARKIN

184

Erosion

It took the sea a thousand years,
A thousand years to trace
The granite features of this cliff,
In crag and scarp and base.

It took the sea an hour one night,
An hour of storm to place
The sculpture of these granite seams
Upon a woman's face.

E. J. PRATT

185

In a Station of the Metro

The apparition of these faces in the crowd;
Petals on a wet, black bough.

EZRA POUND

186

Domination of Black

At night, by the fire,
The colors of the bushes
And of the fallen leaves,
Repeating themselves,
Turned in the room,
Like the leaves themselves
Turning in the wind.
Yes: but the color of the heavy hemlocks
Came striding.
And I remembered the cry of the peacocks.   10

The colors of their tails
Were like the leaves themselves
Turning in the wind,
In the twilight wind.
They swept over the room,
Just as they flew from the boughs of the hemlocks
Down to the ground.
I heard them cry — the peacocks:
Was it a cry against the twilight
Or against the leaves themselves   20
Turning in the wind,
Turning as the flames
Turned in the fire,
Turning as the tails of the peacocks
Turned in the loud fire,
Loud as the hemlocks
Full of the cry of the peacocks?
Or was it a cry against the hemlocks?

Out of the window,
I saw how the planets gathered
Like the leaves themselves
Turning in the wind.
I saw how the night came,
Came striding like the color of the heavy hemlocks.
I felt afraid.
And I remembered the cry of the peacocks.

WALLACE STEVENS

187

Ode to the West Wind

I

O wild West Wind, thou breath of Autumn's being,
   Thou, from whose unseen presence the leaves dead
Are driven, like ghosts from an enchanter fleeing,

Yellow, and black, and pale, and hectic red,
   Pestilence-stricken multitudes: O thou
Who chariotest to their dark wintry bed

The wingèd seeds, where they lie cold and low,
   Each like a corpse within its grave, until
Thine azure sister of the Spring shall blow

Her clarion o'er the dreaming earth, and fill   10
   (Driving sweet buds like flocks to feed in air)
With living hues and odours plain and hill:

Wild Spirit, which art moving everywhere;
Destroyer and Preserver; hear, oh, hear!

II

Thou on whose stream, mid the steep sky's commotion,
   Loose clouds like earth's decaying leaves are shed,
Shook from the tangled boughs of Heaven and Ocean,

Angels of rain and lightning: there are spread
   On the blue surface of thine airy surge,
Like the bright hair uplifted from the head   20

Of some fierce Maenad, even from the dim verge
    Of the horizon to the zenith's height,
The locks of the approaching storm. Thou dirge

Of the dying year, to which this closing night
    Will be the dome of a vast sepulchre,
Vaulted with all thy congregated might

Of vapours, from whose solid atmosphere
Black rain, and fire, and hail, will burst: oh, hear!

III

Thou who didst waken from his summer dreams
    The blue Mediterranean, where he lay,   30
Lull'd by the coil of his crystalline streams,

Beside a pumice isle in Baiae's bay,
    And saw in sleep old palaces and towers
Quivering within the wave's intenser day,

All overgrown with azure moss and flowers
    So sweet, the sense faints picturing them! Thou
For whose path the Atlantic's level powers

Cleave themselves into chasms, while far below
    The sea-blooms and the oozy woods which wear
The sapless foliage of the ocean, know   40

Thy voice, and suddenly grow grey with fear,
And tremble and despoil themselves: oh, hear!

IV

If I were a dead leaf thou mightest bear;
   If I were a swift cloud to fly with thee;
A wave to pant beneath thy power, and share

The impulse of thy strength, only less free
   Than thou, O uncontrollable! If even
I were as in my boyhood, and could be

The comrade of thy wanderings over Heaven,
   As then, when to outstrip thy skyey speed   50
Scarce seemed a vision, I would ne'er have striven

As thus with thee in prayer in my sore need.
   Oh, lift me as a wave, a leaf, a cloud!
I fall upon the thorns of life! I bleed!

A heavy weight of hours has chained and bowed
One too like thee: tameless, and swift, and proud.

V

Make me thy lyre, even as the forest is:
   What if my leaves are falling like its own!
The tumult of thy mighty harmonies

Will take from both a deep, autumnal tone,   60
   Sweet though in sadness. Be thou, Spirit fierce,
My spirit! Be thou me, impetuous one!

Drive my dead thoughts over the universe
   Like withered leaves to quicken a new birth!
And, by the incantation of this verse,

Scatter, as from an unextinguished hearth
   Ashes and sparks, my words among mankind!
Be through my lips to unawakened earth

The trumpet of a prophecy! O Wind,
If Winter comes, can Spring be far behind?

PERCY BYSSHE SHELLEY

In November

The hills and leafless forests slowly yield
To the thick-driving snow. A little while
And night shall darken down. In shouting file
The woodmen's carts go by me homeward-wheeled,
Past the thin fading stubbles, half concealed,
Now golden-grey, sowed softly through with snow,
Where the last ploughman follows still his row,
Turning black furrows through the whitening field.
Far off the village lamps begin to gleam,
Fast drives the snow, and no man comes this way;
The hills grow wintry white, and bleak winds moan
About the naked uplands. I alone
Am neither sad, nor shelterless, nor grey,
Wrapped round with thought, content to watch and dream.

ARCHIBALD LAMPMAN

189

The Mowing

This is the voice of high midsummer's heat.
  The rasping vibrant clamour soars and shrills
  O'er all the meadowy range of shadeless hills,
As if a host of giant cicadae beat
The cymbals of their wings with tireless feet,
  Or brazen grasshoppers with triumphing note
  From the long swath proclaimed the fate that smote
The clover and timothy-tops and meadowsweet.

The crying knives glide on; the green swath lies.
  And all noon long the sun, with chemic ray,
  Seals up each cordial essence in its cell,
That in the dusky stalls, some winter's day,
  The spirit of June, here prisoned by his spell.
  May cheer the herds with pasture memories.

SIR CHARLES G. D. ROBERTS

Indian Summer

Along the line of smoky hills
    The crimson forest stands,
And all the day the blue-jay calls
    Throughout the autumn lands.

Now by the brook the maple leans
    With all his glory spread,
And all the sumachs on the hills
    Have turned their green to red.

Now by great marshes wrapt in mist,
    Or past some river's mouth,
Throughout the long, still autumn day
    Wild birds are flying south.

WILFRED CAMPBELL

Stopping by Woods on a Snowy Evening

Whose woods these are I think I know.
His house is in the village though;
He will not see me stopping here
To watch his woods fill up with snow.

My little horse must think it queer
To stop without a farmhouse near
Between the woods and frozen lake
The darkest evening of the year.

He gives his harness bells a shake
To ask if there is some mistake.
The only other sound's the sweep
Of easy wind and downy flake.

The woods are lovely, dark and deep.
But I have promises to keep,
And miles to go before I sleep,
And miles to go before I sleep.

ROBERT FROST

192

Plucking the Rushes

Green rushes with red shoots,
Long leaves bending to the wind —
You and I in the same boat
Plucking rushes at the Five Lakes.
We started at dawn from the orchid-island:
We rested under the elms till noon.
You and I plucking rushes
Had not plucked a handful when night came!

An anonymous Chinese poem
translated by ARTHUR WALEY

193

The River-Merchant's Wife: A Letter

While my hair was still cut straight across my forehead
I played about the front gate, pulling flowers.
You came by on bamboo stilts, playing horse,
You walked about my seat, playing with blue plums.
And we went on living in the village of Chokan:
Two small people, without dislike or suspicion.

At fourteen I married My Lord you.
I never laughed, being bashful.
Lowering my head, I looked at the wall.
Called to, a thousand times, I never looked back.   10

At fifteen I stopped scowling,
I desired my dust to be mingled with yours
Forever and forever and forever.
Why should I climb the look out?

At sixteen you departed,
And went into far Ku-to-yen, by the river of swirling
    eddies,
And you have been gone five months.
The monkeys make sorrowful noise overhead.
You dragged your feet when you went out.

By the gate now, the moss is grown, the different mosses,   20
Too deep to clear them away!
The leaves fall early this autumn, in wind.
The paired butterflies are already yellow with August
Over the grass in the West garden;

They hurt me. I grow older.
If you are coming down through the narrows of the river
    Kiang
Please let me know beforehand,
And I will come out to meet you
    As far as Cho-fu-sa.

LI PO
A version by EZRA POUND

194

A Birthday

My heart is like a singing bird
  Whose nest is in a watered shoot;
My heart is like an apple-tree
  Whose boughs are bent with thick-set fruit;
My heart is like a rainbow shell
  That paddles in a halcyon sea;
My heart is gladder than all these
  Because my love is come to me.

Raise me a dais of silk and down;
  Hang it with vair and purple dyes;
Carve it in doves, and pomegranates,
  And peacocks with a hundred eyes;
Work it in gold and silver grapes,
  In leaves, and silver fleur-de-lys;
Because the birthday of my life
  Is come, my love is come to me.

CHRISTINA ROSSETTI

195
Go by Brooks

Go by brooks, love,
Where fish stare,
Go by brooks,
I will pass there.

Go by rivers,
Where eels throng,
Rivers, love,
I won't be long.

Go by oceans,
Where whales sail,
Oceans, love,
I will not fail.

LEONARD COHEN

196

Accidentally Broke

accidentally
broke a teacup —
how good it feels
to break things

ISHIKAWA TAKUBOKU
A version by CARL SESAR

197

On the Move

'MAN, YOU GOTTA GO'

The blue jay scuffling in the bushes follows
Some hidden purpose, and the gust of birds
That spurts across the field, the wheeling swallows,
Have nested in the trees and undergrowth.
Seeking their instinct, or their poise, or both,
One moves with an uncertain violence
Under the dust thrown by a baffled sense
Or the dull thunder of approximate words.

On motorcycles, up the road, they come:
Small, black, as flies hanging in heat, the Boys,   10
Until the distance throws them forth, their hum
Bulges to thunder held by calf and thigh.
In goggles, donned impersonality,
In gleaming jackets trophied with the dust,
They strap in doubt — hiding it, robust —
And almost hear a meaning in their noise.

Exact conclusion of their hardiness
Has no shape yet, but from known whereabouts
They ride, direction where the tires press.
They scare a flight of birds across the field: 20
Much that is natural, to the will must yield.
Men manufacture both machine and soul,
And use what they imperfectly control
To dare a future from the taken routes.

It is a part solution, after all.
One is not necessarily discord
On earth; or damned because, half animal,
One lacks direct instinct, because one wakes
Afloat on movement that divides and breaks.
One joins the movement in a valueless world,   30
Choosing it, till, both hurler and hurled,
One moves as well, always toward, toward.

A minute holds them, who have come to go:
The self-defined, astride the created will
They burst away; the towns they travel through
Are home for neither bird nor holiness,
For birds and saints complete their purposes.
At worst, one is in motion; and at best,
Reaching no absolute, in which to rest,
One is always nearer by not keeping still.

THOM GUNN

198
The Hitchhiker

On that black highway,
where are you going? —

it is in Alberta
among the trees

where the road sweeps
left and right

in great concrete arcs
at the famous resort —

there you stood on
the road in the wind,

the cold wind going
through you and you

going through the country
to no end, only

to turn again at one sea
and begin it again,

feeling safe with strangers
in a moving car.

JOHN NEWLOVE

199

Saturday Night

Every five minutes they turn,
with their tires like sirens,
tusking the dirt up on the creek road,
and drive back through town —

> slowing down on Main Street, manoeuvring
> between the farmers' cars, hooting
> at girls on the pavement who reply
> with little hen movements, laughing, waiting.

The boys sport leather jackets and Levis,
but that's their underwear,
the car is their real clothing:
at Taylor's Corner they turn again,
their Hollywood mufflers
making sounds furious, derisive, vulgar —
like a bear growling and breaking wind,

> and roar through Main Street again.

ALDEN NOWLAN

The Fights

What an elusive target
the brain is! Set up
like a coconut on a flexible stem
it has 101 evasions.
A twisted nod slues a punch
a thin gillette's width
past a brain, or
a rude brush-cut to the chin
tucks one brain safe under another.
Two of these targets are   10
set up to be knocked down
for 25 dollars or a million.

In that TV picture in the parlor
the men, who linked move to move
in a chancy dance,
are abstractions only.
Come to ringside, with two
experts in there! See
each step or blow pivoted,
balanced and sudden as gunfire.   20
See muscles wriggle, shine
in sweat like windshield rain.

In stinking dancehalls, in
the forums of small towns,
punches are cheaper but
still pieces of death.

For the brain's the target
with its hungers
and code of honor. See
in those stinking little towns,   30
with long counts, swindling judges,
how fury ends with the last gong.
No matter who's the cheated one
they hug like a girl and man.

It's craft and
the body rhythmic and terrible,
the game of struggle.
We need something of its nature
but not this;
for the brain's the target   40
and round by round it's whittled
til nothing's left of a man
but a jerky bum, humming
with a gentleness less than human.

MILTON ACORN

The Improved Binoculars

Below me the city was in flames:
the firemen were the first to save
themselves. I saw steeples fall on their knees.

I saw an agent kick the charred bodies
from an orphanage to one side, marking
the site carefully for a future speculation.

Lovers stopped short of the final spasm
and went off angrily in opposite directions,
their elbows held by giant escorts of fire.

Then the dignitaries rode across the bridges
under an auricle of light which delighted them,
noting for later punishment those that went before.

And the rest of the populace, their mouths
distorted by an unusual gladness, bawled thanks
to this comely and ravaging ally, asking

Only for more light with which to see
their neighbour's destruction.

All this I saw through my improved binoculars.

IRVING LAYTON

Wishes of an Elderly Man at a Garden Party

I wish I loved the Human Race;
I wish I loved its silly face;
I wish I liked the way it walks;
I wish I liked the way it talks;
And when I'm introduced to one
I wish I thought *What Jolly Fun!*

SIR WALTER RALEIGH

The Fisherman

Although I can see him still,
The freckled man who goes
To a grey place on a hill
In grey Connemara clothes
At dawn to cast his flies,
It's long since I began
To call up to the eyes
This wise and simple man.
All day I'd looked in the face
What I had hoped 'twould be   10
To write for my own race
And the reality;
The living men that I hate,
The dead man that I loved,
The craven man in his seat,
The insolent unreproved,
And no knave brought to book
Who has won a drunken cheer,
The witty man and his joke
Aimed at the commonest ear,   20
The clever man who cries
The catch-cries of the clown,
The beating down of the wise
And great Art beaten down.

Maybe a twelvemonth since
Suddenly I began,
In scorn of this audience,
Imagining a man,
And his sun-freckled face,
And grey Connemara cloth,   30
Climbing up to a place
Where stone is dark under froth,
And the down-turn of his wrist
When the flies drop in the stream;
A man who does not exist,
A man who is but a dream;
And cried, 'Before I am old
I shall have written him one
Poem maybe as cold
And passionate as the dawn.'

WILLIAM BUTLER YEATS

204

An Epilogue

I have seen flowers come in stony places
And kind things done by men with ugly faces,
And the gold cup won by the worst horse at the races,
So I trust, too.

JOHN MASEFIELD

205

Selections

from the *Rubaiyat of Omar Khayyam of Naishapur*

Awake! for Morning in the Bowl of Night
Has flung the Stone that puts the Stars to Flight:
   And Lo! the Hunter of the East has caught
The Sultan's Turret in a Noose of Light.

Dreaming when Dawn's Left Hand was in the Sky
I heard a Voice within the Tavern cry,
   'Awake, my Little ones, and fill the Cup
Before Life's Liquor in its Cup be dry.'

And, as the Cock crew, those who stood before
The Tavern shouted — 'Open then the Door!   10
   You know how little while we have to stay,
And, once departed, may return no more.'

Come, fill the Cup, and in the Fire of Spring
The Winter Garment of Repentance fling:
   The Bird of Time has but a little way
To fly — and Lo! the Bird is on the Wing.

With me along some Strip of Herbage strown,
That just divides the desert from the sown,
   Where name of Slave and Sultan scarce is known,
And pity Sultan Mahmud on his Throne.   20

Here with a Loaf of Bread beneath the Bough,
A Flask of Wine, a Book of Verse — and Thou

Beside me singing in the Wilderness —
And Wilderness is Paradise enow.

'How sweet is mortal Sovranty!' — think some:
Others — 'How blest the Paradise to come!'
    Ah, take the Cash in hand and waive the Rest;
Oh, the brave Music of a *distant* Drum!

The Worldly Hope men set their Hearts upon
Turns Ashes — or it prospers; and anon,   30
    Like Snow upon the Desert's dusty Face
Lighting a little Hour or two — is gone.

Myself when young did eagerly frequent
Doctor and Saint, and heard great Argument
    About it and about: but evermore
Came out by the same Door as in I went.

With them the seed of Wisdom did I sow,
And with mine own hand wrought to make it grow;
    And this was all the Harvest that I reap'd —
'I came like Water, and like Wind I go.'   40

There was the Door to which I found no Key;
There was the Veil through which I might not see:
    Some little talk awhile of ME and THEE
There was — and then no more of THEE and ME.

The Moving Finger writes; and, having writ,
Moves on: nor all thy Piety nor Wit
    Shall lure it back to cancel half a Line,
Nor all thy Tears wash out a Word of it.

EDWARD FITZGERALD

Dirge Without Music

I am not resigned to the shutting away of loving hearts in
    the hard ground.
So it is, and so it will be, for so it has been, time out of
    mind:
Into the darkness they go, the wise and the lovely. Crowned
With lilies and with laurel they go; but I am not resigned.

Lovers and thinkers, into the earth with you.
Be one with the dull, the indiscriminate dust.
A fragment of what you felt, of what you knew,
A formula, a phrase remains, — but the best is lost.

The answers quick & keen, the honest look, the laughter,
    the love,
They are gone. They have gone to feed the roses. Elegant
    and curled
Is the blossom. Fragrant is the blossom. I know. But I do
    not approve.
More precious was the light in your eyes than all the roses
    in the world.

Down, down, down into the darkness of the grave
Gently they go, the beautiful, the tender, the kind;
Quietly they go, the intelligent, the witty, the brave.
I know. But I do not approve. And I am not resigned.

EDNA ST VINCENT MILLAY

And Death Shall Have No Dominion

And death shall have no dominion.
Dead men naked they shall be one
With the man in the wind and the west moon;
When their bones are picked clean and the clean bones
    gone,
They shall have stars at elbow and foot;
Though they go mad they shall be sane,
Though they sink through the sea they shall rise again;
Though lovers be lost love shall not;
And death shall have no dominion.

And death shall have no dominion.   10
Under the windings of the sea
They lying long shall not die windily;
Twisting on racks when sinews give way,
Strapped to a wheel, yet they shall not break;
Faith in their hands shall snap in two,
And the unicorn evils run them through;
Split all ends up they shan't crack;
And death shall have no dominion.

And death shall have no dominion.
No more may gulls cry at their ears   20
Or waves break loud on the seashores;
Where blew a flower may a flower no more
Lift its head to the blows of the rain;

Though they be mad and dead as nails,
Heads of the characters hammer through daisies;
Break in the sun till the sun breaks down,
And death shall have no dominion.

DYLAN THOMAS

208

The Isles of Greece

FROM *Don Juan*

The isles of Greece, the isles of Greece!
   Where burning Sappho loved and sung,
Where grew the arts of war and peace,
   Where Delos rose, and Phoebus sprung!
Eternal summer gilds them yet,
But all, except their sun, is set.

The mountains look on Marathon —
   And Marathon looks on the sea;
And musing there an hour alone,
   I dream'd that Greece might still be free;   10
For standing on the Persians' grave,
I could not deem myself a slave.

A king sate on the rocky brow
   Which looks o'er sea-born Salamis;
And ships, by thousands, lay below,
   And men in nations; — all were his!
He counted them at break of day —
And when the sun set where were they?

Must *we* but weep o'er days more blest?
   Must *we* but blush? — Our fathers bled.   20
Earth! render back from out thy breast
   A remnant of our Spartan dead!
Of the three hundred grant but three,
To make a new Thermopylae!

What, silent still? and silent all?
   Ah! no; — the voices of the dead
Sound like a distant torrent's fall,
   And answer, 'Let one living head,
But one arise, — we come, we come!'
'Tis but the living who are dumb.

LORD BYRON

209

All That's Past

Very old are the woods;
 And the buds that break
Out of the briar's boughs,
 When March winds wake,
So old with their beauty are —
 Oh, no man knows
Through what wild centuries
 Roves back the rose.

Very old are the brooks;
 And the rills that rise
Where snow sleeps cold beneath
 The azure skies
Sing such a history
 Of come and gone,
Their every drop is as wise
 As Solomon.

Very old are we men;
 Our dreams are tales
Told in dim Eden
 By Eve's nightingales;
We wake and whisper awhile,
 But, the day gone by,
Silence and sleep like fields
 Of amaranth lie.

WALTER DE LA MARE

Echo

'Who called?' I said, and the words
   Through the whispering glades,
Hither, thither, baffled the birds —
   'Who called? Who called?'

The leafy boughs on high
   Hissed in the sun;
The dark air carried my cry
   Faintingly on:

Eyes in the green, in the shade,
   In the motionless brake,
Voices that said what I said
   For mockery's sake:

'Who cares?' I bawled through my tears;
   The wind fell low:
In the silence, 'Who cares? Who cares?'
   Wailed to and fro.

WALTER DE LA MARE

Death the Leveller

The glories of our blood and state
  Are shadows, not substantial things;
There is no armour against Fate;
  Death lays his icy hand on kings:
    Sceptre and Crown
    Must tumble down,
And in the dust be equal made
With the poor crookèd scythe and spade.

Some men with swords may reap the field,
  And plant fresh laurels where they kill: 10
But their strong nerves at last must yield;
  They tame but one another still:
    Early or late
    They stoop to fate,
And must give up their murmuring breath
When they, pale captives, creep to death.

The garlands wither on your brow;
  Then boast no more your mighty deeds!
Upon Death's purple altar now
  See where the victor-victim bleeds.   20
    Your heads must come
    To the cold tomb:
Only the actions of the just
Smell sweet and blossom in their dust.

JAMES SHIRLEY

What Thou Lovest Well Remains

FROM CANTO LXXXI, *The Cantos*

What thou lovest well remains,
the rest is dross
What thou lov'st well shall not be reft from thee
    What thou lov'st well is thy true heritage
Whose world, or mine or theirs
or is it of none?
First came the seen, then thus the palpable
    Elysium, though it were in the halls of hell,
What thou lovest well is thy true heritage
What thou lov'st well shall not be reft from thee   10

The ant's a centaur in his dragon world.
Pull down thy vanity, it is not man
Made courage, or made order, or made grace,
    Pull down thy vanity, I say pull down.
Learn of the green world what can be thy place
In scaled invention or true artistry,
Pull down thy vanity,
Paquin pull down!
The green casque has outdone your elegance.

'Master thyself, then others shall thee beare'   20
    Pull down thy vanity
Thou art a beaten dog beneath the hail,

A swollen magpie in a fitful sun,
Half black half white
Nor knowst'ou wing from tail
Pull down thy vanity
        How mean thy hates
Fostered in falsity,
        Pull down thy vanity,
Rathe to destroy, niggard in charity,   30
Pull down thy vanity,
        I say pull down.

But to have done instead of not doing
        this is not vanity
To have, with decency, knocked
That a Blunt should open
    To have gathered from the air a live tradition
or from a fine old eye the unconquered flame
This is not vanity.
    Here error is all in the not done,   40
all in the diffidence that faltered.

EZRA POUND

213

Song

FROM *Cymbeline*

Fear no more the heat o' the sun,
  Nor the furious winter's rages;
Thou thy worldly task hast done,
  Home art gone, and ta'en thy wages;
Golden lads and girls all must,
As chimney-sweepers, come to dust.

Fear no more the frown o' the great,
  Thou are past the tyrant's stroke;
Care no more to clothe and eat;
  To thee the reed is as the oak;
The Sceptre, Learning, Physic, must
All follow this, and come to dust.

Fear no more the lightning-flash,
  Nor the all-dreaded thunder-stone;
Fear not slander, censure rash;
  Thou hast finish'd joy and moan:
All lovers young, all lovers must
Consign to thee, and come to dust.

No exorciser harm thee!
  Nor no witchcraft charm thee!
Ghost unlaid forbear thee!
  Nothing ill come near thee!
Quiet consummation have;
And renowned be thy grave!

WILLIAM SHAKESPEARE

214

Song

Adieu, farewell earths blisse,
This world uncertaine is,
Fond are lifes lustfull joyes,
Death proves them all but toyes,
None from his darts can flye,
I am sick, I must dye:
   Lord have mercy on us.

Rich men, trust not in wealth,
Gold cannot buy you health,
Phisick himself must fade.   10
All things, to end are made,
The plague full swift goes bye,
I am sick, I must dye:
   Lord have mercy on us.

Beauty is but a flowre,
Which wrinckles will devoure,
Brightness falls from the ayre,
Queenes have died young, and faire,
Dust hath closed *Helens* eye.
I am sick, I must dye: 20
   Lord have mercy on us.

Strength stoopes unto the grave,
Wormes feed on *Hector* brave,
Swords may not fight with fate,
Earth still holds ope her gate.
Come, come, the bells do crye.
I am sick, I must dye:
   Lord have mercy on us.

Wit with his wantonesse,
Tasteth deaths bitterness: 30
Hels executioner,
Hath no eares for to heare
What vaine art can reply.
I am sick, I must dye:
   Lord have mercy on us.

Haste therefore eche degree,
To welcome destiny:
Heaven is our heritage,
Earth but a players stage,
Mount wee unto the sky.   40
I am sick, I must dye:
   Lord have mercy on us.

THOMAS NASIIE

215
I Give You the End of a Golden String

I give you the end of a golden string;
   Only wind it into a ball,
It will lead you in at Heaven's gate,
   Built in Jerusalem's wall.

WILLIAM BLAKE

Poetry and Ordinary Experience

An Excerpt from an Essay by M. L. Rosenthal, 1974

Life without poetry would, I believe, be very much less worth living. I speak of poetry now as a natural human activity and state of awareness. It is an expression of what one poet, Gerard Manley Hopkins, called 'my sweating self.' It belongs to the world of hunger and sex — a kind of thought, but thought felt as bodily need and energy. Poetry is filled with memories of the physical impact of feelings and sensations, including especially the impact of sound and most especially of the human voice.

John Berryman's 'Dream Song 29,' for instance, begins with a feeling of the *weight* of undefined guilt on a man's heart. Various remembered sensations attach themselves to his 'heavy' feeling, and the voice we hear is of someone who has carried infantile misery into adulthood as an inescapable burden. It is really a mixture of two voices, that of a gravely perceptive, mature person and that of a childlike one who does not always speak grammatically:

> There sat down, once, a thing on Henry's heart
> só heavy, if he had a hundred years
> & more, & weeping, sleepless, in all them time
> Henry could not make good.
> Starts again in Henry's ears
> the little cough somewhere, an odour, a chime.

Now perhaps this is to begin from the wrong end, from poetry in relation to our griefs rather than to our joys. But just as people sometimes weep with happiness, so art measures feeling by its intensity rather than its literal object. Whatever the medium — the painter's oils, the sculptor's marble, the composer's notes and chords, the dancer's own body, or the poet's words — art converts feelings into aspects of that medium, such as shadings of color or a dancer's patterned movements; and the conversion demands a certain degree of intensity. In Berryman's poem about the depression that 'sat down' on 'Henry's heart,' the intensity is almost the same as when Tennyson's speaker in *The Princess* says, in his very different mood of love-ecstasy:

> Now lies the Earth all Danaë to the stars,
> And all thy heart lies open unto me.
>
> Now slides the silent meteor on, and leaves
> A shining furrow, as thy thoughts in me.
>
> Now folds the lily all her sweetness up
> And slips into the bosom of the lake:
> So fold thyself, my dearest, thou, and slip
> Into my bosom and be lost in me.

Many people, I admit, lead very full lives without poetry. It is ludicrous even to mention so obvious a fact. Yet to the poet everything he knows belies that fact. All his experience, all his introspection, flow into a rhythm and design of language. When people say they do not 'get' poetry, it is because they think of language as factual description and the explanation of ideas. They forget the other ways in which they themselves use it — for social cordiality, for cold rejection or irritation, for outcries of pain and excitement, for joking or 'manly' obscenities or 'feminine' hyperbole. Language is like color or space or pure sound. Its realm is both conscious thought and subconscious reaction to life: the touch of other personalities, for instance, and a myriad other sensations and fears and desires. These stimuli, active in every mind, create in all of us a hunger to express ourselves accurately and vividly. Words like 'humorous,' 'racy,' 'dramatic,' 'poignant' reveal that we want our speech to have a life of its own, something much more than flat statement. So the poet is not working out of mere private eccentricity. The poetic process goes on incessantly in the minds of people who would never believe it, who are sure they have neither an interest in poetry nor the ability to grasp it. Carl Sandburg knew and loved this unconscious poetry of ordinary life —

> When I asked for fish in the restaurant facing the Ohio river, with fish signs and fish pictures all over the wooden, cracked frame of the fish shack, the young man said, 'Come around next Friday — the fish is all gone today.'

> So I took eggs, fried, straight up, one side, and he murmured, humming, looking out at the shining breast of the Ohio river, 'and the next is something else; and the next is something else.'

> The customer next was a hoarse roustabout, handling nail kegs on a steamboat all day, asking for three eggs, sunny side up, three, nothing less, shake us a mean pan of eggs.

> And while we sat eating eggs, looking at the shining breast of the Ohio river in the evening lights, he had his thoughts and I had mine thinking how the French who found the Ohio river named it La Belle Rivière meaning a woman easy to look at.

The first impression of this passage, from Sandburg's 'Whiffs of the Ohio River at Cincinnati,' is that he is telling a joke. He begins with an anecdote about the shabby waterfront scene. Soon, however, more lyrical elements are being mixed in with the earthily realistic comic ones. When Sandburg read his poems aloud, he would speak in a slow, rocking chant that gave strong emphasis to the kind of contrast here between a wild folk-buffoonery and the tones of romantic intensity. On the one side we have the prosaic but hilarious echoing of the words 'fish' and 'eggs' and all the American restaurant lingo and slang — 'fried, straight up, one side,' 'shake us a mean pan of eggs.' On the other, we have the glamour and simple delight of the repeated words 'the shining breast of the Ohio.' That phrase is linked with such others as 'evening lights' and 'La Belle Rivière,' which Sandburg pretends to translate into 'a woman easy to look at.' His lightly colloquial, yet suggestive touch of straight-faced mistranslation combines the flippant and the lyrical elements of the poem. So does the counterman's half-clowning, half-prophetic wisdom ('and the next is something else'), and so does the speaker's easy profundity ('he had his thoughts and I had mine').

So this casual-seeming passage is actually a sharply focused impression of a real scene with real people, and, within it, of contrasting elements: the presence of beauty all around the ridiculous and nearly squalid scene. Between the beginning and the end we move from pleasant clowning to an atmosphere of dreaming. Sandburg has created a delicate dance of mood and tone out of materials as familiar and common as the nearest 'diner' or cheap restaurant. The appeal to the eye and the ear, the zest for common realities, in this poem make it like a tall tale or a certain kind of comic strip. It reflects the relish for incongruities found in all folk and popular humor. By the end, though, its increasingly heightened atmosphere brings something subtler and more moving into play.

Let me take another example, plainer and less exuberant. Robert Frost's 'The Investment' grows out of the lives of New England dirt farmers of an earlier generation. Its first two stanzas, whose phrasing is saturated with the harsh necessity of those lives, are the strongest. The poem grows weaker in its closing six lines, when the speaker draws apart from the people whose lives he has presented to us in order to speculate on them:

> Over back where they speak of life as staying
> ('You couldn't call it living for it ain't')
> There was an old, old house renewed with paint,
> And in it a piano loudly playing.
>
> Out in the plowed ground in the cold a digger,
> Among unearthed potatoes standing still,
> Was counting winter dinners, one a hill,
> With half an ear to the piano's vigor.
>
> All that piano and new paint back there,
> Was it some money suddenly come into?
> Or some extravagance young love had been to?
> Or old love on an impulse not to care —
>
> Not to sink under being man and wife,
> But get some color and music out of life?

The first two lines of this sonnet have always given me great pleasure and are the main reason I thought of 'The Investment' just now. They have such a truthful, spontaneous sound, grim and wry and witty all at once, that we know they come directly out of the farm country Frost writes about. The man or woman talking this way might never call it poetry, yet he or she would be as aware as any conscious poet of style and rhythm and nuances of phrasing. Such speech has a tradition behind it. It plays with shadings of meaning ('staying' and 'living'). It is colored by brutal experience, but softened against bitterness by irony and momentarily cheerful candor. The slightly drawling pace of the first line is balanced by the mock-thoughtful briskness of the witticism in the second, with the speaker playing a character role of smart countryman and coming down hard on the words 'living' and 'ain't.'

To the person speaking in these two lines, or at least in the second, there is the release of expressing his own inner dissatisfaction in the salty, humorous phrasing of an art form: a sly, paradoxical, compressed comment on life. The form enables him to avoid self-pity. It gives the statement a springing life of its own and makes it a piece of wisdom, like a biblical proverb. Many proverbs and folk sayings, like much racy ordinary speech and many jokes, have this kind of impersonality that they share with art generally. Cruel, demeaning attitudes may be imbedded in them — as, for instance, in the saying 'Fish and visitors stink after three days' — but even in this disagreeable instance the achievement of an unexpected association in the form of a witticism that is also a human insight almost makes us forget the nastiness.

Back, though, to 'The Investment' — look for a moment at the three lines beginning the second stanza. Nothing could be simpler than these descriptive lines; they give us the literal scene of the farmer standing amid the potatoes he has just dug up. The words 'plowed' and 'digger' and 'unearthed' speak of his hard work. The phrase 'Out in the plowed ground in the cold' gently reveals his exposed, elemental existence. That he was 'counting winter dinners' shows his relative poverty, for each little mound of potatoes equals one family meal. There is a colloquial literalness in 'winter dinners,' and the phrase, though used by an observer, speaks for the farmer himself at the same time. It shows both his hard lot and his sturdy providence. The language, in fact, though that of an observer — perhaps a neighbor, perhaps the poet himself — who is recalling an experience, also manages to project the digger's own private thoughts. At least, this is so in the first eight lines if we disregard the rhyme and meter and the one word 'vigor.' We stand there with him, knowing what he was thinking about and what he was listening to. The passage gives us sharply clear pictures for the eye, while the loud piano music fills an otherwise silent scene. That is to say, Frost's language isolates these sense impressions in such a way as to make them suggest just how a whole way of life felt to the people living it.

The rest of the poem, giving the 'moral' as it were, is less effective. It rather hammers away at us about why these poor folk, in their 'old, old house,' have invested in new paint and a piano. The speaker clearly prefers the last of the possible explanations he suggests, and certainly it expresses the deep human need to make life more than a routine animal struggle for survival — to redirect and transcend it through giving it 'color and music.' My main objection to this ending is that it is such an obvious comment from 'outside,' whereas the first eight lines find just the right language from 'inside' the scene. The ending loses the unsentimental compassion with which the poem started, its high spirits triumphing over a low condition. As soon as the letdown begins and the poem becomes talkative rather than concretely alive, the rhyme and rhythm become awkward too. The reason is that they call attention to themselves as part of a coldly contrived device for winding up the poem. In Sandburg's 'Whiffs of the Ohio River at Cincinnati,' the speaker keeps himself in the scene, blending his own mood and language with those of the people around him so that the feeling that emerges contains all the tones that have built into it. In Frost's poem the speaker does this only to a tiny extent and loses touch to a great degree. It was what was discovered in the digger's life and mind, in its own terms, essentially, that made the beginning so much more telling than the end.

But my purpose in quoting 'The Investment' was not really to criticize it in detail. If I may return to something elusive and infinitely suggestive in this poem, let me quote its first two lines once more:

> Over back where they speak of life as staying
> ('You couldn't call it living, for it ain't')

One reason I love these lines is that they show how much poetry is present in the voices of people to whom it would hardly occur that this could be so. The fullness of life, of the way we all feel and the way we all speak in unselfconscious moments, is the very stuff of poetry. The touchstones of our lives, and therefore of art, are vivid experiences and strong needs either gratified or thwarted. At this moment I can see from my window, after a spring rain, four orange-breasted, speckle-backed robins poking into the high wet grass. I can turn to erotic dreaming — a memory, say, of a white shoulder just above my head at some happy moment. I can summon up harsher memories: a scream from a vast apartment building late at night on a Chicago street as I passed by, or the voice of a union organizer rising hysterically in the same city after strikers were shot down outside a steel mill many years ago. Of such sights and dreams and recollections, shared by millions of people, poetry is made.

I want to stress this point. Too often poetry is thought to be impossibly far apart from ordinary human existence. Anyone's mind is a teeming gallery of sensations and memories. Housewife, murderer, plumber, schoolboy, each has a mind full of blue or gray skies, the touch or absence of love, the give and take of conversation, the filth and

excitement of cities (or the seasonal shiftings of country existence or the nervous sameness of the suburbs). We all know
the taste of things sweet or bland or sour, we all have known
rage, we all feel the passion to recall even a painful past. A
rich confusion of awareness underlies all human feeling, and
the language for it surges all around us. The poet reaches
into that rich confusion toward the wellspring of the surging
speech of life. He must, through language alone, catch a tone,
a perception, a quality of sensation and arrange a whole poem
around the impulse of energy so captured.

Frost at his best was one of the masters of the art of
making metrical verse based on natural speech. He used his
art to catch life on the run and then tried to hold the whole
sense of it intact within a formal frame. The urge to make
poetry has a good deal to do with such a purpose. That is
why all real poetry, even when difficult or complex, has so
much to say that comes from the depths of normal life. It is
always in touch with the intrinsic music of our everyday
world. More than that, it reveals and identifies the realiza-
tions that make life the surprising, often exhilarating, often
terrifying condition it truly is.

As soon as one gets a glimpse of this rooting of poetry in
everything we know and feel and are, it stops being something alien and formidable. Or let's say it is neither more
nor less alien and formidable than dreaming at night or
arising in the morning into more conscious existence. It is
an invitation to see keenly into what our dreams and
thoughts are about, like the invitation that Frost extends to
us in his little poem 'The Pasture,' which introduces each
of his collected editions.

> I'm going out to clean the pasture spring;
> I'll only stop to rake the leaves away
> (And wait to watch the water clear, I may):
> I shan't be gone long. — You come too.

I'm going out to fetch the little calf
That's standing by the mother. It's so young
It totters when she licks it with her tongue.
I shan't be gone long. — You come too.

This is poetry that has a love affair with life. 'The Pasture' takes us out into the midst of country things as they are. And though the ordinary life of most of us today may be very far from the poem's rural scene, the pictures of the clear pasture spring and of the cow with her calf are powerfully suggestive even for city dwellers. The speaker is happily anticipating what he is going to *see*, but he is also going forth into the world's continuing tasks. You can never clean the pasture spring once and for all, nor will the calf remain forever just as it is now. Since the poem introduces the whole book, it is probably meant also as an invitation to come along to whatever a lifetime of writing will have discovered. But meanwhile, and first of all, we have the gentle urging to companionship in the literal chores of the new season. Nothing rare is promised, yet such isolation of ordinary sense impressions is sweetly rare indeed. Frost makes a song of his invitation, using a refrain and simple rhymes. The poem reaches gaily into the marvels of the commonplace, with only a just possible hint of the lifetime of labor required to clean the pasture springs and fetch the calves and do all the other chores season after season. The irony, from that point of view, of 'I shan't be gone long' is virtually hidden in the warm strength, the friendly, plain, colloquial speech that invites us to plunge into the realities of the physical world.

The marvels of the commonplace, which of course includes circumstances that are superficially dull or routine, are always present to the subconscious mind at least. The normal mind can discover them merely by paying attention to what goes on within itself in response to the realities all around. As Marianne Moore writes in 'The Mind Is an Enchanting Thing,' it is also, and more accurately, an 'enchanted thing,'

> like the glaze on a
> katydid-wing
>> subdivided by sun
>> till the nettings are legion.
> Like Gieseking playing Scarlatti . . .

It reflects and refracts the light from the world around it like the glaze on the insect's wings. More than that, it actively interprets and arranges the reality it experiences, like a piano virtuoso playing a lovely piece of music. And it is itself physical, a living function of the body that is a composite organ of all the senses:

> the mind
> feeling its way as though blind,
> walks along with its eyes on the ground.

The thought I am insisting on here is that an essential ingredient of poetic vision and genius is present in all minds. First of all, poetry draws deeply on experiences we have all had. We may not all be familiar with the art of Scarlatti or of Gieseking, it is true, but we have all at some time felt we were hearing beautiful music beautifully played. We have all observed the way a katydid-wing (or a dragonfly-wing) creates a brilliant design out of sunlight. We have all felt our minds groping into the essence of what we are experiencing in the way Miss Moore describes. What the ordinary reader shares with a very subtle poet like Marianne Moore is so important that it would be impossible for anyone to write at all without it. I am not saying that this fact makes the achievement of any poet perfectly easy to grasp. One may have to go along with a demanding set of associations; and one may have to follow the sound of a speaking voice in elusively varied modulations and intricately patterned rhythms. But the associations are actual human associations, the voice is that of a human mind like our own, and the rhythmic patterning in a good poem reinforces the other qualities.

Wallace Stevens, for instance, is generally held to be a somewhat difficult poet, and in certain respects he is. But if I quote the closing lines of his most famous poem, 'Sunday Morning,' it will be seen that he is expressing a sense of life felt by anyone who has ever opened his eyes and looked about him. The question raised in 'Sunday Morning' is whether we can accept without dismay the fact of a world without God. This is, after all, a question that has disturbed modern man and has strongly affected history. Stevens does not examine it theoretically. Instead, he imagines the state of mind of a moderately self-indulgent, moderately meditative woman who on Sunday morning is a little troubled by thoughts of death and a little guilty, or at least uneasy, at her neglect of the Sabbath. These are feelings so common they hardly need explanation and yet so real they cannot be ignored. They emerge in a manner that allows us to see the poem in two possible ways. We may see it as a sort of internal dialogue between two aspects of the woman's own inner self, or we may read it as an implied dialogue between the woman and the poet, who imagines overhearing her thoughts and who comments on them — as if she were delivering a monologue on the stage and he listened and then addressed his own remarks about it to the audience. Either way, the poem begins with the woman's natural longing to have her life, with all its richness and possibilities, persist forever. And then the position is more and more ardently advanced — either by the woman taking a fuller look at reality or by the poet — that the only choice possible is a sensuous, tough-minded idealizing of life as it is, made all the more desirable by the finality of death. The poem is at once exquisite in the way it unfolds and very close to the way many people think and feel. In the eleven lines that close the final stanza, Stevens gives a picture of man in his universe that reflects a widespread modern viewpoint:

> We live in an old chaos of the sun,
> Or old dependency of day and night,
> Or island solitude, unsponsored, free,
> Of that wide water, inescapable.
> Deer walk upon our mountains, and the quail
> Whistle about us their spontaneous cries;
> Sweet berries ripen in the wilderness;
> And, in the isolation of the sky,
> At evening, casual flocks of pigeons make
> Ambiguous undulations as they sink,
> Downward to darkness, on extended wings.

We have been brought to this point in the poem by a series of shifts of focus and tone. At the beginning, we see the woman in her home, relaxing of a Sunday morning. We follow the drift of her mind as she turns from sheer enjoyment and reluctantly begins to meditate. Because of the circumstances and her mood, presented in vivid detail, her thoughts turn to religion and to the double meaning of the Crucifixion: the blood, suffering, and death of the man Jesus, and the promise of Paradise he brought. The ideas of 'Sunday Morning' sometimes grow subtle and elusive, but the images are almost always boldly clear and strike familiar notes: 'late coffee and oranges in a sunny chair,' 'gusty emotions on wet roads on autumn nights,' 'this dividing and indifferent blue' (the sky). When the images are less elementary in their reference, they still evoke familiar associations. The religious meaning of Sunday summons up 'the holy hush of ancient sacrifice' in the woman's mind. Romantic young girls 'stray impassioned in the littering leaves.' At the thought of death, the woman's mood changes 'as a calm darkens among waterlights.' Stevens does not ordinarily use folk speech the way Sandburg, or even Frost, does, but he takes a great deal of strength from the sensuous immediacy of his images. They appeal at the level of reverie, which has infinitely more to do with our bodies and emotions than with logical argument. By the end of the poem the thinking is deliberately primitive, except for its rejection of any place for the supernatural in the world that we know.

The closing passage — already quoted — begins with the blunt statement that 'We live in an old chaos of the sun.' The earth is an 'island solitude' in space, 'unsponsored' and 'free' because it has no Creator. (The phrase 'of that wide water' in the fourth line of the passage refers to an earlier use of the words 'wide water' in the first stanza. There the woman's mind goes back, in imagination, across the ocean to Palestine in the time of the Crucifixion.) 'Free' of God, our condition is still 'inescapable,' bound by death's inevitability. Suddenly, now, the poem turns from the trapped feeling of these thoughts to an emphasis on certain of earth's beautiful realities: the deer that 'walk upon our mountains,' the quails' 'spontaneous cries,' the 'sweet berries,' the flights of 'casual flocks of pigeons' earthward. Their presence, like our own, is a kind of miracle though not a divinely inspired one. In this context the word 'ambiguous,' used for the undulations of the pigeons, expresses both a general thought and a precise observation. The general thought is simply that life's purpose, if it exists at all, is extremely unclear but that nevertheless we cannot help reading affirmative values into life itself. This double idea is implied by the observation that the pigeons, as they 'sink downward,' do make ambiguous movements that suggest they might change their course. Also, they extend their wings to control their sinking movement, and that act of controlling power gives the impression of something triumphant ('extended'). It is almost as though they were about to soar upwards, away from the darkness and the associations of death.

Does the impression *prove* anything? Of course not. The whole poem, despite the ideas it suggests, merely balances sets of images and feelings against one another. These are images of life's pleasures, images of the dream of God's presence among us, and images of loss and deprivation. Lyric poets often handle the sense of life's being disastrous by finding a suggestion of affirmation in the very language they choose to show their despair. To 'sink downward to darkness on extended wings' is a perfect example. So too is the description through most of the closing stanza, of the delights the earth has to offer us. Such language enables the poet to 'control' destiny, as it were, through seeing it affirmatively: an assertion of desired power very close to what happens in primitive ritual.

Stevens performs this 'ritual' in a more sophisticated way earlier in the poem, preparing us for his final simplifications. For instance, in the third stanza he provides a whimsical mock-theological argument, at once fanciful and half serious, to justify his call for a secular, hedonistic approach to life. Stevens uses the word 'Jove' in speaking of God — a usage that allows him to combine pagan and Christian references as though he were at liberty to construct his own

version of such sacred tales as the Greek account of the rape
of Leda by Zeus and the New Testament account of Mary's
virgin pregnancy:

> He moved among us, as a muttering king,
> Magnificent, would move among his hinds,
> Until our blood, commingling, virginal,
> With heaven, brought such requital to desire
> The very hinds discerned it, in a star.
> Shall our blood fail? or shall it come to be
> The blood of paradise? . . .

Because both pagan and Christian tradition report that in
the past divine beings impregnated mortals, we are now
ourselves divinities by heritage. Paradise is, if only we fulfill
ourselves, the physical universe we inhabit — or so we
must insist.

As for the other Paradise of which various religions
speak, where there is no aging and no death but only 'im-
perishable bliss,' Stevens devotes a stanza of sophisticated
argument to it as well. That Paradise, he says, is 'like our
perishing earth' except that it is static and insipid, a mere
interruption before maturing of nature's cycle. But we *need*
the whole cycle of life as it is, for

> Death is the mother of beauty, mystical,
> Within whose burning bosom we devise
> Our earthly mothers waiting, sleeplessly.

Without change and death our sense responses, our dreams
and desires, and our imaginations could never be felt so
keenly as they are now. And so the poem proposes a kind
of ritual that is not really religious and yet celebrates a
'boisterous devotion to the sun' — 'not as a god, but as a
god might be.' We belong to 'the heavenly fellowship/Of
men that perish and of summer morn.' It is only a step

from this to the very simple vision, at the end, of man and the rest of nature existing, miraculously, precariously, in 'an old chaos of the sun.'

This simple vision was implicit in the poem from the start, but it had to be sifted through the psychological and philosphical complexities presented in the woman's mind and examined in the dialogue. Even the parts of the poem I have called sophisticated are centered on elementary or primitive pictures. There is the picture of Jove 'commingling' with human beings — that is, wandering among them and having sexual intercourse with them. There is the picture of a Paradise with the earth's own familiar fruits, the same landscapes, the same colors and atmosphere, except that it cannot change. Most striking of all, there is the picture of 'our earthly mothers waiting, sleeplessly' beyond the grave — not a matter of religious faith but a piercing expression of normal human grief and desire.

Almost inevitably, then, the sensuous, emotional, and tonal texture of a poem of real interest has a primal clarity regardless of any overlay of intellectuality. Most painters paint far better than they philosophize; so do most poets. 'Paint' is of course only a hint of what the poet does in a line like 'Sweet berries ripen in the wilderness' or in lines like

> And, in the isolation of the sky,
> At evening, casual flocks of pigeons make
> Ambiguous undulations as they sink,
> Downward to darkness, on extended wings.

What such lines present to the eye and the other senses is a focusing, such as we have all observed again and again without really seeing it sharply in just this way, of nature in action. They remind us, always surprisingly, of how dependent art must be on what it is given by common experience.

There is one blindingly obvious, very powerful psychological factor in all this. This factor is the common human longing not to let go of experience. We linger, for instance, over a beautiful scenic view, fixing it in our memories, noting more and more of its depths and shadings, considering and reconsidering it. We want to have it and keep it. But we do the same thing, usually less consciously, with less beautiful views, with persons and incidents in the ordinary course of life, and indeed with whatever somehow involves us. Even more to the point, we cannot really part with anything or anyone we love, and indeed we already long for what we have quite as much as for what we have lost. Every time we turn, as we must, from what we are attached to, the parting seems too abrupt.

This unavoidable longing of ours, pervasive and compelling, is an active motive for artistic creation. In poetry it is the urge to find language sensitive enough to evoke the impact that external realities have made on our feelings and awareness. If we go back now to the passage at the end of 'Sunday Morning' (beginning 'We live in an old chaos of the sun'), the sharpness of its longing has such force that it turns the poem's surface meaning right around. Surely the whole poem is less an argument for secular hedonism — though it is that too — than an attempt to cope with an overwhelming sense of loss at life's transience. The speaker's passion is to fix everything he can experience or imagine in language so keen it cannot perish. That passion — to remember and retain what inevitably we must lose — is the most powerful source of art. It is why the ancient Greeks called Mnemosyne, their goddess of memory, the mother of the Muses.

The Continuity of Poetry

An Excerpt from an Essay by Elizabeth Drew, 1933

2.

. . . what we are accustomed to regard as the spirit of an age in the past, is very frequently the spirit of a poet, or poets, who, when they were writing, were in conscious revolt from their age. As I. A. Richards says: 'the poet is the point at which the growth of the mind shows itself.' Poets such as Chaucer, or Donne, or Dryden, or Wordsworth and Coleridge, by the force of their individual vision and creative power, appear to change the whole current of literature. So it is over and over again in the history of art. The great poet revolts from the past, and re-creates the elements of life and thought into fresh organic structures. It is not that the material of his experience is any different from that of his age in general, but the *way* he experiences it — the 'style' he gives it — these make of it a new thing. Then, when the poet has become 'recognized' by the age, which means that the age has recognized itself in the poet, and that 'point' at which the growth of the mind has showed itself has become generalized, then in a flood comes 'the spirit of the age'. All the imitable qualities in the poet's matter and manner rapidly become a fashion, and remain so until again a new vision and a new synthesis happen. It is not until the whole movement belongs sufficiently to the past to be seen in just perspective that we are alive to it. For as Donne said of his portrait, so it is true of a poet and his poetry:

> 'Tis like me now, but I dead, 'twill be more
> When we are shadows both, than 'twas before.

3.

What then is the course of our own literary history? Whence did it come and where is it now and whither is it going? How have individuals and public opinion interplayed within it? What different facets of man's consciousness have been illumined by it? In what perspectives have the elements of poetry arranged themselves: what syntheses have been achieved: what harmony results? Here is matter for many more books, but perhaps we can see enough of the past to feel its essential unity with the present.

Modern man in England emerges at the Renaissance. Even Chaucer, with his sanity and his humour, his pity and his tolerance, his keenness of external observation and his flashes of insight, lacks something. His attitude is one of acceptance of life as it is:

> What is this world? What asketh men to have?
> Now with his love, now in this colde grave
> Allone, with-outen any companye.
> Thanne is it wisdom, as it thinketh me,
> To maken vertu of necessitee,
> And take it wel.

And we can perhaps illustrate best what it is that Chaucer lacks, by a quotation from an Elizabethan poet — Sir John Davies.

> I know my body's of so frail a kind
>   As force without, fevers within, can kill;
> I know the heavenly nature of my mind,
>   But 'tis corrupted both in wit and will;
>
> I know my soul hath power to know all things,
>   Yet is she blind and ignorant in all;
> I know I am one of nature's little kings,
>   Yet to the least and vilest thing am thrall.

> I know my life's a pain and but a span,
>   I know my sense is mocked in everything;
> And to conclude, I know myself a man,
>   Which is a proud, and yet a wretched thing.

It is the note of challenge to life that is lacking in medieval literature; the knowledge of the freedom of the individual to explore the mystery of its own being. The Renaissance saw the birth of the critical and analytical mind, and hence the birth of the poetry of personal relationships. The poets no longer write of man in relation to a fixed scheme of cosmic, religious or chivalrous values, they write of the direct experiences of individual men in relation to God, to nature, to knowledge, to each other, to women. And this analytical spirit, young and experimental in Spenser and the sonneteers, and maturing gradually in the great dramatic movement of the age, comes to its complete point of self-consciousness in John Donne (1573-1631). Donne, like Bacon, took all knowledge for his province, but he has little interest in knowledge as such. He is a great poet — that is, he brings all he has learnt and read and thought into direct kinship with his emotional experience. His love of woman, and later his love of God, is knit up with the whole of his apprehension of the sensuous and intellectual worlds. It is one with all the elements of the physical universe, with all the professional terminology of the court, of the law, of the church, of trade, of the sciences: with cynicism and with ecstasy, with lust and with mystical passion, with anger, fear, jealousy, disgust, and with perfect peace.

THE SUN RISING

> Busy old fool, unruly sun,
> Why dost thou thus,

Through windows and through curtains call on us?
Must to thy motions lovers seasons run?
    Saucy pedantic wretch, go chide
    Late school-boys, and sour prentices,
Go tell Court-huntsmen, that the King will ride,
Call country ants to harvest offices;
Love, all alike, no season knows, nor clime,
Nor hours, days, months, which are the rags of time.

    Thy beams, so reverend and strong
    Why shouldst thou think?
I could eclipse and cloud them with a wink,
But that I would not lose her sight so long:
    If her eyes have not blinded thine,
    Look, and tomorrow late, tell me,
Whether both the Indias, of spice and mine,
Be where thou leftst them, or lie here with me.
Ask for those Kings whom thou saw'st yesterday,
An thou shalt hear, All here in one bed lay.

    She is all States, and all Princes, I,
    Nothing else is.
Princes do but play us; compar'd to this
All honour's mimic; All wealth alchemy.
    Thou sun art half as happy as we,
    In that the world's contracted thus;
Thine age asks ease, and since thy duties be
To warm the world, that's done in warming us.
Shine here to us, and thou art everywhere;
This bed thy centre is, these walls, thy sphere.

For a generation after Donne's death almost every minor
poet wrote like Donne. Sophisticated love poetry and inti-
mately personal religious poetry were the two popular
channels of expression, and although of course the personality of each poet colours his work — and the age of

Herrick and Herbert, Vaughan and Marvell, Carew and
Lovelace, is an age of great charm and originality of personality — yet through them all persist those qualities in Donne
which could be imitated; the fashion of using esoteric images, and of combining their use with a colloquial use of language, in which speech rhythms were blended with those of
the written word. Then, while Milton was creating new organic rhythms of thought and words in the loneliness of su-
preme genius, the reaction against the 'metaphysicals' came
from another quarter. The new king (Charles II) and his
court brought back all the new French ideals of writing from
his exile — the ideals of clarity and directness of presentation
and 'a close, naked, natural way of speaking' in both verse
and prose. Again one man, John Dryden, born in the year
that Donne died, imposed a new approach to experience and
a new formal technique upon poetry. Its elements appeared
to him to have become distorted and disrupted by the arti-
fices of the metaphysical 'conceit':

> Since that the thing we call the world,
> By chance on atoms is begot,
> Which though in daily motions hurl'd
>   Yet weary not,
>   How doth it prove
> Thou art so fair and I in love?

So sang the metaphysical poet, and was prepared to prove it
in any number of complicated ways. Dryden's vision saw a
very different world. It was a world mapped and planned
by a practical intelligence, by a masculine ideal of sanity
and discipline. It rested upon a scheme of thought which
accepted certain premises about the nature of God and
man, and ordered the rest of the universe accordingly. Its
great controlling force was the rational faculty in man's na-

THE CONTINUITY OF POETRY

ture, and the great civilizing power of poetry must support and further that force. Just as the social and intellectual forces of the later Renaissance seemed to become incarnated in Donne, so the social and intellectual forces of the Restoration seemed to become incarnate in Dryden. Profound social changes were in the air. The Civil War had been fought and the middle-class had emerged triumphant — a middle-class which represented a huge new potential reading public. Man in general, after all the turmoil and unrest of the war wanted again to become a social animal: he wanted an orderly, stable, safe way of life. He congregated in towns; he became urban and gregarious; he invented the coffee house as a centre for business and culture and gossip; his standards of literature became mundane and bourgeois; 'I hold it very indecent,' said Shaftesbury, in 1711, when Dryden's creation of the new values had again turned into the general fashion of thought of the day, 'I hold it very indecent that a man should publish his meditations or solitary thoughts. Those are the froth and scum of writing, which should be unburdened in private and consigned to oblivion, before the writer comes before the world as good company.' It is not surprising that the popular poetic figure of Shaftesbury's day should be Pope, 'the wicked wasp of Twickenham', the most brilliant purveyor of social gossip who has ever written verse, and whose wit and point and lucidity and exquisite precision of statement made him the perfect artist for the age whose ideal of a writer was that he should be 'good company'.

But as was again natural, behind this fashion of urban and common-sense poetry, the forces were gestating which were to embody themselves in the great figures of Wordsworth and Coleridge, and afterwards to decline gradually into the general fashion for romantic verse of the middle and late Victorian Age.

The new creation of poetic values, while it was in complete revolt from the eighteenth century ideal, was again different from that of the Renaissance and of Donne, and to our modern eyes, not only different, but definitely inferior. Great poetry, as we have said, depends on the association of the whole man with the material of his poem. The poet is neither an intellectual nor an emotional being alone; he feels his thoughts and thinks his sensations as it were. If only a part of him is involved in the creation of his symbols — only his senses or only his intellect or only his emotions — his poetry will fail of being great poetry. And the failure of nineteenth century poetry, when it does fail, is precisely in this narrowing of the responses of the poet. When Wordsworth is a great poet, when he is writing the Lucy poems or *The Solitary Reaper*, when Coleridge creates *The Ancient Mariner*, when Keats writes anything, almost, when Shelley writes the *Ode to the West Wind*, when Tennyson writes *Break, break, break*, or Browning *Meeting at Night*, they are great poets. When they are not writing these poems and some others like them, their response to their material tends to lose that fusion of all the activities within them, and to become limited to the reflective and moralizing activity they possess. Instead of being analytical they become ruminative. As T. S. Eliot says, 'the possible interests of a poet are unlimited; the more intelligent he is the better; the more intelligent he is the more likely that he will have interests: our only condition is that he turn them into poetry, and not merely meditate on them poetically.' Henry King (1592-1669) turns flowers and life and death into poetry.

A CONTEMPLATION UPON FLOWERS

Brave flowers, that I could gallant it like you
And be as little vain,

You come abroad and make a harmless show,
And to your beds of earth again;
You are not proud, you know your birth
For your embroidered garments are from earth.

You do obey your months, and times, but I
Would have it ever spring,
My fate would know no winter, never die
Nor think of such a thing;
Oh that I could my bed of earth but view
And smile, and look as cheerfully as you.

Oh teach me to see death, and not to fear
But rather to take truce;
How often have I seen you at a bier,
And there look fresh and spruce;
You fragrant flowers, then teach me that my breath
Like yours may sweeten and perfume my death.

But when Wordsworth writes:

One impulse from a vernal wood
May teach you more of man,
Of moral evil and of good,
Than all the sages can.

he is meditating on flowers poetically. It is a question of
the 'message' of the poem being implicit or explicit;
whether the moral nature is fused with the rest of the nature of the poet, or whether it stays outside to give its comment on the material of the poem. It is present as much in
A Contemplation upon Flowers as in *The Tables Turned*, but
one is a beautiful little poem and the other is a sermon in
verse. Matthew Arnold, indeed, unconsciously revealed the
weakness of the ideals held by himself and his age when he
defined poetry as 'criticism of life'. Poetry and criticism are
different functions of the consciousness. Poetry apprehends

and creates; it is concerned with seizing the whole nature of an experience: criticism is concerned with drawing conclusions from it, with speculating upon it, with trying to comprehend it, with interpreting it.

> Flower in the crannied wall,
> I pluck you out of the crannies,
> I hold you here, root and all, in my hand,
> Little flower — but *if* I could understand
> What you are, root and all, and all in all,
> I should know what God and man is.

Poetry creates the flower and criticism tries to understand it.

4.

This tendency to meditate poetically about life instead of creating poetry, was fostered by a change in the relationship between the poet and his environment, which began in the eighteenth century and has progressed steadily ever since. A poet is a member of the society he lives in, just as everyone else is, and it is common knowledge that the potentialities of the individual develop more easily and harmoniously if he feel himself in step with the modes of life and thought around him; if he is at home in his environment, physical, intellectual and emotional. If the major forces and interests of an age are with the poet he can develop much more fully and freely than if they are against him. In the history of English society during the sixteenth and seventeenth centuries, and up to the middle of the eighteenth century, the major forces and interests at work were national, religious and political. Now these ideals and enthusiasms are those in which the whole of a man can be involved, without repression or limitation, and the ages when they held the field are the ages when poetry flourished in a more general way than it has ever since flourished. There was a definite place for poetry in the interests of the age. The poets drew strength and nourishment from the national atmosphere they breathed; it was stimulating and vital. But Milton is the last great poet whom it fed, and the change can be traced from the time of Dryden. At first the interests themselves remained the same, but the stream ran ever more shallow and narrow compared with the full and spacious Elizabethan spirit. It was clear that with the introduction of more sternly rational values, and with the huge new bourgeois reading public, prose would usurp much of the old popularity of poetry. Real poetic inspiration ran underground, and when it next burst out in great individual figures it found itself in an alien environment. The major forces at work in society were rapidly shifting. Vitality had passed from religious interests, and the direction and character of national and political issues had changed. The main currents were industrial and financial, and as the Victorian age developed, they became more and more centred in the progress of science. Byron belonged enough to the general spirit of his times to use his whole talents in satirizing it, and to lose his life in a bid for a new freedom. Shelley flung his whole self into revolt and attempted to create a counterforce which might overthrow the current standards. But the genius of Wordsworth, Coleridge and Keats found nothing in the common interests of the community which could feed their inspiration, nor has any poet since done so. Tennyson bent his genius to please the taste of his age, but he drew no nourishment from it: rather it impoverished him. Browning, like Walt Whitman, had so much animal vitality, such perfectly functioning glands and nerves, that it was of little moment to him what environment he lived in. But the minor Victorian poets were pure individualists, each working his own vein: engrossed by personal religious experience, like Patmore, or Hopkins, or Christina Rossetti; escaping into a world of experience ruled over by 'that Lady Beauty', worshipped by Rossetti or Swinburne; or musing sadly in a cultivated and intelligent way like Arnold or Clough.

The same tendency continued in the new generation of the early twentieth century, but was pushed still further. The domain of poetry had become smaller and smaller. Poetic drama was dead, and the novel had usurped the place of epic and narrative verse. There was still poetry — exquisite poetry very often — written in the old tradition, and an age in which Housman and Hardy and Bridges, Yeats and de la Mare, Robert Frost and Edward Thomas, Edna St. Vincent Millay and Edwin Arlington Robinson were writing can hardly be called a very barren age. But it is nevertheless impossible to read any of these poets today and not to feel that they belong to an age that is passing, and that their rhythms are those of a swan song. Not that there were yet any signs of a new poetry in which the poet identified himself with the spirit of a new civilization. Rather he isolated himself still further, for no longer did he regard himself as the guardian of those spiritual and moral values in life which the growth of the industrial and scientific interests of the world at large were threatening. All the young intellectual bent was towards 'pure poetry', the poetry which, as Gautier said, 'proves nothing and tells nothing'. There was a wave of new interest in the formal 'organization' of Art, but as far as material went the youthful possessor of the poetic vision felt more and more driven in upon himself. His main preoccupation became psychological, the creation of detached moments of experience for their own sakes, unrelated to any social or moral significance. Never

before had man been so aware of his own consciousness, or
so fascinated by its intricacy.

> To penetrate that room is my desire,
> The extreme attic of the mind, that lies
> Just beyond the last bend in the corridor.

5.

The 'point' at which the new psychological growth of the
mind showed itself was in the poetry of T. S. Eliot. Here
we feel a definite impact between a wide and sensitive intelligence and the values of the Romantic Revival in its last
stages. In the early poems and *The Waste Land* that rebellion
is implicit. Eliot found a technique which, with the barest
economy in the use of language, was nevertheless a verbal
equivalent to his experience of personal challenge to the
immediate past, to his sense of exile in the present, to the
emotional and intellectual flavour of his apprehension of
life on all sides of his nature.

Eliot's poetry is very difficult, and it seems inevitable that
the poetry of the future will be difficult for the present
generation of readers. It is Eliot who has made readers
aware of where one great difficulty lies. We have become so
used to only certain of our mental processes — the logical
ones — rising to the level of expression in language, that
the task of adjusting and accommodating the attention to
respond in a new way to new material is a very hard one.
And beyond that, modern poetry becomes increasingly difficult to read because not only have we to adjust our responses to the reception of very much more complex mental
and emotional experiences, but we live in an age when new
knowledge has altered the whole conception of the universe, just as it did at the Renaissance. . . .

Notes and Questions on the Poems

The sequence of the poems often traces out several different patterns at once. The particular 'clusters' of poems singled out below are not the only groupings worthy of attention.

Poems 1 to 4

The first four poems each celebrate the poet's joyous response to the natural world in different ways.

1. *Fern Hill*

See the notes on ambiguity (p. 491), pastoral poetry (p. 513), symbol (p. 505), and transferred epithet (p. 527).

Thomas recalls the days he spent as a boy on a farm in Wales. The poet's techniques include: playful twisting of stock phrases, such as three variations on 'happy as the day is long' in lines 2, 11, and 38; repetition of simple images with cumulative effect; unobtrusive use of the creation story from Genesis to suggest the innocence of the young child, the fresh creation of the world with each new day in the child's life, and the eventual loss of this idyllic world. **l. 3 dingle** A small secluded ravine. **l. 9 windfall light** It is typical of Thomas to achieve such a multiplicity of meanings in a single phrase. The words can suggest any one of the following images, any combination of them, and may go far beyond: the subdued atmosphere at twilight as both the light and the wind fade together; the reflected patches of rosy sky and green foliage; the colours of the apples blown prematurely from the trees in autumn; the distinctive grey-green colour of the sky at twilight, as the barely disturbed water reflects the darkened sky and the bordering foliage; shafts of light, like rivers, between the rows of trees in the orchard; the unexpected wealth added by this experience. **ll. 10-18 green, golden** The green is not only the grass, but the poet's youth and the joy of fresh experience. The gold is the sun, the source of life, and the blessing of God. **ll. 11, 13, 14, and 15** The opening words of these lines repeat those of the first stanza, thereby suggesting the child's sense of permanence and security. **l. 25**

nightjars Nocturnal birds so-called because of a whirring noise that they make. **l. 26 ricks** Haystacks. **l. 39** Each day presents a freshly created world; also, the child is reborn with each new day. Cf. ll. 32-33. **l. 40** Although Thomas revised this poem at least seventeen times, he was always dissatisfied with one word in this line. Can you identify the word and explain his dissatisfaction? **ll. 53-54** An effective realization in imagery of the paradoxical relationship of growth and decline. The sea's chains are the tides, controlled by the circling moon.

2. *There Was a Boy* from *The Prelude*

See the note on pastoral poetry (p. 513).

Wordsworth drew together his childhood memories in *The Prelude*, a remarkable long poem that illustrates the gradual shaping of the individual by the experiences and environment of early life. The excerpt from Book V (ll. 364-388), given here, was also published separately. It is difficult to be certain whether Wordsworth, at this stage in his life, believed in pantheism or in divine immanence. The pantheist describes God in terms of the spirit of Nature; a believer in divine immanence describes Nature in terms of God who pervades it. **l. 2 Winander** The scene is Lake Windermere (Wynander's lake) in the English Lake District. **ll. 19-25** Wordsworth felt that, in such moments of deep communion, Nature impressed its patterns on his mind and imagination.

3. *A Field of Light*

See the notes on cadence (p. 518) and juxtaposition (p. 508).

Roethke traces states of feeling by depicting the very delicate nuances of a natural setting. The landscape of the first part suggests isolation and stagnancy, and an incapacity for a sensuous response to the beauty around him. The poet is driven to ask himself whether he has ever denied the forces of life by 'cursing the sun.' Immediately he is carried back in memory to earlier scenes, in which he had felt himself drawn to dark and enclosed vegetation, dank and rotting in the absence of sunlight. Even there, he recalls, he had celebrated his delight in the natural world. Fortified by this memory, he moves in the third part to a joyful affirmation of personal and natural well-being.

l. 43 the lovely diminutives Roethke is enthusiastic about the myriad forms in nature — particularly small plants, animals, and inanimate objects.

4. *I Taste a Liquor Never Brewed*

See the note on poem 76 (p. 396) for a comment about Dickinson's unconventional punctuation and format.

Dickinson celebrates her joyous response to intimate aspects of the natural environment. In contrast to the simple pleasures she is celebrating, she conjures up a series of vivid images of exotic conditions. Compare this poem with the three others by Dickinson in this collection (pp. 119 and 121) to get a sense of her inimitable style.

Questions: Poems 1 to 4

    (a)   Compare the response of the four poets to their natural environments.

    (b)   Compare the effects achieved by the language, rhythm, and imagery of these poems.

    (c)   Compare the way that Thomas and Wordsworth recollect their childhoods. What are the outstanding differences in style?

Poems 5 to 7

Each of these poems comments on a lack of harmony with or appreciation of the environment.

5. *Depression in Namu, B.C.*

Namu A small town on an inlet of Queen Charlotte Sound in British Columbia. How does Purdy's attitude to nature differ from the attitude implicit in the previous grouping of poems? Would you call this attitude negative?

6. *Snake*

See the notes on free verse (p. 520) and imitative harmony (p. 525).

Lawrence uses his reactions to the snake to expose what he sees as a conflict between the values and standards of natural man and those imposed by 'civilized' life. The suggestiveness of the symbols, the extremely evocative imagery, and the internal dialogue blend to recreate both the physical experience and the spiritual crisis. **l. 4 carob** An evergreen with dark reddish berries, native to the Mediterranean region. **l. 18** Note that Lawrence mentions the forked tongue but not the fangs. **l. 21 Etna** A famous active volcano near Taormina, on the east coast of Sicily, where Lawrence lived for a time. **ll. 22-24** Is the significance of black and gold normal? **l. 66 the albatross** In Coleridge's 'Rime of the Ancient Mariner,' a sailor was punished for having wantonly killed an albatross, a large sea-bird. He was sentenced to wander, telling the story of his sin and of his redemption by love. It is interesting to compare Coleridge's and Lawrence's treatments of wanton brutality and its symbolic overtones.

7. *To a Fat Lady Seen from a Train*

See the note on the triolet (p. 527).

Questions: Poems 5 to 7

   (a)   Select images from each of these poems that express the poet's appreciation of natural beauty.

   (b)   What is the relationship between the poet's mood and the landscape in each poem?

   (c)   To what extent does each poet rely on sensual appeal in order to make a point?

Poems 8 to 12

These poems use a transitory environment as the setting for the poets' reflections about their destiny.

8. *Baseball*

See the note on extended metaphor (p. 505).

Mazur begins the poem by stating that the 'game of baseball is not a metaphor' and 'not really life.' Does she maintain this distinction throughout the poem? Pick out several gently amusing insights into human behaviour that enrich the poem. **ll. 27-28 the farmer that Auden speaks of in Breughel's Icarus** A reference to Auden's poem 'Musée des Beaux Arts.' **ll. 51-52 our guys look like Sennett cops** Mack Sennett was a producer of a series of silent films in which good and bad guys alike bumped into each other, fell down, chased around frantically, and engaged in other ridiculous antics. The Keystone Cops were particularly popular figures of fun.

9. *Walking Around*

See the notes on free verse (p. 520) and image (p. 501).

Neruda's evocation of realistic and surrealist images is very much like effects produced in psychic films.

What does the last line contribute to the impact made by the poem?

10. *I Know Where I'm Going*

Although claims have been made stating that this song originated in Ireland, the source of the poem is now fairly well established as Scotland. **ll. 13-14** In northern climates in earlier days a 'fair' complexion was considered attractive, a dark complexion less desirable.

11. *Waterloo Express*

l. 7 pariah The reference is to any outcast of society.

12. *The Road Not Taken*

See the note on extended metaphor (p. 505).

What is the significance of taking the road 'less travelled by'? Why has this decision 'made all the difference' to the speaker of the poem?

Questions: Poems 8 to 12

    (a)   What personal values are expressed in each poem?
    (b)   How does geographic reference help convey the feelings and concerns expressed?
    (c)   How does the form of each poem contribute to the mood?

Poems 13 and 14

'Ulysses' and 'Ozymandias' focus on heroes and journeys in far-away lands.

13. *Ulysses*

See the notes on blank verse (p. 494), climax (p. 494), and dramatic monologue (p. 497).

The speaker is the Greek hero Ulysses of the epic poem *The Odyssey*. Ulysses has returned home to his kingdom of Ithaca and his faithful wife Penelope after ten years of fighting in the Trojan War and ten further years of adventurous wandering. Having ruled his kingdom for three years, he now realizes he is aging and longs for his days of former glory. **l. 10 Hyades** A V-shaped cluster of stars that were supposed to indicate rainy weather when they rose with the sun. **ll. 19-21** A sustained metaphor that crystallizes the philosophy of Ulysses. **l. 23 unburnish'd** A reference to his sword, which has become dull-coloured from disuse. The image is used to represent Ulysses' inaction. **l. 53 men that strove with Gods** The gods took sides and joined in actual combat during the Trojan War. **l. 63 the Happy Isles** According to ancient belief, a land where warriors who had died honourably and received proper burial rites assumed the form they had in the prime of life. **l. 64 Achilles** The greatest Greek fighter in the Trojan War, killed by an arrow that struck him in the heel. After his death, his armour was awarded to Ulysses.

How sympathetic are you to Ulysses as he is portrayed in the poem?

14. *Ozymandias*

See the notes on the sonnet (p. 522), symbol (p. 505), and synechdoche (p. 526).

Why has Shelley used a reporter and a far-away setting to make his point?

Questions: Poems 13 and 14

    (a)   The subjects in both poems are men of stature. What characteristics do you find in each man that are admirable or less than admirable?

(b) Both poems convey a sense of dignity. What features of each are responsible for this impression?

(c) How is a sense of bygone times achieved in each poem?

(d) What do the references to the setting contribute to each poem?

Poems 15 to 18

These poems are portraits of ordinary individuals and everyday life.

15. *A Peasant*

l. 1 Prytherch Pronounce *y* as *u* in but; *th* as in then; and *ch* as in the Scottish word loch. **l. 3 gap of cloud** The tops of the Welsh hills are frequently enveloped in mist. **l. 7 clods that glint** The turned edge of the furrow is polished by the ploughshare.

Why does Thomas change the level of diction part way through the poem?

16. *The Village Master* from *The Deserted Village*

See the note on irony (p. 507).

ll. 1-2 What do these two lines contribute to our reading of what follows? **furze** A low prickly evergreen shrub with yellow flowers.

17. *Sir Penny* from *Carmina Burana*

See the notes on invective (p. 507), irony (p. 507), and rhyme (p. 524).

'Sir Penny' is one of the poems in a thirteenth-century anthology entitled *Carmina Burana*. It is also called *Benediktbeuern Songs* because, in 1803, it was found in the monastery of Benediktbeuern in Upper Bavaria. Most of the selections are in German or Latin, although some are of obvious English, French, or Italian origin. **ll. 7-8** Sir Penny's operations, although breaking codes of justice, cannot be challenged by church courts of law. **l. 15 Dives** Dives was the rich man in the St Luke account of the rich man and Lazarus. **ll. 36-40 ablative, datives, genitives** These grammatical terms refer to three of the cases in Latin syntax that indicate by means of a suffix added to a noun the relationship of that noun to other words in the sentence. The ablative case indicates the agent responsible for an action; the dative establishes the indirect object or the recipient of an action; and the genitive shows possession or ownership of something. **l. 48 soldi** Italian coins of little value.

18. *The Unknown Citizen*

See the notes on irony (p. 507) and satire (p. 522).

l. 26 Eugenist A scientist who specializes in determining conditions that will produce a 'superior' race of people.

Which features relate this poem to relatively contemporary times rather than to an earlier period of history? Are any of the details no longer quite appropriate for their intended purpose?

Questions: Poems 15 to 18

(a) Describe the basic tone of each poem. What other tones (if any) are present?

(b) To what extent does the form contribute to the tonal impression in each poem?

(c) What comments are the poets making about the society of their time?

(d) Do any of the poets suggest possibilities for improvement in their societies? Do you think that there is any value in poets commenting on the political and social issues of their times?

Poems 19 to 21

These satirical portraits are light and humorous.

19. *Impromptu on Charles II*

See the note on satire (p. 522).

Charles II, proclaimed King of Scotland, parts of Ireland, and England after the execution of his father Charles I, reigned from 1660 to 1685. In his struggles with Parliament he was always having to make compromises and engage in secret negotiations. Rochester, formerly influential at court, had fallen out of favour with Charles.

20. *Salutation*

See the notes on modernist poetry (p. 510) and satire (p. 522).

Pound accuses his generation of being both 'smug' and 'uncomfortable.' What evidence does he offer to support his charge?

21. *You Hear That Fat Frog*

See the notes on the haiku (p. 500) and satire (p. 522).

Questions: Poems 19 to 21

(a) What relationship does each poet establish with the reader?
(b) Look up the biographies of each poet, and decide to what extent you think the tone of each poem reflects what you know about the respective poet.

Poem 22

The original Japanese characters, transliteration, and versions by three different translators are shown for this haiku by Issa.

22. *My Grumbling Wife*

By comparing the English versions and sensing the feeling of each, the strategic importance of the choice and placement of single words in haiku poetry and in all poetry becomes apparent. Notice how the mood and focus varies from one version to the next.

Questions: Poem 22

(a) Examine the three poems by Issa in this collection (pp. 33, 34, and 174). Can you sense the 'taste' of Issa's poetry and distinguish his work from that of other haiku poets?
(b) Try writing your own version of 'My Grumbling Wife' from the transliteration. Compare your version with those of your classmates to determine what causes the different impressions you make.

Poems 23 and 24

In each poem a woman has been without her husband for many years. The cause of the feelings of despondency, however, is quite different.

23. *An Old Woman's Lamentations*

Translated very freely from *Le Grand Testament* by François Villon, the name adopted by the French poet Montcorbier (1431-c. 1484). His sardonic, ribald, but very moving lyrics were championed by many writers in the first decades of the present century. Do you find any evidence of Synge's Irish background in the poem?

24. *Penelope's Despair*

Penelope is the wife of the Greek hero Ulysses, as described by Homer in *The Odyssey*, Books XXII and XXIII. See Tennyson's poem 'Ulysses' (p. 22). The poem shows Penelope's possible reaction to the return of her husband after many years away. **ll. 14-17** While Ulysses was away from home for twenty long years, a multitude of suitors, insisting that Ulysses must no longer be alive, settled in Penelope's home and tried to induce her to select one of them as a husband. She was able to put off a decision by saying that she would choose one of them when she finished the tapestry she was weaving daily. Each night she secretly undid the day's work, and the suitors were held off until her husband finally did return. How does Penelope's picture of Ulysses compare with Ulysses' own image of himself as he speaks in Tennyson's poem?

Questions: Poems 23 and 24

(a) What is the attitude of the wife to the husband in each poem?

(b) How does the point of view from which the comments are made (first person, third person) affect the impression made by each poem?

(c) In each poem we have a detailed physical description of one character. How are we, the readers, affected by these pictures?

Poems 25 to 27

These three poems are studies of mood.

25. *Little Green Tree*

See the note on archetype (p. 492).

The mood and form of this poem are derived from the blues. In the six-line stanza of the traditional blues, lines 1 and 2 are repeated as lines 3 and 4, as in 'Good Mornin' Blues':

> *I woke up this mornin'*
> *With the blues all round my bed.*
> *Yes, I woke up this mornin'*
> *With the blues all round my bed.*
> *Went to eat my breakfast*
> *Had the blues all in my bread.*

How has Hughes adapted the form?

26. *Lines* from 'The Garden of Proserpine'

See the notes on archetype (p. 492), rhyme (p. 524), and sound (p. 524).

Proserpine The beautiful daughter of Jupiter and Ceres (in Greek mythology, Persephone, daughter of Zeus and Demeter). While walking in her garden, Proserpine was carried off by Pluto to be made queen of the Underworld. Her mother persuaded Jupiter to ordain that Proserpine return to earth twice a year. With each sojourn on earth she brought prosperous harvests to the world. The myth represents the cycle of planting and harvest.

Notice how the balance and cadence of phrases suggest that Swinburne's statements are beyond doubt. The patterning of vowels and consonants, the rhyme scheme, and the placing of masculine and feminine endings make this stanza form a remarkably appropriate medium. Swinburne was praised for his technical facility. Do you find it pleasing or overdone?

27. *The Hitherandthithering Waters Of* from *Finnegan's Wake*

See the notes on archetype (p. 492), portmanteau words (p. 514), and sound (p. 524).

Finnegan's Wake, the long novel on which Joyce spent seventeen years, is ostensibly the recreation of a single night's dream. The dreamer is H. C. Earwicker (Eire-wicker, or dweller in Ireland), keeper of a tavern in Dublin. His dreams revolve around his family — his wife, Anna, his two sons, Shaun and Shem, and his daughter Iseult — and around minor incidents in his waking life. By developing an intricately punning dream-language of his own, drawn from many languages, and by expanding the major figures in the novel into universal symbols of masculinity and femininity, Joyce contrived to make all time and all space his subject-matter.

This excerpt is taken from a dialogue between two Irish washer-women who, in the dream, are rinsing out Earwicker's 'dirty linen' in the River Liffey, which runs through Dublin. They stand on opposite banks discussing Earwicker's family; as day flows into night they move gradually down the widening stream, so that it becomes increasingly difficult to communicate from one bank to the other. In an astonishing feat of verbal orchestration, Joyce recreates the drowsiness of the washerwomen as their senses are invaded and overcome by the night-sounds about them, until finally they are metamorphosed into a stone and a tree-trunk. **ll. 1-2 chittering . . . bawk talk** A reference to the thin sounds and sudden reverses of direction of the bats and mice that are particularly active at twilight. 'Bawkie' is an old word for a bat. **ll. 4-5 my foos won't Moos** An early draft of this line read 'My feet won't move.' Joyce changed 'move' to 'moos' in order to draw on the German word 'Moos' meaning 'moss.' The suggestion is that the woman's feet have become mossy, as though she were a stone or a tree. The change from 'feet' to 'foos' deepens the effect of the dream-like chant, in which all things flow into one another and seem to sleep. **ll. 5-6 elm . . . Shaun or Shem** Shaun (Sean; in English, 'John') is the blond heroic son of Anna and Earwicker, and the builder of social order. Shem (a Hebrew name, given, for example, to Noah's eldest son) is dark, introverted, and brooding. In his dream

Earwicker frequently thinks of Shaun as a tree (an elm) and Shem as a stone. As the washerwomen discuss the two sons, they find their own feet taking root and their bodies growing heavy. **l. 6 Livia** The dreamer identifies his wife Anna with the River Liffey, casting the name of the river in a form suited to a Roman matron. Earwicker's full name for his wife is Anna Livia Plurabelle. **daughtersons** In this dream-world masculine and feminine characteristics are frequently transferred from one sex to the other.

Questions: Poems 25 to 27

    (a)   Which do you find more effective: a direct statement of mood or the suggestion of mood by imagery?

    (b)   Compare the use of imagery in the three selections.

Poem 28

A series of kaleidoscopic images traces the feelings and thoughts of the anti-hero, Prufrock, in this episode of his disenchanted life.

28. *The Love Song of J. Alfred Prufrock*

See the notes on allusion (p. 490), conceit (p. 495), dramatic monologue (p. 497), imagery (p. 501), irony, (p. 507), juxtaposition (p. 508), and modernist poetry (p. 510).

The title is calculated to convey the dissonance and wry flavour that penetrate the poem. 'J. Alfred Prufrock' is a grotesquely unsuitable name for a singer of love songs; and it is not until we have read almost a hundred lines that we find reason to call the poem a love song.

The speaker, Prufrock, invites a companion to accompany him on a journey through run-down city streets. The strollers are at once impelled to consider an 'overwhelming question'; but Prufrock refuses to take the question up, suggesting instead that his companion and he continue on their way to visit a lady friend. They soon arrive, and the remainder of the poem is occupied with images of the banal and futile existence in the home of Prufrock's friend; and with the doubts, hesitations, and self-recriminations of Prufrock himself, who is paralyzed before the momentous question that he cannot even articulate. The total impression of desperation and spiritual fatigue can be sensed directly in Prufrock, and indirectly in his society, which has produced only slums for the lonely men in shirtsleeves and sterile sophistication for the well-to-do. The poem is filled with references to inconsequential activities, such as taking tea or marmalade, engaging in banal conversation, or measuring out one's life with coffee spoons.

The key to reading this poem lies in recognizing its tone. Prufrock has the awareness and sensitivity to see through pretence, whether other people's or his own; but he has not the resolution necessary to shake off his apathy. Hence he speaks in a tone of self-deprecating irony. It is that element that provokes the deliberately childish rhythms and mocking rhymes:

Oh, do not ask, 'What is it?'
Let us go and make our visit.

Every effort of Prufrock to compare himself with great figures of the past is defeated by the same self-irony. Is he like John the Baptist, martyred by a cruel woman? At once he has the humiliating thought: how would *his* head, with its bald spot, look on a platter? No, he has nothing of the prophet in him.

The Italian epigraph is from Dante's *The Inferno*, XXVII, 61-66. These are the words of a damned soul who addressed Dante during his descent into Hell. 'If I believed my answer were being made to one who could ever return to the world, this flame would shake [i.e., this soul would speak] no more; but since, if what I hear is true, never from this abyss did living man return, I answer thee without fear of infamy.' The epigraph suggests that the poet considers himself and his readers to be living in a hell on earth. **ll. 2-3** This audacious conceit, one of the most famous in modern poetry, not only provides a setting, but establishes the clinical, unromantic atmosphere of a poem that dissects a diseased society. **l. 10 an overwhelming question** Prufrock's obsession with this question, which he cannot bring himself to ask, returns in lines 30, 45, 80, and 93. It becomes increasingly ominous throughout the poem, but we never learn what the question is. **ll. 13-14 Michelangelo** The Florentine artist Miche-langelo Buonarroti (1475-1564), noted for the massive virility of his work. This juxtaposed couplet, with its inane rhyme, suggests vividly the debasing of great art to the status of a conversation piece for dilet-tantes. Life in the home of Prufrock's friend is characterized by such conversations. **ll. 15-22** What is the sustained metaphor in these lines? **ll. 23-37 there will be time, works and days** Phrases taken from *Works and Days*, a didactic poem by Hesiod, a Greek poet thought to have lived about the end of the eighth century B. C. It describes a de-pressed peasantry and a decadent aristocracy and gives advice on such matters as worthy and unworthy effort, choosing a wife, and lucky and unlucky days. What are the functions of this allusion? **l. 51** What fact about his life is Prufrock summing up so effectively? **l. 52 a dying fall** An allusion to the opening lines of *Twelfth Night*. **ll. 70-74** At the begin-ning of his only attempt to speak out directly, Prufrock trails off into si-lence (l. 72). He recognizes his ignoble lack of purpose, seeing himself as a crab scuttling away at every fright. **l. 92** A reworded allusion to the love poem 'To His Coy Mistress,' ll. 41-42 (p. 233). All time and space would be condensed into one small sphere if the question were asked. **ll. 94-95 Lazarus** Apparently a blending of two Biblical allusions. One is to John II: 1-44, where the brother of Martha and Mary, raised by Christ from the dead, returns to the grim world that he had left for a time. In the other, Luke 16: 19-31, a beggar is not allowed to return from the land of the dead to warn the rich about damnation. **ll. 96-98** What is the final fear that paralyzes Prufrock? **ll. 111-119** Prufrock wonders idly if he might be compared to Hamlet, who was also tortured by in-decision and spiritual malaise, but he rejects the idea and speaks of himself in terms that suggest Polonius. **l. 117 Full of high sentence** In Chaucer's description of the Clerk of Oxenford in the *Canterbury Tales*, this phrase is used in commendation. Here Eliot used it to sug-gest pompous bombast. **l. 121** The fashion of having cuffs on trousers was new. Prufrock would like to be stylish.

Questions: Poem 28

    (a) Who might Prufrock's companion be?
    (b) It is impossible to know precisely what 'overwhelming' ques-

tion Prufrock has tried to ask and failed. Can you suggest some of the elements it might include?

(c) Justify your favorable or unfavorable response to any verse paragraph in the poem.

Poems 29 to 35
These seven poems are expressions of the poets' feelings toward loved ones.

29. *A Kiss*
See the note on the triolet (p. 527).

30. *Western Wind*
This is a segment of a song written in the fifteenth century. How does it evoke such powerful feelings?

31. Sonnet XVIII: *Shall I Compare Thee to a Summer's Day?*
See the note on the sonnet (p. 522).

While Shakespeare's sonnets were probably written between 1592 and 1601, the precise date of each is impossible to establish, as they were published only in a pirated and slipshod edition in 1609. Scholars have not identified with certainty the young man whose friendship the poet treasures, or the woman with whom he is infatuated. In any case the sonnets are valued, not primarily for their biographical information, but for the cumulative power of their emotional statement and imagery. **l. 8 untrimm'd** Divested of ornament. **l. 10 ow'st** Ownest. **l. 12 to time thou grow'st** You acquire the same duration of life as time itself.

32. Sonnet XXX: *When to the Sessions of Sweet Silent Thought*
See the notes on extended metaphor (p. 505), the sonnet (p. 522), and poem 31.

l. 1 sessions This term introduces a sustained metaphor drawn from courtroom procedure. **l. 7 cancell'd** Paid, as a debt. Note the continuing imagery of business and finance. **l. 9 grievances** Troubles, griefs; legal complaints. **foregone** Long since past. **l. 10 tell** Count; recount.

33. *Sonnet: How Do I Love Thee?*
See the note on the sonnet (p. 522).

This poem comes from the sequence *Sonnets from the Portuguese*, dedicated to fellow-poet Robert Browning before their marriage.

34. *You Never Touch*
See the note on the tanka (p. 527).

l. 5 the Way Possibly Zen Buddhist philosophy. What picture emerges of the person whom the speaker is addressing?

35. *The Ill-Tempered Lover*
See the note on invective (p. 507).

The thirteenth poem in a sequence of the same name. **l. 4 Sebastian** A Christian martyr, killed by Roman archers. The death of St Sebastian is the subject of many well-known paintings.

Questions: Poems 29 to 35
- (a) What feature of love is being addressed in each poem? How would you describe the mood of each poem?
- (b) What differences do you find between the ways in which Shakespeare and Elizabeth Barrett Browning handle the sonnet form?

Poems 36 to 38
These poems deal with 'madness' and thus are able to reveal the soul without the protection of reason.

36. *The Song of the Mad Prince*
Why has the prince become mad? What effect does the question-

and-answer format have on the mood of the poem? What effect is conjured up by the sound of the words in the second-last line?

37. *Tom O' Bedlam's Song*

These two stanzas are taken from a much longer poem, which occurs in a number of versions of varying lengths.

Tom O' Bedlams were wandering beggars who were either mad or pretended to be so. The name Bedlam comes from the Hospital of Saint Mary of Bethlehem, an asylum for the insane in London in the sixteenth and seventeenth centuries, which was miserably overcrowded and discharged many of its patients to beg in the streets. Snatches of their street cries are woven into the refrain of this song. **l. 4 Moons** The moon was often associated with madness; hence the word lunatic from the Latin word *luna*, meaning 'moon.' **ll. 13-15** The irrational arithmetic reflects his tortured mind. **l. 14 enragèd** Mad. **ll. 6-20** Disturbed and ironic references to the wards and cages of Bedlam, and to the barbarous treatment of the insane that was usual at the time.

38. *The Mad Gardener's Song*

How do you account for the widespread appeal of Carroll's brand of nonsense verse?

Questions: Poems 36 to 38
   (a)   How is the impression of madness created in each poem?
   (b)   What do the mad visions in 'The Song of the Mad Prince' and 'Tom O' Bedlam's Song' have to do with the speakers' earlier lives?

Poem 39

This playful poem is an excellent example of the limerick form.

39. *A Man Hired by John Smith & Co.*

See the note on the limerick (p. 508).
The poem is a play on abbreviations. Read the full word

represented by the abbreviation 'Co.' Then read 'tho' and 'do' as if they were similar abbreviations.

Poems 40 to 42

Each of these poems moves with a narrative thread through a supernatural world.

40. *The Lines of the Hand*

Pick out the details in the poem that seem amusing at first, but have a threatening overtone. **l. 5 Boucher** François Boucher (1703-1770) was a French painter whose work depicted the elegance and gaiety of the courts of Louis XV and Louis XVI.

The opening scene and the final scene are connected by the narration. What are some possible relationships between the letter and the revolver? For example, did the man send or receive the letter? What sense can be made of the details of the path traced by the wandering line? How does the title fit into the puzzling scenario? What features would rank this selection as a prose poem?

41. *The Twa Corbies*

See the note on the ballad (p. 493).

This version of the poem is Scottish. There are several English versions. What is suggested about the cause of the knight's death?

42. *Sir Patrick Spens*

See the note on the ballad (p. 493).

This ballad is one of eighteen known versions. Some versions mention the King of Scotland's daughter, who was to be either taken to Norway or brought back from Norway by Sir Patrick Spens for her betrothal. **l. 1 Dumferling** A town on the east coast of southern Scotland, and a favourite residence of the Scottish kings. **ll. 24-26** It is a popular belief still that when the crescent moon is seen with the remainder of the disk faintly outlined, a storm will follow.

Questions: Poems 40 to 42

    (a) An element of the unknown is suggested in each of the three poems. In which poem does it seem most important to the effectiveness of the poem?

    (b) What pictures from each poem remain vivid in your mind?

Poems 43 to 48

The focus of these poems is the celebration of the imagination, including a variety of arts.

43. *You'd Better Believe Him*

See the note on the fable (p. 500). Can you justify the sub-title, 'A Fable'?

Why do you think the poem begins with a verb and no subject? What do you think is the prosecution's attitude at the end of the poem? What do you think makes this *tour de force* work? To which of the previous seven poems is this one most akin?

44. *The Artist*

In what way is Mr. T like the man in the previous poem? **l. 14 entrechat** A dance movement in which the person leaps into the air and repeatedly claps the feet together or crosses the legs. Do you find that the form of the poem adds to its effectiveness?

45. *The Six Strings*

See the note on extended metaphor (p. 505).

The instrument referred to is presumably a Spanish guitar. What different impressions do you have of the style of today's guitar music?

46. *Song for Saint Cecilia's Day, 1687*

See the notes on accentual verse (p. 521), imitative harmony (p. 525), and imitative rhythm (p. 525).

Saint Cecilia was a Christian martyr who has traditionally been associated with music. When the Academy of Music was founded at Rome in 1584, she was made the patron saint of church music.

Dryden wrote this poem as the libretto for a musical performance.
ll. 1-15 The account of creation in Genesis is united with the Platonic
conception of an eternal order underlying finite existence and revealing
its nature most fully in the harmonies of music and mathematics. **l. 8
Then cold . . . dry** A reference from medieval natural philosophy to
the four elements: earth, air, fire, and water. **l. 15 The diapason . . .
Man** A swelling burst of harmony, here achieving its climax in the creation of human life. **l. 17 Jubal** 'The father of all such as handle the
harp and organ' (Genesis 4: 21). **l. 48 Orpheus** A legendary Greek bard,
who, by the power of his music, could charm animals and trees into
following him. **l. 56 spheres** According to a doctrine accepted by Plato,
the earth stood at the centre of nine concentric, transparent spheres that
carried the planets and stars. As the spheres revolved they produced
harmonies in which the eternal Order was revealed more fully than on
earth. Only those who qualified by understanding and proper living
could hear the music of the revolving spheres. **ll. 61-63** Compare these
line to I Corinthians 15: 52.

To what extent do you agree or disagree with the claims Dryden
makes about the evocative powers of specific musical instruments?

47. *On First Looking into Chapman's Homer*

See the notes on extended metaphor (p. 505) and the sonnet
(p. 522).

When John Keats was twenty-one years old, he and a friend came
upon a translation by the Elizabethan poet George Chapman of Homer's *The Iliad* and *The Odyssey*. The two friends, enchanted, sat up
most of the night reading aloud to each other from these treasures of
ancient literature, which they had been unable to read in the original
Greek. In the early morning Keats walked home and wrote this sonnet, which he delivered to his friend's door before he went to bed.
Keats came to a whole new experience of literature with his reading
of Homer. **ll. 1-4** In the past, literature had given him insight into
other times and places. **Apollo** This celebrated Greek god was a master musician and the god of truth. **l. 1 Cortez** Actually, Balboa, not
Cortez, discovered the Pacific Ocean in September, 1513. The point of
the comparison is not lost by having an incorrect name. Cortez was

another conquistador, living at the same time, whose exploits centred around Mexico and the Aztecs. Try substituting the correct name in l. II. How is the notion of 'travelled' in l. I developed throughout the poem?

48. *Ode on a Grecian Urn*

See the notes on apostrophe (p. 492), ode (p. 512), paradox (p. 512), and pastoral poetry (p. 513).

Keats's imagination was fired by the display of Grecian urns and friezes from the Parthenon, which he saw in the British Museum. With these in mind, he traces the scenes depicted around the curved surface of an antique urn. **ll. 3-4** The essence of history is conveyed more tellingly by the scenes depicted on the urn than by a written description. **l. 7 Tempe** A Thessalonian valley celebrated for its beauty, cool shade, and birdsong. **Arcady** A mountainous district in Greece idealized as a place of pastoral contentment. **l. 41 Attic** Here, referring to the purity and simplicity of classical Greek art. **brede** An old form of 'braid.' The effect is of an interwoven design.

In the first three lines of 'Ode on a Grecian Urn' Keats addresses the urn as 'a bride of quietness,' 'a foster-child of silence and slow time,' and a 'sylvan historian.' Which references in subsequent lines justify each of the three titles? What do you find significant about Keats's use of language in this ode? What other features of the poem are responsible for its emotional appeal?

Questions: Poems 43 to 48

(a) What claims does each poet make for dance, music, visual art, and the power of imagination?

(b) What is the relationship of actual life and ideal life in each poem in this cluster?

Poems 49 to 51

In these poems the poets are concerned with their own fulfilment as artists rather than celebrating the art form as a means of expression.

49. *Sonnet: When I Have Fears*

See the notes on persona (p. 514) and the sonnet (p. 522).

Keats wrote this poem in 1818, the year his brother, whom he had been nursing, died from tuberculosis and three years before his own death from the same disease. Having a premonition that he, too, would die an untimely death, he expresses his fear that he will not live long enough to articulate his poetic vision and celebrate his love for Fanny Brawne.

50. *Selections* from *Song of Myself*

See the notes on free verse (p. 520) and persona (p. 514).

Song of Myself consists of 52 poems embodying a wide range of sensuous and spiritual experience. By revealing the most personal details, real and imagined, of his life, Whitman intended to become the voice of the American people.

[Poem 1] In this manifesto of his aims and assumptions Whitman declares that he has the breadth of vision and the disinterested concern for all things, good and bad alike, necessary to a great poet. The declaration is reinforced by his cumulative rhetoric with its appositional phrases (in lines 7, 8, 9, and 11) and its nominative absolute construction (in lines 6 and 10.).

[From Poem 6] **l. 11 Kanuck** A French Canadian. **Tuckahoe** A Virginian. **Cuff** A black American.

[From Poem 33] Whitman has already declared that he is qualified as a poet by his capacity for identifying with all humanity. Here, in the white heat of imagination, he takes upon himself the sufferings of the martyred slave and fireman. **l. 18 inspired** Inhaled.

[Poem 52] The last poem in the series. Whitman evaluates himself and his poetry, convinced that both will continue to exist. **l. 8 jags** Shreds.

51. *A Supermarket in California*

See the note on transferred epithet (p. 527).

Ginsberg has been called the heir to Whitman. What similarities and differences do you observe in their work? **ll. 5-6 dreaming of**

your enumerations A reference to a feature of Whitman's style. **l. 7
penumbras** Shadows as cast by an eclipse, where some light comes
through. **l. 9 Garcia Lorca** See the biography (p. 471) and 'The Six
Strings' (p. 63). **l. 32 Charon** An aged boatman in Greek and Roman
mythology who ferried the souls of the dead across the River Lethe.
l. 34 Lethe The river of forgetfulness that separated the underworld
from the world above.

What is Ginsberg saying about himself in his references to Whitman?

Questions: Poems 49 to 51
  (a) What kind of fulfilment does each poet seek for himself?
  (b) Each poet has his own kind of language. Characterize the lan-
       guage of each.
  (c) What similarities and differences in style do you find in the
       three poems?

Poems 52 and 53

These selections reflect the poets' feelings on poetic survival.

52. *Sonnet* LV: *Not Marble, Nor the Gilded Monuments*

See the notes on the sonnet (p. 522) and poem 31 (p. 379).

Shakespeare's boast that he will achieve immortality in his verse
echoes the Latin poets Ovid and Horace. **l. 6 broils** Embroilments,
tumults. **l. 7 Mars** The god of war. **l. 13 the judgment that** The
day of judgment when; or, the decree on judgment day that.

53. *On His Books*

See the notes on internal rhyme (p. 506) and pun (p. 514).

Question: Poems 52 and 53
  (a) Both Shakespeare and Belloc seem reasonably confident of
       their literary achievements. Do you think they have avoided
       appearing smug? If so, how did they manage it? If you feel
       there is any smugness, what features give you this impression?

Poem 54

The focus of this humorous poem is the menacing aspects of childhood.

54. *Jim*

See the notes on parody (p. 513), polysyllabic rhyme (p. 524), and wit (p. 528).

Belloc's wit has full play in this parody of the Victorian 'cautionary tale,' which presents young readers with 'Dreadful Examples and Edifying Conclusions' intended to persuade them to lead virtuous lives. 'Albert and the Lion' is another well-known dialect version of the same story.

Questions: Poem 54

    (a)   Why do you think this poem has remained popular with adults as well as children?

    (b)   How does Belloc create humour in his poem?

Poems 55 to 57

These poems strike an apprehensive note about the future of youngsters as they face adulthood.

55. *Nursery Rhyme of Innocence and Experience*

See the note on didactic poetry (p. 497).

The title of the poem alludes to Blake's famous series, *Songs of Innocence and of Experience*. The jingly rhyming of the poem is incongruous with Blake's poems. We expect a light poem, but omens of impending sorrow appear. What effect do these omens have as the poem develops? What point do you think is being made about childhood? What role does the sailor play in the overall statement of the poem?

56. *Rite of Passage*

What future does Sharon Olds suggest lies ahead for her son and the others at the party? Is she saying anything about the basic nature of males? What is a 'rite of passage'? Explain the paradox in the last line.

57. *Backdrop Addresses Cowboy*

The poem operates on two levels, which interface to make an overall comment on the unsavory nature of North American life. The poem opens with a spoof on the traditional cowboy film in which good guys overcome villains in violent shootouts, then ride off into the sunset in search of new adventures. Then Atwood touches more enigmatically on the effects of the promotion of violence. By using the backdrop, the artificial stage setting for westerns, Atwood suggests that our romantic version of how the west was settled is a sham and that today's 'heroic developers' are carrying on the tradition of desecration that underlay the bravado of the western films.

What is the significance of the words 'backdrop,' 'porcelain grin,' and 'papier-mâché' in establishing the message of the poem? What kind of interaction takes place between the speaker and the person addressed?

Questions: Poems 55 to 57

(a) All of these poems use a first person speaker. What is each speaker's attitude toward the evolution from childhood to adulthood?

(b) In your opinion, which poem conveys the most apprehension? Support your viewpoint.

Poems 58 to 62

The horrifying aspects of war dominate this group of poems.

58. *Death of the Ball Turret Gunner*

See the notes on imagery (p. 501) and sound (p. 524).

Ball Turret Gunner In World War II, the gunner who sat in the small bubble-shaped enclosure on the underside of the bomber.

59. *APO 96225*

The title refers to a military postal address. What has the poet succeeded in saying in general about the relationship between soldiers at war and the families back home? Was the exchange of letters a good way to make his point?

60. *Strange Meeting*

See the notes on accentual verse (p. 521), connotation (p. 495), consonance (p. 525), and near-rhyme (p. 511).

This visionary meeting takes place, not in the hell that sinners enter after death as in Dante's *The Inferno*, but in a hell created by war and imposed on innocent people. The poet's warning is urgent and explicit. **l. 3 Titanic wars** Wars waged by the Titans, mythical giants imprisoned underground by Jupiter. **groined** A groined roof consists of intersecting vaulted arches that can give the impression of being scooped out of the stone. With what other meanings does Owen invest the word here? **l. 5 fast** Fixed, bound. **l. 38 cess** This word achieves its force in the poem by evoking a number of connotations. Among them are the following: cess-pool, swamp or bog, and luck, as in the phrase, 'Bad cess to you.'

61. *Naming of Parts*

See the note on juxtaposition (p. 508).

What do the intervening references to the gardens and the repetition of the phrases contribute to the effectiveness of the poem?

62. *War on the Periphery*

This deceptively simple poem reflects on the tensions of civilian life in the years following World War II. What is the effect of the rhyme pattern and rhythmic pattern on the poem's message?

Question: Poems 58 to 62
(a) Compare the treatment of the theme of war in the poems by Jarrell, Rottmann, Owen, Reed, and Johnston.

Poems 63 to 68
This group of poems touches on many different facets of family relationships.

63. *Lullaby*
See the note on the Akan people (p. 454).
Repetition of sentence forms and of whole lines is an important feature of many folk poems. What effect does the repetition have on your reading of the poem?

64. *To a Sad Daughter*
See the notes on enjambment (p. 499) and free verse (p. 500).
l. 23 Casablanca A 1942 film of international intrigue with Humphrey Bogart and Ingrid Bergman. **l. 25 Creature from the Black Lagoon** A 1954 science-fiction movie with many visual gimmicks. **l. 28 siren** In classical mythology the sirens lived on an island in the sea. They sang so enchantingly that they lured passing sailors to their death. **l. 54 forsythia** See 'Forsythia' (p. 126). **l. 81 annunciation** A proclamation. The forsythia announced the coming of spring. In the Christian story, the Annunciation was the announcement to the Virgin Mary of the coming of Christ. What hopes does Ondaatje have for his daughter?

65. *Girl's-Eye View of Relatives*
See the note on the triolet (p. 527).
l. 5 Why does McGinley call the terrors 'romantic'?
Is the triolet form particularly suited to what is said about sisters?

66. *Home After Three Months Away*

See the notes on internal rhyme (p. 506) and near-rhyme (p. 511).

The speaker, who has been undergoing treatment for mental illness, tries to take up the threads of his home-life again. **l. 13 levee** The morning ceremony at which sovereigns received select visitors as they prepared to rise from bed. **l. 28** A self-mocking allusion to Matthew 6: 28.

67. *Once Upon a Time*

Forms of repetition are used for effect in this folk-type poem.

68. *Anyone Lived in a Pretty How Town*

See the note on convention (p. 496).

The anonymity of Cummings's hero is expressed in his name, 'anyone.' The cycle of his life is traced in fanciful, generalized terms. **l. 4** This line is typical of Cummings, both in its unconventional syntax and its ability to communicate an abstract idea. The use of verb forms where nouns would be expected stimulates close attention to what is being said. The negative form, balanced immediately by the positive, suggests anyone's unreflecting passage through the negative and positive experiences of life. Why does Cummings change the order of the items in his repeated lists?

Questions: Poems 63 to 68

(a) Describe the feelings expressed for the child in the poems by the Akan, Ondaatje, Lowell, and Okara.

(b) What views communicated in 'Girl's-Eye View of Relatives' are also present in 'To a Sad Daughter'?

(c) What similarities do you find in 'Lullaby' and 'Once Upon a Time'?

(d) What similarities do you find in 'War on the Periphery' and 'Anyone Lived in a Pretty How Town'?

Poems 69 to 72

These four poems are related to the Bible.

69. *To Every Thing There Is a Season*

The Authorized Version of the Bible, published in 1611 at the direction of King James I, was the work of a committee of eminent scholars and theologians. As the most widely read and memorized book in English, it had a penetrating influence on the language and on subsequent poetry and prose from John Donne and John Milton to Robert Bringhurst and Dylan Thomas. Rolling, dignified rhythms, parallelism, and natural imagery formed its literary style.

What are some of the possible outcomes of accepting the philosophy stated in these lines?

70. *Deuteronomy*

The story of Moses and Aaron leading their people out of bondage in Egypt to find The Promised Land is told in the book of Deuteronomy in the Old Testament and retold in this poem. The language imagines the understanding and feelings of Moses, who was chosen to be the instrument of God. Bringhurst has been able to reproduce the original incidents and details from the Bible, but has introduced various features that support a first person point of view. Examine these features and comment on their effectiveness.

71. *Lines* from the Prologue to the *Canterbury Tales*

Canterbury Tales, Chaucer's most ambitious work, concerns a party of pilgrims travelling to the shrine of St Thomas à Becket at Canterbury. To make the journey more amusing, they tell stories. Chaucer wrote a general prologue to introduce the situation and characters, then linked the stories by passages of lively narrative. **l. 8 Ram** The zodiacal sign of Aries, the ram. According to the astrological system of the time, Aries was dominant in the month following March 12. **l. 13 palmeres** Palmers. Originally, pilgrims who wore crossed palm leaves after a journey to the Holy Land. The word was extended to include any religious votary or pilgrim. **l. 17 martir** Becket was martyred in 1170 as an outcome of a church-versus-state struggle with Henry II. His shrine soon became popular for pilgrimages. **l. 18 seeke**

Sick. The identical rhyme, here between 'seke' and 'seeke,' was an acceptable convention in Chaucer's day.

72. *St Yves' Poor*

St Yves, a monk, lived in Brittany in the thirteenth century. As a lawyer he was reputed to be a zealous defender of widows and orphans. **Yves** Pronounce 'Eves.' **l. 5 rheumed** With running eyes; here, possibly rheumatic. **l. 27 Michael** St Michael commanded the heavenly army in the war against Satan. The story can be found in Books V and VI of *Paradise Lost*. **ll. 30-45** Cf. Matthew 25: 31-46. **l. 51 rapt** Oblivious of the outer world; consumed in a trance or vision.

Questions: Poems 69 to 72

    (a)   Although poems 69 to 71 are concerned with religious beliefs, they have an air of matter-of-factness rather than of ecstasy or fervour. Why is this atmosphere sought? How is it established?

    (b)   What elements contribute to the mood of religious fervour of 'St Yves' Poor'?

    (c)   What dicta from 'To Every Thing There Is a Season' are exemplified in 'Deuteronomy,' 'Lines from the Prologue to the *Canterbury Tales*,' and 'St Yves' Poor'?

Poem 73

This poem is about religious beliefs, in particular, the nature of good and evil.

73. *Heaven and Hell*

See the note on the Netsilik people (p. 475).

The Inuit are storytellers. They each make up their own personal tales that are their 'property' from then on. No one else may repeat or pass on the story — unlike the traditional Scottish ballads that were handed down in various versions. As a result, a decidedly personal flavour to the 'theological dogma' is apparent in the poem despite the fact that this version of an afterlife obviously has elements in common with the 'mythologies' of other religions. The poem was collected at the time of Knud Rasmussen's expeditions to the Arctic region in the 1920s. It was translated by Edward Field and published in the 1970s. **l. 10 angatoks** Healers and religious leaders. They are believed to receive insights while in a state of trance.

Questions: Poem 73
  (a) What similarities and differences do you find between this account of an afterlife and other accounts with which you are familiar?
  (b) Which details in the poem make it a personal testament?

Poems 74 and 75

In both poems the poets wonder how God can allow evil and suffering to exist.

74. *The Tyger* (An Early Draft)

See the note on imagery (p. 501).

In this early draft of the poem, the controlling image is of heating metal in a furnace and forging it into a durable form. Notice the extent to which this image has been retained in the final version. Consider the significance of the alternative in line 4 and suggest the reason for the final wording.

74. *The Tyger* (The Final Version)

See the notes on metaphor (p. 503), paradox (p. 512), and symbol (p. 505).

ll. 17-18 Probably a reference to the story of the insurrection of Lucifer and his forces, which resulted in their expulsion from heaven and the first presence of evil on earth. Lucifer was the name sometimes given to the morning star. The description of the glinting rays of light and the morning dew becomes part of the symbolism of good and evil that permeates the poem. Blake has made effective use of repetition with variation.

75. *Then the Lord Answered Job Out of the Whirlwind*

See the note on poem 69 (p. 393) for a comment about the Bible.

Struck by a series of catastrophes, Job has asked God to show just cause for his suffering. When he rejects the oversimplified view of three friends who claim that the Lord always rewards the good and punishes the wicked, Job is given an overwhelming experience of the presence of God. This brings, not an explanation of the existence of evil, but confidence in God's power and concern. The author conveys the overwhelming experience of God's presence by the press of unanswered questions that the Lord asks Job. **l. 23 Pleiades** A group of stars named after the seven daughters of Atlas. **l. 24 Orion** One of the most conspicuous constellations in the heavens, identified by the three bright stars that form Orion's belt. **l. 25 Mazzaroth** The signs of the Zodiac. **l. 26 Arcturus** A giant star in the constellation Boötes; the name sometimes given to the Great Bear.

Questions: Poems 74 and 75

(a) What is the effect of the unanswered questions in 'St Yves' Poor,' 'The Tyger,' and 'Then the Lord Answered Job Out of the Whirlwind'?

(b) What is the difference between the cause of human suffering as presented in 'Heaven and Hell' on the one hand, and 'The Tyger' and 'Then the Lord Answered Job Out of the Whirlwind' on the other?

Poems 76 to 78

Emily Dickinson's unique way of looking at life and her distinctive imagery and rhythms are apparent in this group of poems.

76. *Apparently With No Surprise*

None of Dickinson's poetry was published during her lifetime. Her earliest editors were unable to believe that the radical punctuation in her manuscripts, including the many dashes, expressed a serious artistic intent. Hence they standardized the format. For many decades this poem appeared in the following version:

> *Apparently with no surprise*
> *To any happy flower,*
> *The frost beheads it at its play*
> *In accidental power.*
> *The blond assassin passes on,*
> *The sun proceeds unmoved*
> *To measure off another day*
> *For an approving God.*

All four poems by Emily Dickinson in this anthology are printed in her format. Which version do you find more effective?

77. *The Last Night That She Lived*

See the notes on consonance (p. 525), near-rhyme (p. 511), and poem 76.

78. *Within My Garden, Rides a Bird*

See the notes on consonance (p. 525), near-rhyme (p. 511), and poem 76.

The poem conveys Dickinson's impression of a hummingbird. Years later she rewrote the twenty-line poem, distilling the images to a mere eight lines:

> *A Route of Evanescence*
> *With a revolving Wheel —*
> *A Resonance of Emerald —*
> *A Rush of Cochineal —*
> *And every Blossom on the Bush*
> *Adjusts its tumbled Head —*
> *The mail from Tunis, probably,*
> *An easy Morning's Ride —*

ll. 13-16 An extreme ellipsis. The poet and her dog wonder whether they actually saw the bird or whether it was merely an apparition in 'the Garden in the brain.'

Questions: Poems 76 to 78
    (a)   How would you characterize Dickinson's style?
    (b)   What do you find simple and what do you find complex or profound in the poems?

Poems 79 to 82

These poems use oral techniques to make statements about aspects of our environment.

79. *Mushrooms*

See the notes on internal rhyme (p. 506), near-rhyme (p. 511), and symbol (p. 505).

The poem achieves the effects of a science-fiction film, depicting the magical way in which mushrooms appear and suggesting horror-story images. Compare the mood of the last three lines with that of the opening twelve lines. **ll. 26 and 31-32** See St Matthew 5: 5 'Blessed are the meek; for they shall inherit the earth.'

80. *Natural Prayer*

See the notes on concrete poetry (p. 495) and sound poetry (p. 526).

The listener/reader is subsumed into the poem by sound impressions and conditioned associations as the essence of bees is revealed in this paean of praise. The poem is from Rosenblatt's collection *Bumblebee Dithyramb*, where he explores the universe of bees.

81. *Forsythia*

See the note on concrete poetry (p. 495).

'Forsythia' could be said to epitomize concrete poetry. The shape of the poem on the page depicts the subject; the letter-blossoms spell it out; the morse-code stems repeat the letters; and the vase and base provide commentary on forsythias as the harbingers of spring.

82. *& So the Little Fieldmouse Said*

Many of Patchen's poems take this form — handwritten comments accompanied by deliberately child-like drawings. They make reference to matters that preoccupy thoughtful individuals in today's world. The disparity between the simplicity of the drawings and language and the vastness of the subject addressed add poignancy to the poem. Is this poem a dramatic monologue? See p. 497.

Questions: Poems 79 to 82

    (a)   What do 'Within My Garden, Rides a Bird,' 'Mushrooms,' and 'Natural Prayer' have in common?

    (b)   What do 'Apparently With No Surprise' and 'Forsythia' have in common?

    (c)   How do you feel about the contribution made to poetry by the techniques of such poems as 'Natural Prayer,' 'Forsythia,' and '& So the Little Fieldmouse Said'?

Poems 83 to 85

These poems use water imagery to express gravity.

83. *The Swimmer's Moment*

See the note on symbol (p. 505).

The whirlpool, a highly dramatic symbol with a wide range of meanings, tests the courage and quality of a person's life. What kinds of defeat and spiritual death can be undergone by those at the edge of the whirlpool and within its vortex? Who are the people who reach the estuary? From which side of the vortex does the poet speak?

84. *Not Waving But Drowning*

See the note on symbol (p. 505).

The rhythm and rhyme pattern underscore the matter-of-fact statements in the poem. An almost off-hand mood that gives way to shock is created as we realize the importance of the symbolic situation. In your opinion, are any phrases in the poem particularly touching?

85. *Dover Beach*

See the note on the dramatic monologue (p. 497), imagery (p. 501), and rhythm (p. 515).

Arnold evokes the loneliness and despair of his time, which accompanied, he says, a loss of faith in the certainty of religion. Personal constancy in love remains as his last hope. **ll. 3-8** The chalk cliffs of Dover and the coast of France are only twenty-one miles apart. **l. 15 Sophocles** A Greek tragedian of the fifth century B. C. His writing depicts the tragic suffering of noble characters who have encountered the impersonal laws that order the universe. He dwells on the value and the transience of all human achievement. **l. 16 Aegaean** The arm of the Mediterranean Sea to the east of Greece.

Questions: Poems 83 to 85

    (a)   Compare the view of life expressed by the speakers and the significance of the water imagery in these poems.

    (b)   Poets frequently adopt a 'persona,' or poetic personality, that may or may not resemble their everyday character. What persona do you find in each of the three poems?

Poem 86

Wordsworth reflects on his life-long response to the natural environment.

86. *Tintern Abbey*

Wordsworth composed this poem and held it in his mind while enjoying a four-day ramble through the Wye Valley in Wales with his sister Dorothy. On reaching Bristol, he wrote it down exactly as it stands. One of Wordsworth's recurrent themes was the growth of the individual spirit under the influence of nature. Natural scenes often aroused in him a visionary power, and he recorded such scenes, not simply for themselves, but because of the effects they had induced in him. **l. 21 some Hermit's cave** The hermit in eighteenth-century and early nineteenth-century literature conventionally suggested solitude in a natural setting. **ll. 28-29 blood . . . heart . . . mind** For Wordsworth, images of natural beauty affect the feelings and emotions more immediately than they do the intellect. But they are impressed into the depths of the poet's being, to the extent that later recollection restores him, as did the original experience itself, in times of despair over the degradation of the world men create. **l. 49** Transcending his physical being as he contemplates his deep memories of natural beauty, the poet attains a mystical insight into the spirit that animates the natural world. **ll. 65-111** Wordsworth distinguishes three stages in his relationship with nature. In boyhood (ll. 73-74), he had shown an unreflecting delight in outdoor physical activity. As a young man (ll. 65-72, 75-83), he had turned from the city to the natural landscape with a hungry longing for something as yet dimly apprehended. At the time of writing this poem (ll. 83-111), maturity has brought a deeper, more satisfying communion. **l. 74 animal movements** Instinctive, unreflecting physical activity. **ll. 106-107** For Wordsworth, half our experience is derived from external nature and half from the senses and imagination that shape and animate what is perceived.

Questions: Poem 86

    (a)   Wordsworth does much more than describe natural scenery. He explains its importance to him. What does he say about the importance of nature to him emotionally, intellectually, and spiritually?

    (b)   What does Wordsworth say is his sister Dorothy's role in the experience he describes in this poem?

Poems 87 to 90

These poems share a pastoral theme.

87. *The Shepheardes Lament*

(Several stanzas of the original poem, *The Shepheardes Calender: December*, have been omitted from this excerpt.) See the note on pastoral poetry (p. 513).

In order to create the pastoral atmosphere, Spenser deliberately used language that was already archaic when the poem was published in 1579. The twelve eclogues or pastoral poems in the *Calender* take their titles from the twelve months. Against the background of the countryside at different times of the year, shepherds discuss such themes as love, poetry, religion, or allegiance to Queen Elizabeth. The December poem is, appropriately, a lament of one shepherd, Colin Clout (often identified with Spenser), over the waste of his life. **l. 11 in the fan be fynd** Be driven off in threshing. **l. 26 stounde** Noise; also, time of trial or pain.

88. *Branwell's Lament* from *A Suit of Nettles: June*

See the note on pastoral poetry (p. 513).

A Suit of Nettles, like *The Shepheardes Calender*, comprises twelve poems. The speakers in the modern poem, however, are geese in an Ontario farmyard. This lament is spoken by Branwell, whom the poet Reaney describes as 'the slightly ridiculous figure of melancholy itself, wrapped up in a suit of nettles he has put on in order to emphasize his sorrow at a fair goose's inattention.' In his morbid state, Branwell has been haunted by visions of a weasel and of an owl, here thought of as the bird of melancholy. **l. 1 I am like a hollow tree** To what extent is this simile developed throughout the rest of the poem? Note the two related elements in the imagery of the containing and that which is contained. **l. 22** At the June solstice, sunset occurs at its most northerly point on the horizon; thereafter the days grow shorter. **ll. 24-25** The owl and weasel that plague him are the emanations of a sick mind; a possible parallel with the harpies (harassers of classical mythology). **l. 26 fair** Perhaps a country fair where animals are exhibited. **l. 27 bittern** A small heron that frequents marshy land and makes a curious pumping sound.

Comment on the form used in the first four stanzas and the change of form in the final stanza.

89. *The Country North of Belleville*

Purdy's pastoral landscape is the rough northern hinterland toward the east end of Lake Ontario, a far cry from the manicured settings of the traditional pastoral. He describes the features of the countryside where he grew up and offers a litany of the places that left their imprint on his imagination. In commenting on the satisfactions and defeats experienced by those who once lived north of Belleville, he is probably also assessing his own life. Purdy conveys both toughness and sensitivity through his imagery, his style of writing, and his interesting use of dashes instead of periods. **l. 10 Sisyphus** In classical mythology, Sisyphus, King of Corinth, having offended Zeus, was punished by having to forever push a rock uphill, which forever rolled back down on him.

90. *My '48 Pontiac*

The three poems by Purdy in this anthology (pp. 9, 142, and 145) should provide a 'feeling for Purdy' — his chief interests, style, and emotional range. What links this poem with traditional pastoral poetry? The old Pontiac, the object of his tenderness, stands for more than itself, of course. Image after image suggests that the parameters of concern are being extended to include a sampling of the daily disasters and eventualities that sadden our lives. **l. 18 Tyrannosaurus Rex** This whimsical reference to the extinct dinosaur helps establish the idea that past, present, and future all coexist. What other references in the poem relate to this notion?

Questions: Poems 87 to 90

    (a)   What elements of the pastoral convention are common to these poems? How have Reaney and Purdy treated the convention in modern terms?

    (b)   What loss is grieved over in each of the poems?

Poems 91 to 95

Fanciful humour with a slightly cutting edge links these poems.

91. *The Dancing Cabman*

What does the dead aunt have to do with the situation described so graphically in the poem?

92. *Cheerio My Deario*

See the note on allusion (p. 490).

Archy the cockroach used Don Marquis's typewriter at night to relate his adventures with Mehitabel, an alleycat who claimed to be a reincarnation of Cleopatra. Archy typed by leaping off the carriage and striking a key with his head. Unfortunately, he could not work the shift key to create upper-case letters. Could it be considered a dramatic monologue? See p. 497. **l. 1 boss** Don Marquis. **ll. 12-15 king tutankhamen** An Egyptian pharaoh who lived some thirteen centuries before Cleopatra. **l. 49 sisters of uncharity** An unflattering reference to the uncharitable gossips who have made life difficult for Mehitabel. The Sisters of Charity are an order of nuns founded by St Vincent de Paul; they devote themselves largely to charitable works in education and nursing. **l. 73 anvil chorus** A rhythmic, hammering chorus from Verdi's opera *Il Trovatore*; in Mehitabel's vivid slang, the 'sisters of uncharity' of lines 45-49. **ll. 77-80** The sisters of uncharity have had local groups meeting all through history.

93. *Indian Summer*

Many of Dorothy Parker's short stories, which were written before the major thrust of the women's movement, display this same irreverent sense of a woman's relationship with a male partner. What is the significance of the title?

94. *The Constant Lover*

What signal is given to us by the opening phrase?

95. *The Braw Wooer*

l. 22 Dalgarnock A seventeenth-century village in the border country of Scotland. Ordinarily a tryst is a prearranged meeting of lovers; here, however, the meeting is unplanned.

Questions: Poems 91 to 95

(a) 'Indian Summer,' 'The Constant Lover,' and 'The Braw Wooer' are all love poems, but they do not treat love in the same way. What is the particular situation and atmosphere presented in each love poem?

(b) How is incongruity used to effect in 'The Dancing Cabman' and 'Cheerio My Deario'?

Poem 96

In this poem, the poet comes to the disheartening realization of how time affects 'enduring' love.

96. *As I Walked Out One Evening*

See the note on the ballad (p. 493).

Auden frequently used the image of the British industrial town to suggest the unsatisfactory quality of the social life that men create for themselves. Here, the clocks of the town speak a far more sombre message than does the lover. The style is typical of Auden, with its sardonic wit and cryptic descriptions that demand great agility from the reader. **ll. 41-56** Auden, like many modern poets, makes amusing and ironic use of nursery rhymes and well-known children's stories. **l. 45 raffle** Sell by raffle; or riffle through, as with the pages of a book. **l. 47 Lily-white Boy is a Roarer** A reference to the ancient number-song, 'Green Grow the Rushes — O': 'Two, two, the lily-white boys, clothèd all in green — O.' In the very early versions of the song, the lily-white boys were assistants to a Druid priest; in the later Christian version, they were taken to be Jesus Christ and John the Baptist. A roarer is a street rowdy.

Question: Poem 96

(a) Compare the traditional ballad represented by 'The Twa Corbies' (p. 58) and 'Sir Patrick Spens' (p. 59) with the literary ballad represented by 'As I Walked Out One Evening.' Refer to any other ballads with which you are familiar.

Poems 97 to 99
Each of these poets mourns the passing of happier times.

97. *The Sick Rose*
See the note on symbol (p. 505).

This poem of Blake's, like his other poems in this anthology (pp. 114, 116, 281, 333), leaves readers to interpret the meaning of the symbol it presents.

98. *Tears, Idle Tears*
A song from the long poem *The Princess*, Part IV. The song was written at Tintern Abbey (cf. 'Tintern Abbey,' p. 132), which held many memories for Tennyson.

99. *Selections* from *In Memoriam*
See the notes on elegy (p. 498) and lyric (p. 509).

In Memoriam, which Tennyson wrote over a period of seventeen years, expresses his despair after the death of his friend Arthur Hallam, and the conflict of his doubt with his religious faith as he considers the suffering and waste in nature and the survival of the species rather than the individual. The sequence of 133 poems of varying lengths is unified by developing imagery and themes. The recurring celebration of Christmas, New Year's Day, and Easter, over a period of three years, affords Tennyson a series of vantage points from which to consider his grief and the progress of his meditation. Why is the metre unusual for an elegiac poem?

[VII] The house is Hallam's former residence.

[LIV] Theories of evolution were much disputed in Tennyson's day. Here he tries to assure himself that the struggle and suffering in nature have some ultimate purpose. **l. 7 void** Here, space containing no ordered matter and hence devoid of God's active presence. **l. 8** A deliberately vague image for the creative process.

[CXV] **l. 2 quick** Living plants considered collectively; often, a hawthorn hedge.

[CVIII] The poet sees a purpose working itself out in the slow processes that produced human beings, and he concludes that people must continue by their own moral effort the labour of evolving a higher form of life. **l. 26 Faun** In Roman mythology, a pleasure-loving, minor deity of nature, part man, part goat.

[CXXIII] Despair and faith are in precarious balance throughout the first hundred poems of *In Memoriam*. Here Tennyson realizes that, in the perspective of geological time, nature is shadowy and transient. It is, therefore, partly on the basis of evolution, not in contradiction of it, that he comes to rely on his intuition of the universe as fundamentally spiritual. Hallam has died; but Tennyson is able to affirm that in some higher sphere the friends will be reunited. **l. 12** This line can be understood in at least three ways: I cannot, by mere thought, rid myself of what I have been thinking; I cannot think that Hallam's friendship will never be present again; I cannot conceive the thought 'Farewell.'

Questions: Poems 97 to 99

    (a) What differing views of nature does Tennyson present in *In Memoriam* CXVIII and CXXIII?

    (b) What mood is conveyed in each poem?

    (c) What do you find different about Blake's and Tennyson's use of symbols?

Poems 100 and 101

These poems by John Donne are about death and mourning.

100. *A Valediction: Forbidding Mourning*

See the notes on conceit (p. 495) and metaphysical poetry (p. 510).

Donne wrote this poem to his wife just before departing from England on a diplomatic mission to France. In the first six stanzas a series of images evokes an emotional response to changes in the physical world. The last three stanzas develop a single conceit, which has become one of the most famous in English poetry. **Valediction** A farewell address. **ll. 1-8** Donne draws a comparison between the gentle parting of a godly man from life on earth to a higher life beyond and the peaceful severance of the physical companionship of the husband and wife, which will enable their relationship to enter a more exalted state. **l. 8 laity** Church members as distinct from the clergy. **ll. 9-12** A contrast between earthquakes (equated with physical love), which bring harm and fear, and the vibration of the spheres (equated with the communion of a higher love), which produces heavenly harmony. In the Ptolemaic system the universe is conceived of as a series of rotating spheres, one inside another, with the earth at the centre. **ll. 13-16** Earthly love cannot survive separation because its very life depends on physical presence. **ll. 17-20** An image based on the refinement of metals by the removal of impure elements. **ll. 21-24** When gold is beaten into gold leaf the surface is extended, but the metal is not broken. **ll. 25-36** This conceit presents the image of a pair of compasses, of which one foot remains in a central position while the other maintains a fixed relation to it in tracing out a circle.

101. *Death*

See the notes on paradox (p. 512) and the sonnet (p. 522).

Donne harnessed the concentrated power of the sonnet, traditionally used for love poetry, to express the complexities and the emotional impact of his religious convictions. **ll. 1-2** See I Corinthians, 15: 51-55. **l. 11 poppy** The poppy as the source of opium, a drug that induces drowsiness.

Questions: Poems 100 and 101

    (a)   What elements are typical of Donne's metaphysical style?

    (b)   How do Donne's religious beliefs affect his attitude toward death?

Poems 102 to 106

Each of these poems reflect on nighttime in very different ways.

102. *The Last Hour of Faustus*

Marlowe's play, *The Tragical History of Dr Faustus*, was written about 1590 in London. According to legend, the scholar Faustus sold his soul to Mephistopheles, an emissary of Lucifer (Satan), in return for twenty-four years of unlimited power. Now, in the last scene of Marlowe's tragedy, comes the reckoning. **l. 4 ever-moving spheres** The Pythagoreans taught that the earth stood at the centre of nine transparent spheres, one inside another, which rotated ceaselessly, carrying the planets and stars. **l. 10** From Ovid: 'Run slowly, slowly, horses of the night.' How does the pace of the Latin line affect the meaning of the words? **ll. 13-21** Faustus becomes more and more remote from God. He is facing the fact of his imminent damnation. He has made his unholy pact with Lucifer and is incapable of accepting God's mercy. His half-prideful conviction of his own damnation is much stronger than his awareness of grace. Notice that at line 15 Faustus addresses Christ directly. Yet to whom is line 16 addressed? **l. 42 metempsychosis** Transmigration of souls, a doctrine taught by Pythagoras. At death, the soul of one creature passed into the body of another, not necessarily of the same species. In each successive life on earth the soul earned a higher or lower position in the scale of creation. **l. 58 books** Books of evil magic.

103. *Welsh Night* from *Under Milk Wood*

See the note on cadence (p. 518).

Under Milk Wood is a play for voices, first broadcast in its final form by the BBC on January 25, 1954. This selection is the opening, spoken very gently by a narrator. The evocative language and cadence of the prose make it scarcely distinguishable from poetry. **Milk Wood** An imaginary Welsh seaside town. **l. 5 sloeblack** The blue-black colour of the sloe, a small wild plum. **l. 7 dingle** A narrow valley or shady glen. **ll. 7-8 Captain Cat** One of the inhabitants of Milk Wood. **l. 14 Llaregyb** Pronounce with a voiceless 'l,' stress the middle syllable, and pronounce 'gyb' as in Gibbon. **l. 17 bombazine** A fine fabric used for mourning clothes. **ll. 18-19 mintoes** Mints. **l. 19 four-ale** A cheap mild ale; here, probably, a tavern. **l. 20**

domino As quiet as one of the pieces in a game of dominoes in the bar. **ll. 20-21 Ocky Milkman . . . Dai Bread** Ocky the milkman, and Dai (David) the baker. Pronounce Dai as 'die.' **l. 26 neddying . . . snuggeries** Neddy is commonly a child's name for a donkey. A snuggery is a small cosy place, especially a parlour in a tavern. What effects are achieved by the juxtaposition?

104. *Reason Has Moons*

What is it that delights and gives wisdom to the poet, while confusing the calculations of the rationalist?

105. *Hymn to Diana*

Diana is the chaste goddess of the moon and the hunt. **l. 4 wonted** Accustomed. **l. 5 Hesperus** The evening star. **l. 9 Cynthia** Another name for Diana.

Questions: Poems 102 to 106
  (a) Night has a special fascination for poets. What is its significance in each of the poems in this group?
  (b) Compare the speakers' attitudes to religious hope in 'Death' and 'The Last Hour of Faustus.'
  (c) Compare the moods created in each of the five poems.

Poems 107 to 109

These short poems convey special feelings related to the slow passage of finite time.

109. *Climbing Mount Fuji*

See the notes on haiku (p. 500) and symbol (p. 505).

Question: Poems 107 to 109
  (a) The poems in this group are all short, but they are not slight. What does each say about fate?

Poem 110

This poem explores a close friendship through the dramatic un-folding of a tragic accident.

110. *David*

'David' describes graphically an incident in which two friends challenge a yet unscaled peak in the Rocky Mountains — The Finger. The less experienced climber brings about the death of his friend. The poem is very convincing, with realistic place names and technical terms related to geology and mountaineering. As the poem progresses, the vivid descriptive phrases indicate a changing relationship between the landscape and the young men. **l. 16 above timber** Above the stands of large trees. **l. 21 Skree** Rock debris accumulated at the bottom of a mountain cliff. **l. 23 larches' edge** The borderline above which the larches — smaller conifers, sometimes known as tamarack — no longer grow. **l. 24 juniper** A low evergreen shrub. **l. 25 gentian and saxifrage** Gentian is a generic term for several species of wild flowers that generally have a blue flower. Saxifrage is a low plant with a yellow flower that commonly grows on mountainsides. **l. 29 arête** The sharp-edged crest of a ridge in a mountain range. **ll. 47-48 the slicing pipe of invisible pika** A narrow slot in the land formation inhabited by the rabbit-related pika. **ll. 50-52 read the scroll . . . Cambrian waves** David pointed out the outlines in the rocks of extinct marine arthopods, a sub-species of crustaceans that lived in the Paleozoic era and reached their greatest numbers in the Cambrian era. At that time the Rockies were beneath the ocean. **l. 53 col** A pass between two peaks in a mountain chain. **l. 56 a dint in the scarp** An indentation in the steep side of the cliff. **l. 72 marten** An animal larger than a weasel, sometimes called a sable. **l. 82 Bighorns** Rocky Mountain sheep. **moraine** An accumulation of earth and stones carried and finally deposited by a glacier. **l. 86 seracs** Pinnacles of ice among the crevasses (deep openings) in the side of a glacier. **l. 88 the chimney** A steep and narrow crevice in the face of a cliff. **l. 103 the cirque** A deep amphitheatre-like space in the wall of a glacier, caused by erosion. **l. 155 traverse** The cliff that they had crossed. **l. 157 bergschrund** A series of crevasses near the head of a

glacier. **l. 159 névé** Partly compacted granular snow forming the surface of the upper part of a glacier.

Questions: Poem 110

    (a)   Foreshadowing is a subtle suggestion in a work of literature
           of an incident or set of details that occurs later. Where do you
           find instances of foreshadowing in 'David'?

    (b)   The poem is about the friendship of two young men. How is
           the warmth of the friendship made evident?

    (c)   What attitude toward nature is demonstrated in the poem?

Poems 111 and 112

Each of these poems by Milton has an afflicted speaker who addresses God.

111. *On His Blindness*

See the notes on allusion (p. 490), the sonnet (p. 522), and Milton's
biography (p. 474).

The poem gains richness and depth through its use of multiple
meanings. In line 2, for example, the world is dark both to the blind
poet and in its ignorance. **ll. 3-8** See Matthew 25: 14-30. **l. 7
day-labour** See John 9: 4. **l. 8 fondly** Foolishly. **l. 11 his mild yoke**
See Matthew 11: 30.

112. *Hail, Holy Light* from *Paradise Lost*

See the notes on cadence (p. 518) and the epic (p. 499).

The first two books of *Paradise Lost* have described Satan and his
cohorts in the darkness of Hell after their revolt against God. At the
end of Book II Satan, on a mission to earth, has re-passed the bound-
aries of Hades and caught a glimpse of the celestial light. This passage, the opening of Book III, serves to translate the reader to the
radiant glory of God's world. It is also a great lyrical statement, in the
midst of the narrative, concerning Milton's physical blindness and the
inner light he has been granted. **l. 6 effluence** A flowing out. **l. 14
Stygian Pool** See *Paradise Lost* II, ll. 575-581. The River Styx was one

of the four rivers of the underworld. The shades of the departed were ferried across it to Hades. **ll. 17-21 Orpheus** A legendary Greek poet and musician who descended to Hades when his wife Eurydice died. He so pleased the god Pluto with his music that he was allowed to lead Eurydice back to life. Because he looked back during their ascent from Hades, contrary to the condition imposed by Pluto, she was lost to Orpheus forever. **l. 30 Sion** Zion, the holy mountain of Israel; for Milton, the home of the Muse that inspired the prophets and writers in the Judaeo-Christian tradition, and which he identified with the Holy Spirit. **ll. 35-36 Thamyris** A poet whom the Muses blinded. **Maeonides** Homer, the blind Greek epic poet. **Tiresias** A Theban who was granted the gift of prophecy when he lost his sight. **Phineus** A blind prophet whom Jason and the Argonauts met.

Scan lines 1 to 6. How has Milton adapted the iambic pentameter? See the notes on cadence (p. 518) and syncopation (p. 517).

Questions: Poems 111 and 112

(a) In 'Hail, Holy Light' and 'On His Blindness' what levels of significance are given to darkness and to light?

(b) What attitude to affliction is expressed at the end of each poem?

Poems 113 to 116

This group of poems offers four distinct impressions of nature.

113. *God's Grandeur*

See the notes on assonance (p. 525), consonance (p. 525), ellipsis (p. 498), internal rhyme (p. 506), the sonnet (p. 522), and sprung rhythm (p. 521).

Hopkins blends emotional and intellectual perception in his forceful imagery, unorthodox and highly compressed syntax, and in the suggestive power of his phrases. He wrote elsewhere of 'the contemplation of the Holy Ghost sent to us through creatures. . . . All things therefore are charged with love, are charged with God and if we know how to touch them give off sparks and take fire, yield drops and flow, ring and tell of Him.' As in the poem, Hopkins describes the immanence of the Holy Spirit in terms of both fire and liquid. **l. 1 charged** In the sense of electrically charged; also, given the responsibility of. **l. 2 shook foil** Hopkins wrote to the poet Robert Bridges: 'I mean foil in its sense of leaf or tinsel . . . Shaken gold foil gives off broad flares like sheet lightning and also, and this is true of nothing else, owing to its zigzag dints and creasings and network of small many cornered facets, a sort of fork lightning too.' **ll. 3-4** The reference is to the emergence of gleaming oil from olives crushed in a press (many religious uses for this oil are described in the Old Testament); or, to the crushing of oil from oil-bearing shale, by the weight of the rock above it. **l. 4 reck** Take heed of, modify one's behaviour on account of. **rod** The symbol of God's authority, with a secondary reference to the miraculous rod of Moses that brought forth the spring of water from the rock. Cf. ll. 10 and 12. **ll. 7-8** An intensely compressed statement of an ironic situation. What has unnaturally bared the soil? When people are no longer in their natural barefoot state, how does their relation to nature change? **l. 9 spent** Used up completely; exhausted, without further energy. **l. 10** The compression of the line suggests the new life that is ready to surge forth. **ll. 13-14** For the image of the Holy Spirit as a gently brooding dove, see Matthew 3: 16-17.

114. *Hurrahing in Harvest*

See the notes on alliteration (p. 525), metaphor (p. 503), the sonnet (p. 522), and sprung rhythm (p. 521).

'The *Hurrahing* sonnet was the outcome of half an hour of extreme enthusiasm as I walked home alone one day from fishing in the Elwy,' wrote Hopkins in a letter of 1878. Some of his most joyous poems were composed in 1877, the year of his ordination as a Jesuit. **l. 4 Meal-drift** The drifting clouds are compared to grain ground into meal. The image continues the parallel between field and sky. **l. 5** An allusion to Psalm 121. **l. 6 glean our Saviour** Search for and gather some indication of the presence of Christ. **ll. 7-8** An overwhelming response comes, more wonderful than any afforded by human love. **l. 9 world-wielding shoulder** In this very complex metaphor, the hills that surround the field are likened to the shoulder of Christ.

The myth of Atlas supporting the burden of the world on his shoulders is transferred to Christ, with the added connotation of His bearing the sins of the world. **l. 13** Hopkins scanned this line as follows: 'The héart réars wíngs bóld and bólder.' **l. 14 half hurls earth for him** The beholder, dizzied with emotion, feels released from the earth; or, Christ's burden (l. 9) is taken away by the joy of the beholder.

115. *Snow*

This poem is an attempt to understand with the senses and feelings a fundamental truth about our experience of the world. The element of surprise is used effectively, both in diction and in the choice of detail. **l. 3 collateral** Situated side by side.

116. *The Lonely Land*

The visual drama of Canada's northland challenges the poet to recreate it in language and rhythm. Apart from explicit statement, how has Smith suggested the strength and desolation of the northland?

Questions: Poems 113 to 116

   (a)   Select images from these poems that express each poet's appreciation of natural beauty.

   (b)   Does the poet gain any insight that goes beyond the appreciation of nature? If so, to what extent is nature the source of the insight?

   (c)   What is the relation between the poet's mood and the landscape?

   (d)   Wordsworth said that poetry 'takes its origin from emotion recollected in tranquillity.' Hopkins declared that 'Hurrahing in Harvest' was written at a peak of direct emotional experience. What features in his poem reflect what Hopkins said about his writing? (See the notes on 'Tintern Abbey' [p. 400] for more information about Wordsworth's style of writing.)

Poems 117 to 123

The focus of this group of poems is homeland and the immigrant experience.

117. *Thoughts from Underground*

See the note on persona (p. 514).

Margaret Atwood wrote a sequence of poems entitled *The Journals of Susanna Moodie*, including 'Thoughts from Underground' and 'The Immigrants,' a year and a half after reading *Roughing It in the Bush* and *Life in the Clearings* by Susanna Moodie, one of Canada's earliest literary figures. Moodie came to Canada in 1832 with her husband and child. They settled north of what is now Cobourg, then near what is now Lakefield, and finally in the town of Belleville. Having grown up in Suffolk, England, she was unaccustomed to the rugged country-life she encountered in her first years in Canada. She described the hardships, both physical and mental, in her two books.

Atwood's sequence of poems *The Journals of Susanna Moodie* is written in the persona of Moodie. Atwood writes about Moodie's arrival in Canada, her various ordeals during seven years in the bush, the move to Belleville, her old age, and even beyond her death. Each poem stands on its own as well as being a part of the continuing saga.

'Thoughts from Underground' is one of the late poems, when Susanna Moodie is trying to reconcile her conflicting reactions to her life in Canada. What are her feelings about the land and about Canada's progress from a pioneer country to a more civilized state?

118. *The Immigrants*

See the notes on persona (p. 514) and the preceding poem.

In this poem, the persona of Moodie speaks as a person who has become part of Canada. She speaks about 'other' immigrants. Nevertheless, what do you feel she is saying about her own status?

119. *Autobiographical*

This poem appears in Klein's novel *The Second Scroll*, which symbolizes, in the life of a Jewish scholar, the religious history of the Jewish people. Klein grew up in the Jewish community in Montreal, and this poem conveys the contented absorption of the boy in all aspects of the life of his community. **ll. 1, 86 Jewboy** Klein uses with pride a term often used derisively. **l. 4 goy** Anyone who is not a Jew. A 'Sabbath-goy' is one who performs duties not permitted to a Jew on Saturday, the Jewish Sabbath. **l. 5 Torah** Literally 'the Law,' the five books of Moses. In the Jewish liturgy the Torah is read from a handwritten scroll of leather or parchment, which on certain occasions is carried in procession. **l. 24 Saturday night** The Sabbath ends at sunset, when it is customary to have a social gathering. **l. 29 maariv** The daily evening prayer. **l. 31 Volhynia** A province in southeastern Poland, and a part of the Russian Empire, where many Jews were slaughtered in the fighting that followed the Russian Revolution of 1917. **ll. 34-35** Every week the Jewish youngsters learned Hebrew and portions of the Bible. When their work was satisfactory, pennies were dropped on their books to reward them. **l. 37** Friday night was the occasion of the family ceremony ushering in the Sabbath. The mother would light ritual candles for which she said a blessing. **l. 38 Warsovian** From Warsaw, Poland. **perruque** A wig. Upon marriage an Orthodox Jewish woman customarily cut off her hair to symbolize the fact that she no longer wished to be attractive to men other than her husband. **l. 40** In the middle of the eighteenth century there developed in Polish Judaism a great religious renaissance known as Hasidism. The founding leader was a teacher called Baal Shem Tov, 'Master of the Good Name.' Many stories are told of his miracles. **l. 65 the Haman rattle** In the annual festival of Purim, Jews celebrate their salvation from destruction at the hands of Haman, the chief minister of King Ahasuerus. As part of the celebration, the story, as told in the book of Esther, is read in the synagogue and the young people mark the reading of the name Haman by waving rattles. **l. 66** The Torah is divided into sections for reading on the Sabbath so that it is finished once a year. Simchas Torah — 'the Joy of the Law' — is the day on which the reading is both completed and begins again with the first chapter of Genesis. It is an occasion for celebrations.

Klein, as a boy, had the capacity to respond vibrantly to the experiences of his daily life. How do the memories of these experiences affect him as he recalls them? How does he feel about his Jewish background?

120. *This Landscape, These People*

See the notes on extended metaphor (p. 505), imagery (p. 501), and simile (p. 503).

Note the extraordinary power of the sensory images throughout the poem. **l. 2 Putney Heath** The north end of a large park area near London. Wimbledon of tennis fame occupies the south end of the park. A heath is an open, level area with uncultivated shrubbery. **ll. 25, 39-49** These lines may refer to Pakistan's struggle for independence from India. Ghose, as a young boy at the time, may have witnessed the strife.

Why is the museum reference in stanza three so effective? Which features of life in London and life in Bombay are counter-balanced? What is achieved by the references to the rope in the poem?

121. *Bans O' Killing*

See the notes on didactic poetry (p. 497), dub poetry (p. 498), and Louise Bennett's biography (p. 456).

Only recently have dialects been recognized as legitimate expressions of the culture and attitudes of the people who use them. Bennett, who is a learned scholar and fluent in 'standard' English, is able to marshal a sound argument, using her Jamaican English to reflect the wit and pride of Jamaicans. Having the poem read aloud by someone who is reasonably at ease with Jamaican English provides a sense of its intent and point of view. **Bans O'** A lot of. **ll. 2-4** They say you are taking many English oaths to do away with dialect. **l. 5 Mass Charlie** Mr Charlie. A Jamaican term used to refer to a white man. **l. 7 gwine** Going to. **ll. 9-11** If you compare the Jamaican language with the English language, then why are you not going to feel inferior? **l. 13 Kean** Can't. **Linstead Market** A Jamaican folk song. **l. 14 Wata come a me y'eye** Water wells up in my eyes. A line from the popular Jamaican song 'Liza.' **ll. 15-16 Auld lang syne, Coming thru de rye** Scottish dialect songs. **l. 21** Let them try turning to language. **l. 23 gawn** Ago. **ll. 25-27 Lancashire, Yorkshire, Cockney, broad Scotch, Irish brogue** Various British dialects. **l. 28 me** My Jamaican dialect. **ll. 31-32 Chaucer, Burns, Lady Grizelle,**

Shakespeare Bennet is saying these British poets wrote in 'dialect.' **l. 35 fine** Find. **l. 37 dah-read** Read. **l. 39 drop a 'h'** Dropping an initial 'h' of a word when speaking is sometimes considered substandard English.

'Wit,' 'humour,' and 'variety' (ll. 33-34) are terms used in studies of English literature. Show that Louise Bennett's poem demonstrates these qualities. Who is the immigrant in this poem?

122. *What Do I Remember of the Evacuation?*

During World War II, the Canadian government passed legislation that caused suffering and humiliation to Canadians of Japanese ancestry. About twenty thousand Japanese Canadians living in the coastal area of British Columbia were forciably moved to detention camps and their property was taken away without compensation. Some people were exiled even after the war had ended. The injustice of these actions was not officially acknowledged until September 22, 1988. A plan to compensate the victims was agreed to by the National Association of Japanese Canadians. Canada's official apology reads as follows:

> *The Government of Canada, on behalf of all Canadians, does hereby: 1) acknowledge that the treatment of Japanese Canadians during and after World War II was unjust and violated principles of human rights as they are understood today; 2) pledge to ensure, to the full extent that its powers allow, that such events will not happen again; and 3) recognize, with great respect, the fortitude and determination of Japanese Canadians who, despite great stress and hardship, retain their commitment and loyalty to Canada and contribute so richly to the development of the Canadian nation.*

ll. 39-40 How does the adult speaker feel now about her childhood wish? What is the attitude of the young girl toward the situation?

123. *Going to Norway*

The parents agree with their son's urging that they should visit Norway, but they never go. Can you suggest why?

Questions: Poems 117 to 123

  (a) Compare the attitudes of the immigrants toward their home-
       land and their new land in 'Thoughts from Underground,'
       'The Immigrants,' and 'This Landscape, These People.'

  (b) In 'Autobiographical' and 'Bans O' Killing' compare the
       speakers' attitudes toward their own culture.

  (c) Both Bennett and Kogawa speak of outsiders' attacks on their
       ways of life. Compare the feelings implicit in the endings of
       the poems.

Poems 124 to 126

In these three poems the speakers comment on what their home-
lands mean to them.

124. *The Lake Isle of Innisfree*

The longing to lead the life of a hermit, expressed in this lyrical
poem, is popular in literature. **Innisfree** Innisfree is a small islet at
the end of a lake in the area of Yeats's boyhood home near Dublin.
Yeats wrote this poem in London where he had become homesick for
the beautiful countryside of Ireland. **l. 2 wattles** Flexible twigs laid
on the clay surface of a building.

125. *Home Thoughts from Abroad*

See the note on cadence (p. 518).

Probably written in 1845 while the poet was in Italy. **l. 5 brushwood sheaf** Here, the growth of young shoots around the bole of
the elm.

126. *The Farm*

See the note on the haiku (p. 500) and imagist poetry (p. 506).

Is Creeley expressing his love for the farm, his distaste for it, or a
sense of inevitability? Would you class this poem as a haiku?

Questions: Poems 124 to 126
  (a) What is the attraction of the 'other' place in each of the poems?
  (b) Which location seems more real to you?

Poems 127 to 129
Each poem transports the reader to a world that no longer exists, either in point of time or by virtue of changed conditions within individuals.

127. *The Railway Children*
See the note on imagery (p. 501).

The children harbour delightfully unreal perceptions as they respond to their environment. **l. 4 freehand** Writing or drawing done by hand without instruments or measurements. **l. 13** See Mark 10: 17-31 in which Christ blesses children and says that a rich man has as much chance of inheriting life everlasting as a camel would have of passing through the eye of a needle. What is being suggested about the enjoyment of the children?

128. *The White Horse*
See the note on ambiguity (p. 491).

Read the poem aloud to note how important the pause is at the end of the second line. What do you think is transpiring in the moment of silence?

129. *The Flower-Fed Buffaloes*
What is the effect of the repetition of sounds, words, phrases, and structures? **ll. 13-14 Blackfeet, Pawnees** Native people who inhabited the central plains of North America. They have almost disappeared.

Questions: Poems 127 to 129

(a) 'The Railway Children' and 'The Flower-Fed Buffaloes' both look back in time. What use is made of imagery in each poem to convey an impression of the past?

(b) 'The Railway Children' and 'The White Horse' both describe specific moments in time. 'The Flower-Fed Buffaloes' offers more general descriptions. Which treatment do you find more appealing?

Poem 130

The poet surveys the landscape from the point of view of a hawk.

130. *Hawk Roosting*

ll. 2-4 The hawk is content to be momentarily inactive, not in order to engage in wishful imagining, but simply as an expression of impulse. **ll. 15-16** The hawk does not try to justify its behaviour with specious argument; its actions simply indicate its given role in life.

Questions: Poem 130

(a) The contrast between humans and hawk remains implicit as the poem develops. What is the attitude of the poet to the bird?

(b) What different impressions are created when the poet uses the point of view of the creature portrayed as opposed to the point of view of a human observer?

Poems 131 to 134

These poems are portraits of various animals.

131. *Cats*

How do the language and the rhythm of the poem support the poet's contentions?

132. *The Prize Cat*

Pratt said that no reference in this poem to a specific international situation was intended. But since Italy had attacked Abyssinia (Ethiopia) in 1935, shortly before the poem was written, many choose to read it as a powerful comment on this act of aggression. The reference of the poem is multiple: it speaks directly about the blood-lust latent in domestic cats, as well as referring to the behaviour of human beings and of nations. **l. 5 gads** Spurs; here, claws. **l. 12 optic parallels** The fixed gaze of the cat's eyes. **l. 20 whitethroat** A species of North American sparrow with a particularly lovely song; the bird that the cat has trapped.

133. *Birds, Bags, Bears, and Buns*

l. 1 cormorant or shag A fairly large bird with a long neck and large beak, which inhabits seashore areas.

134. *Epigram*

See the notes on the couplet (p. 496) and epigram (p. 500).

Questions: Poems 131 to 134
   (a)   Explain the particular fascination felt by the poet for the cat in 'Cats' and 'The Prize Cat.'
   (b)   How is incongruity used to effect in 'Birds, Bags, Bears, and Buns' and 'Epigram'?

Poems 135 to 138

The following poems are portraits of people.

135. *The Proper Study* from *An Essay on Man*

See the notes on antithesis (p. 492), irony (p. 507), satire (p. 522), and wit (p. 528).

These are the opening lines from the second of the four Epistles that constitute *An Essay on Man*. (The generic term 'man,' as it is used here, has over the past few decades been replaced by a variety of non-sexist terms.) In arguing that human beings must recognize their place in the scheme of things and accept the interdependence of every kind of creature, Pope is endeavouring to dissuade the people of his time from their conviction that they were the centre of the universe. Since 'Man' can rely on neither his reason nor his instinct, he is incapable of ruling the world. **l. 2** One of Pope's many epigrams that have been quoted for centuries. **ll. 2-3** Man is a middle link in the chain of creatures, with imperfect wisdom and uncontrolled power. **l. 5 Sceptic** A person whose philosophic beliefs include a distrust of absolute knowledge. **l. 6 Stoic's pride** Stoics prided themselves on dispassionate acceptance of whatever befell them. **ll. 19-22** A reference to the new physics and astronomy of Newton. **l. 23 soar with Plato to th' empyreal sphere** Plato was an early Greek philosopher (427?-347?) who taught that humanity could move up the scale of being toward the ultimate Good by learning to understand the patterns that govern our lives. **ll. 25-28** A reference to Neoplatonism, which flourished for a couple of centuries in the early days of Christianity and reappeared in the middle ages. Its doctrines and teachings are influenced by Jewish and Oriental concepts.

136. *Zimri* from *Absalom and Achitophel*

See the notes on the couplet (p. 496), invective (p. 507), and satire (p. 522).

In *Absalom and Achitophel*, Dryden used the characters and the story of David, Absalom, and Achitophel from II Samuel 13-19 to form a parallel between that account and the political and religious situation that existed in England at the time of his writing. Dryden considered this particular passage to be 'worth the whole poem' as an example of 'Horatian fine raillery.' (Horace was a famous Latin poet particularly skilled in the art of satire.) Zimri was Dryden's name for George Villiers, Duke of Buckingham, who had written a play ridiculing Dryden. However, when this poem was written, 'Zimri' was in the Tower of London, accused of treason. The Biblical source for his name may be Numbers 25: 6-15, or I Kings 16: 8-20. Other historical sources support Dryden's accusations regarding Buckingham's flightiness and managerial ineptitude.

137. *The Wif of Bathe* from the Prologue to the *Canterbury Tales*
See the note on poem 71 (p. 393).

This portrait from the Prologue is one of Chaucer's lively and good-humoured observations of contemporary life. **Bathe** The town of Bath in England. **l. 4 Ypres, Gaunt** Centres of the thriving Flemish wool trade. **l. 6 offrynge** People went to make their church offering in order of social standing. **l. 15 worthy** Having some social standing; of good reputation. Chaucer uses this word in many ways, sometimes ironically, sometimes seriously. **l. 16 at chirchè dore** The marriage service was conducted outside the church; afterward mass was celebrated at the altar. **ll. 19-22** Pilgrims visited shrines in Boulogne, Galicia, and Cologne, often with no deeper religious motives than those of many tourists today. The cathedral in Santiago de Compostela, formerly the capital of Galicia, exhibited the relics of St James. **l. 24 Gat-tothèd** With teeth set wide apart — variously thought to indicate gluttonous or amorous tendencies, or a desire to travel. **l. 25 amblere** An ambling horse, the most comfortable and the easiest to ride. **l. 26 Y-wympled wel** Well protected with a hood.

138. *Mrs Reece Laughs*
See the notes on satire (p. 522) and wit (p. 528).

Note how the choice of language, rhythmic patterns, and rhymes all contribute to this minor *tour de force* of witty description.

Questions: Poems 135 to 138
    (a)   In most satirical writing, the satirist assumes that acceptable mores or social standards exist by which to judge other people. To what extent do these poets accept the standards of the majority, speaking as an average person, and satirizing an outsider? To what extent are they outsiders mocking a representative of the social norm?
    (b)   Compare the tones of satire in these poems.

Poems 139 and 140
These poems reveal how different people communicate their beliefs in language and by silence.

139. *Silence*

Marianne Moore has built up an impression of a highly unusual personality by subtly welding together several apparently disparate ideas. In their context, the simple concrete details take on a new significance and the simple form of the statements adds further comment. **ll. 2-4** What implication is being made? **ll. 5-7** What is the effect of expanding the simile?

140. *Talk*

How has Borson managed to create an emotional impact with such matter-of-fact statements? Do you agree with her comments?

Question: Poems 139 and 140

(a) Which of the two poems, in discussing everyday human behaviour, is more objective? Which is more compassionate? Support your position with details from the poems.

Poems 141 and 142

These poems convey moods associated with specific points of time and locales.

141. *1958*

MacEwen catches the aura of the period with her vivid sensual images. **l. 3 Palais Royale** A dance-hall in western Toronto. **ll. 29-30 Xenobia, Cat Woman** Heroines in a popular television series of the time. Who is 'you' in the poem?

142. *We Shall Not Escape Hell*

See the biography of Marina Tsvetayeva (p. 486).

Note how effectively the rhythm contributes to the underlying passion of the poem. Tsvetayeva recalls the glamorous activities and the free-spirited lifestyle she and her passionate sisters enjoyed in days gone by. She still expresses a cavalier defiance as she foresees the inevitable hell that assuredly awaits them — either in this life or the next. **ll. 13-14** References to how Penelope foiled her besieging suitors by secretly undoing the weaving at night that she had done during the day, as she waited for the return of her husband Ulysses from the Trojan Wars. She had promised the suitors that she would marry one of them as soon as the tapestry she was weaving was complete. **ll. 6-8** An allusion to the spirits of the damned being ferried across the River Styx by Charon. **l. 12 robbers' camp** Possibly a reference to her group of friends who were able to get illegal supplies despite the restrictive government's vigilance.

Questions: Poems 141 and 142
- (a) Both poems express past pleasures and the prospect of suffering. Compare the values set forth in each poem.
- (b) Where does the speaker in each poem look for help in facing her daily life?

Poems 143 to 149
These poems share the eternal literary theme of love.

143. *Suzanne Takes You Down*
This poem is one of the few modern folk songs with lyrics that stand independently as a poem. **ll. 19-20** A reference to one of the miracles performed by Jesus, as reported in the Book of Matthew 14: 22-33.

What is a person's 'perfect body' (referred to in lines 17, 34, and 52)? How would you touch something with your mind? Is the song about Suzanne or something else?

144. *Passing By*
l. 10 Similarly, my beloved changes her dwelling place.

145. *A Sweet Disorder*

Herrick was one of the best Cavalier lyricists; his poetry is characterized by civilized neatness and grace. Note the difference in style from his contemporaries — Donne (pp. 164 and 166) and Herbert (p. 254). **l. 3 lawn** A shawl made of lawn, a fine linen. **l. 6 stomacher** An ornamental cloth, like a cummerbund, worn under the lacing of a bodice.

146. *Go, Lovely Rose*

See the note on symbol (p. 505).

A charming example of a poem enjoining young ladies not to be bashful, but to realize how short-lived their beauty is, and to enjoy the admiration of lovers before it is too late. The theme was popular in the seventeenth century.

147. *To His Coy Mistress*

Andrew Marvell united the elegant grace of the Cavalier poets with the wittier, more closely packed style of the metaphysical poets. Here he echoes the theme of Waller's poem 'Go, Lovely Rose' (and of many of the Greek and Latin lyricists, whose constant refrain was *carpe diem* — seize the pleasures of the day). **l. 7 complain** Sing a love lament. **l. 10** A popular cliché of Marvell's time: endlessly. **l. 40 his slow-chapt power** The power of time's slow-moving jaws.

148. *She Walks in Beauty*

Composed after Byron's first meeting with his cousin Mrs Robert Wilmot.

149. *Somewhere I Have Never Travelled, Gladly Beyond*

Cummings interweaves symbols that have acquired special significance in the history of love poetry. He also experimented with orthography and syntax, more extremely in some poems than in this one.

Questions: Poems 143 to 149

(a)　Can you account for the appeal of each of the love lyrics in this grouping?

(b)　What characteristics are common to all of these love poems?

(c)　Do you notice any difference between the love poems from the seventeenth century and those from the twentieth century?

Poems 150 to 152

These poems describe visionary landscapes and existence.

150. *Kubla Khan*

See the note on imagery (p. 501).

Coleridge subtitled this poem 'A Vision in a Dream. A Fragment.' It recreates a stream of images that he experienced during a dream. Just before falling asleep he had been reading *Purchas his Pilgrimage* by a seventeenth-century writer, Samuel Purchas. The lines he had been reading were as follows:

> *In Xamdu did Cublai Can build a stately Palace, encompassing sixteene miles of plaine ground with a wall, wherein are fertile Meddowes, pleasant springs, delightful Streams, and all sorts of beasts of chase and game, and in the middest thereof a sumptuous house of pleasure, which may be removed from place to place.*

When he woke up he began writing 'Kubla Khan.' A visitor interrupted at the point where the poem ends; after the visit, Coleridge could no longer recapture the images from the dream. **ll. 39-41** See *Paradise Lost*, Book IV, lines 280 to 282:

> *Where Abassin Kings their issue Guard,*
> *Mount Amara, though this by some supposed*
> *True Paradise, under the Ethiop line.*

l. 54 milk of Paradise Plato's *Ion* 534 a-b refers to Dionysiac women who received milk and honey in their Muses' Paradise. Dionysus, the

429

god of wine and sensual ecstasy, was associated with eternal happiness.

What do you consider to be the function of the imagery in this poem? How do the distinct changes of mood fit together?

151. *The Inferno (Canto Third)* from *The Divine Comedy*

See the notes on the canto (p. 494), the epic (p. 499), terza rima (p. 527), and allegory (p. 506).

The Divine Comedy, written in three parts entitled *The Inferno* (Hell), *Purgatory*, and *Paradise*, is a visionary representation of a spiritual crisis in Dante's own life. He is conducted through Hell and Purgatory by the poet Vergil, the representative of unaided human reason. In Paradise he meets and is guided by Beatrice, a young woman, now dead, whom he had adored and idealized in his youth. She is an emissary of Divine Love.

The Inferno envisages Hell as a great vortex of graduated circles where sinners are punished according to their particular crimes. Cantos I and II describe Dante's meeting with Vergil and Vergil's explanation of the journey that Dante is to take and its ultimate joyous outcome. At the beginning of Canto III the two poets pass through the Gate of Hell.

Although the translator, John Ciardi, has not found it expedient to follow Dante's terza rima exactly, the suitability of the general form for Dante's purpose is quite apparent. **l. 1 City of Woe** Hell is often described as a city. **ll. 4-6** God's attributes are inscribed above the gates. **l. 7 Only those elements . . . wear** The angels, the heavens, and matter in its elemental form. **l. 9 Abandon . . . here** The warning is for the souls of the damned, not for Dante and Vergil. **l. 11 Master** Vergil, Dante's guide. **l. 18** These souls have not lost their intelligence and understanding, but failed to benefit from them by apprehending God and truth. **ll. 32-48** The two poets are passing through a limbo occupied by those souls who never acted positively for good or evil. Cf. Revelations 3: 15-16. **ll. 56-57 that soul . . . Denial** Probably Celestine V, who became Pope in 1294 at the age of eighty, but resigned after five months, convinced that his soul was endangered by the worldly preoccupations of the papacy. He was succeeded by Boniface VIII, whom Dante considered to be a symbol of the corruption of the church. Fearlessly, Dante describes great men of his time as damned souls, frequently mentioning them by name. **l. 68 a wide river** The Acheron, one of the four rivers separating the land of the living from Hell. **l. 80 old man** Charon, the ferryman who, in classical mythology, transported shades of the dead across the Acheron. **ll. 85-90** Charon recognizes that Dante is a living man who normally could not enter the land of the dead. Cf. ll. 124-126. **ll. 122-123** These souls have been condemned by divine justice, which they accept to such an extent that they long for punishment. **ll. 133-134** Dante's swoon shows him susceptible to the grief of Hell. As the poem progresses, it reveals also his strong indignation against evil, especially in the politics, the church of the day, and his proud, visionary zeal for a spiritual reawakening to the divine order governing the universe as he understood it.

152. *The Hollow Men*

See the notes on allusion (p. 490), irony (p. 507), juxtaposition (p. 508), modernist poetry (p. 510), and symbol (p. 505).

Lamenting the loss of ideals and initiative by the civilization that survived World War I, Eliot expresses complete despair. In juxtaposed images the poem conveys the condition of people who are spiritually dead, unable to understand the significance of their lives, and incapable of finding any meaning in transcendant revelation.

Influenced by those liturgical forms of public worship in which some parts of the service are spoken by the congregation and other parts by the priest, the poem begins and ends with a chorus of hollow creatures, huddled together in lamentation. The second section continues with the terrible cry of a single voice, recoiling from this waking nightmare and confessing cowardice and impotence. The third and fourth sections go on to describe the wasteland and river bank that the hollow men inhabit, tormented by religious intimations in which they cannot believe. The poem concludes with a pathetic mixture of nursery rhyme and liturgy, spoken by people in the grip of total spiritual paralysis.

The epigraphs amplify the suggestion of the poem by allusion: — **Mistah Kurtz — he dead** An expression of hopelessness. The phrase is taken from Conrad's novel, *Heart of Darkness*. **A Penny for the Old Guy** In 1605 Guy Fawkes attempted to blow up the House of Commons in London, but was caught and executed. (See the final stanza.) The tradition became that, on November 5 each year, English children would make a stuffed dummy to represent Guy Fawkes and burn it on a bonfire to the accompaniment of fireworks. For weeks beforehand, the children asked for a 'penny for the guy' with which to buy fireworks. The expression here reinforces the allusion to stuffed men.

l. 14 death's other Kingdom Eliot refers to his conviction that there are two kingdoms of death — one for those who have already died, one for those who are spiritually dead while physically alive. 'Death's other Kingdom' is probably the eternal life after death that awaits those who have led a deep and courageous spiritual life on earth. It is opposed to 'death's dream kingdom' (l. 20), which is presumably the death in life of the hollow men, those who are without faith and without the ability to act. They are tormented by intimations of a truth that might save them, if only they had the courage to face it. **l. 19 Eyes I dare not meet in dreams** The eyes of those who have gained eternal life. They are the 'direct eyes' of line 14, which challenge the pretence of the hollow men. **ll. 22-28** The interpretation of these lines is uncertain. The difficulty is created by the word 'there' in lines 22 and 24. Does it refer to the world of the hollow men (l. 20) or to the world of those who have faced death triumphantly (l. 14)? In either case the vision is tantalizingly oblique and incomplete. **l. 23 column** The column is often an expression of spiritual aspirations. **l. 28 star** A symbol of eternal life. The phrase 'fading star' indicates the remoteness of such reality from the hollow men. Compare the later references to the star. **l. 32 Such deliberate disguises** The rat's coat (tailcoat?), crowskin (tall black hat?), and crossed staves make up a scarecrow's clothing, recalling the image of the stuffed men. The crossed staves also suggest the emblem of Christ's crucifixion, implying that, for the hollow men, religious observance is a 'deliberate disguise,' an evasion of truth. **l. 38 twilight kingdom** A third kingdom, probably a place of transition from life to death, where individuals must finally face reality. The twilight king-

dom is probably the valley (of the shadow of death) of lines 54 and 55.
l. 39 the dead land Death's dream kingdom. **ll. 39-51** The hollow
men erect stone images, idols for worship. In their few moments of authentic spiritual activity, they might be able to express real tenderness to
one another, but each is isolated and alone. Hence they continue to utter prayers in fear to the stone images, even though the images are now
broken. **l. 54 this valley** The valley of the shadow of death. See Psalm
23. **l. 63 tumid** Swollen. Here, the impression is one of foulness. The
river is often pictured as separating life from death, as the Styx and the
Jordan. **l. 61 Sightless** Without vision of truth or of what lies beyond
death. **l. 63 perpetual star** Cf. the fading star of line 28 and the dying
star of line 54. **l. 64 Multifoliate** Here, many-petalled. **rose** A traditional symbol; here, for the transcendant realities of religion. **ll. 68-98**
These lines portray the struggle in the hollow men between religious
affirmation and a deliberately mindless despair. **l. 68 Here we go
round** . . . This parody of a nursery rhyme, juxtaposed with the fragment of the Lord's Prayer, suggests the utter desperation of people
without beliefs. See the discussion of these lines under juxtaposition
(p. 508) and allusion (p. 490). **l. 76 the Shadow** The shadow of death.
The fear of purposelessness in life and oblivion in death paralyses every
response of the hollow men. **l. 98** Even in their last hour the hollow
men achieve, not tragic dignity, but pathetic weakness.

Questions: Poems 150 to 152

   (a) Compare 'The Hollow Men' and *The Inferno* with respect to
        (i) the afflictions of the people amongst whom the speaker in
        each poem finds himself (ii) and the position of the speaker
        in each poem in relation to his environment.

   (b) Compare the moods established at the end of 'Kubla Khan,'
        The Inferno, and 'The Hollow Men.'

   (c) Comment on the use of imagery in each poem.

Poems 153 to 158

This group of poems extols the goodness of people and the blessed
aspects of life.

153. *I Think Continually of Those Who Were Truly Great*

See the notes on accentual verse (p. 521) and symbol (p. 505).

This poem develops through the use of symbols. **l. 3 suns** Source of light and life. **l. 5 touched with fire** As inspired prophets. **l. 10 springs** Waters of life. Compare Moses' rod that brought water from the rock in the wilderness.

154. *Great Things*

l. 3 Spinning Cycling. **Weymouth** A seaport town in Dorset, the county in which Hardy was born.

155. *The Choice* from 'A Dialogue of Self and Soul'

This excerpt is the second part of a debate within the poet's mind, in which he balances the implications of reincarnation against those of an afterlife. Reincarnation would mean accepting the conditions of earthly life, which Yeats found increasingly bitter: violent hatreds, physical prostration, and a frustrated love affair seemed ample cause for giving up his life with relief. Yet, after bitterly enumerating his trials, Yeats decides that he would 'live it all again.' **ll. 22-24** For fifteen years Yeats had loved Maud Gonne, a prominent Irish actress and revolutionary. She married a man whom Yeats despised, but she wanted to keep the poet as a friend. **ll. 25-27** Yeats thought it possible, from his studies in the occult, that the soul relived its past life immediately after death; when the soul had 'followed to its source' its entire life, it could achieve forgiveness and consequent reincarnation.

156. *Virtue*

See the notes on conceit (p. 495) and metaphysical poetry (p. 510).

l. 11 closes A multiple pun. The box of spring must eventually be closed; its sweets — the 'sweet days and roses' — must be locked away in death. With reference to music, 'closes' also meant concluding cadences. **ll. 13-16** This elaborated comparison is a metaphysical conceit. Seasoned wood does not warp or bend, but actually improves with age. Similarly, the soul matured by virtuous living does not die, but achieves a greater vitality when freed from the body. The poet elaborates the simile further. Living plants and trees may finally die and decompose to form coal; the soul, however, attains its fullest life after death.

157. *Though I Speak With the Tongues of Men and of Angels*

See the notes on imagery (p. 501) and poem 69 (p. 393).

Notice the extensive use of concrete images and symbols. It is interesting to compare the 1611 translation of this passage with modern translations. **l. 11 Charity** Christian love.

158. *Prayer*

How has the mood of gentleness been achieved? Who might 'her' be in the last third of the poem?

Questions: Poems 153 to 158
   (a) What aspects of religious belief inform each poet?
   (b) How do the language, imagery, and rhythm contribute to the mood of each of the poems?

Poems 159 and 160

These two poems express personal feelings about religious beliefs. See the note on the Nootka (p. 476).

Question: Poems 159 and 160
   (a) What aspect of the culture of the native people of Canada is reflected in the two poems?

Poems 161 to 165

This group of poems evokes a realization that a hidden and mysterious world lies deep within each person.

161. *An Absolutely Ordinary Rainbow*

The poem operates on two levels — firstly, it is a recognition of the reality and dignity of the personal sorrow that each individual suffers, and, secondly, it is a suggestion of the godhead in human beings, since the incident described may be implicitly connected with the suffering of Christ. The setting is Sydney, Australia. **ll. 1-2 Repins, Lorenzinis** Fashionable restaurants. **l. 3 Tattersalls** A club where bets can be placed on the day's races. **l. 5 the Greek Club** A private club. **l. 6 Martin Place** A pedestrian mall. **l. 7 George Street** A downtown shopping street. **l. 47 Pitt Street** A downtown shopping street.

Besides the use of place names, what features contribute to the sense of realism that pervades the poem? The last line is a masterpiece of concrete detail conveying a profundity of meaning. How does it elevate the significance of the incident to a higher level? Why is the title appropriate for the poem?

162. *Common Magic*

The poem provides a series of evocative and sympathetic pictures of commonly observed behaviour patterns in all walks of life.

163. *Richard Cory*

What general conclusions can you draw from the specific incident described?

164. *My Last Duchess*

See the notes on dramatic monologue (p. 497), juxtaposition (p. 508), and persona (p. 514).

The speaker is almost certainly modelled upon Duke Alfonso II (b. 1533) of the aristocratic Este family in Italy. He married Lucrezia de Medici of Florence when he was twenty-five and she was fourteen. Three years later she was dead, many people suspecting that she had been poisoned. Shortly thereafter the Duke began negotiations for the hand of Barbara, niece of the Count of Tyrol. The incident takes place in a picture gallery of the Duke's palace at Ferrara, a city in northern Italy. This poem illustrates Browning's effective use of all the resources of the dramatic monologue. **l. 3 Frà** *Frater*, a brother; that is, a member of a religious order. Frà Pandolf and Claus of Innsbruck (l. 56) are imaginary artists. **l. 56 Innsbruck** A town in the Austrian Tyrol near the Italian border. **ll. 54-56** What innuendoes make the Duke's remark more revealing than he intends?

165. *The Child Who Walks Backwards*

Crozier is addressing a social problem, the extent and seriousness of which the public is just beginning to recognize. **l. 30** Note the pun on 'lies.' How has the poet kept the poem from becoming sentimental? At what point in your reading of the poem did you begin to suspect the truth?

Questions: Poems 161 to 165

   (a)   What message is implicit, but not overtly stated, in each of these poems?

   (b)   Which poem has the greatest emotional impact on you? How do you account for this effect?

Poems 166 to 168

These poems offer insights into human dilemmas.

166. *It's Good to Be Here*

The poem presents a surprising view of an unwanted or unplanned child. How did the title strike you after reading the poem as compared to before you read it?

167. *Weakness*

What effect do the comparison in line 5 and the detail of lines 15 and 16 have on the poem?

168. *Coyote Pup Meets the Crazy People in Kootenay National Park*

Kootenay National Park In the Rocky Mountain Range in southeast British Columbia. **l. 11 'nectine** Presumably a lethal substance. **l. 13 the .270** The size of the firearm he carries. **ll. 29-30** What is being implied by the comments on communication in these lines? **ll. 33-35** The topics of conversation are about aspects of their work as rangers and their means of communication with the outside world.

Why place the incident in a national park? What is the effect of the word 'crazy' in the title? What kind of people are the rangers?

Questions: Poems 166 to 168

- (a)   In what way is the attitude expressed at the end of 'It's Good to Be Here' similar to and different from that at the end of 'Coyote Pup Meets the Crazy People in Kootenay National Park'?
- (b)   How does the level of language used in each poem affect your response as a reader?
- (c)   Pick out images in each poem that make a particularly strong impression on you.
- (d)   What is the speaker's attitude to the victim in each of the three poems?

Poems 169 to 172

These poets recognise the nobility of the ordinary members of society and the downtrodden.

169. *I've Tasted My Blood*

ll. 1-3 There could be an allusion to lines from Blake's 'The Tyger' (p. 116). **ll. 14-16** Many of Acorn's playmates, he says, died in Europe in World War II. Little mounds of earth are voided by earthworms on the surface of the ground above their burial sites.

170. *SOS*

SOS In the days of telegraph communication and Morse code, the distress signal that meant 'Save Our Souls.'

What shift in meaning occurs in the phrase 'come in' as the poem progresses? Do you find the format used in the poem as effective as a series of polemic statements?

171. *John Henry*

See the note on the ballad (p. 493).

John Henry was a six-foot tall, two-hundred pound folk hero. He was 'of pure African blood,' a prodigious singer, and the best hammer man engaged in laying the Chesapeake and Ohio Railroad in West Virginia between 1870 and 1873. The introduction of power-operated machinery at this time gave rise to the incident described in the song. **l. 3 De Big Bend Tunnel** A mile and a quarter long and the biggest tunnel attempted up to that date. It was drilled through the face of a mountain. **l. 7 steam drill** John Henry has been swinging a ten-pound hammer in a nineteen-foot arc to come down on the head of a steel drill. **l. 36 shaker** The man who holds the drill as it is being struck by the hammer and turns it after each blow.

172. *Questions from a Worker Who Reads*

Brecht, a Marxist, believed in the dignity of the working class and the value of education for working people. What assumptions is the worker questioning in the way history is usually recorded? If the questions were taken seriously, how might the writing of history change?

Questions: Poems 169 to 172

(a) Each of the poems in this group draws attention to the plight of the underdogs of society. Which poem makes the strongest impact on you? Why does it affect you so strongly? If none of the poems moves you personally, explain why.

(b) What moods are expressed in each poem?

Poem 173

Blake presents his point of view by means of vivid concrete images.

173. *London*

ll. 1, 2 chartered The streets were given a legal identity, named, and the names placed on maps. The Thames River has had its course and depth charted.

Question: Poem 173

(a)   What is Blake's impression of London in his time?

Poems 174 to 177

Each poem represents a vision of idyllic life.

174. *The Peace of Wild Things*

l. 4 wood drake The male wood duck is the most highly colourful North American species of duck. **l. 5 the great heron** The great blue heron, one of the largest and most impressive of the inland water birds. **l. 11**   The line has layers of meaning: his belief that the world is in a state of grace (spiritual goodness) frees him from worry; and his state of contentment is provided by the grace (kindness) of the world.

175. *The Shepherd to His Love*

See the note on pastoral poetry (p. 513).

l. 2 prove Experience; try. **l. 8 madrigal** An intricate part-song popular with the Elizabethans; here, any pastoral music. **l. 11 kirtle** Skirt. **l. 21 Meat** Food in general. **l. 25 swains** Rustic lovers.

176. *The Nymph's Reply*

See the note on pastoral poetry (p. 513).

l. 7 Philomel A poetic name for the nightingale. In the Greek myth, Philomela was assaulted by her brother-in-law, Tereus, who cut out her tongue so that she could not reveal his crime. The gods, pitying her, turned her into a nightingale.

177. *Raleigh Was Right*

See the note on pastoral poetry (p. 513).

Williams expands on each point made in 'The Nymph's Reply' by Sir Walter Raleigh.

Questions: Poems 174 to 177

    (a)   How does each poet characterize pastoral life? Which poets distinguish between the ideal world and reality?

    (b)   What is the basis for the choice each poet makes in favour of the pastoral life?

Poems 178 to 180

These imagist poems vividly portray sensory moments with sparse language and non-metric rhythms.

178. *The Term*

See the note on imagery (p. 501).

179. *This Is Just to Say*

See the note on imagery (p. 501).

180. *Variations on a Theme by William Carlos Williams*

See the notes on imagery (p. 501) and parody (p. 513).

Which features of the imagist William Carlos Williams is Koch parodying?

Questions: Poems 178 to 180

    (a)   Do you see any similarities between these poems and the haiku form? See the notes on the haiku (p. 500) and poems 21, 22, and 109.

    (b)   Compare the use of imagery in Williams's poems with the imagery in Pound's 'In a Station of the Metro' (p. 294).

Poems 181 to 183

The following poems are concerned with impressions of enduring time.

181. *In Time of 'The Breaking of Nations'*

This poem was written in 1915, during World War I, although the incidents are recalled from forty years earlier. **l. 9 wight** Young man. The archaic word stresses the timelessness of love.

182. *Sonnet* CXVI: *Let Me Not to the Marriage of True Minds*

See the notes on the sonnet (p. 522) and poem 31 (p. 379).

l. 4 remover One who ceases to love; literally, one who moves away. **l. 8 worth's . . . height** Mariners determine a star's distance above the horizon for purposes of navigation; they cannot, however, calculate its mystical or occult value.

183. *An Arundel Tomb*

See the notes on imagery (p. 501) and irony (p. 507).

In medieval times it was common for members of the nobility to be buried in the church they patronized and to have a likeness carved on the cover of the horizontal stone tomb. Observe how Larkin leads the reader from glancing casually at details of the tomb to philosophizing about time, ideals that have been lost, and the lasting importance of love. **Arundel** A small town in West Sussex, England. The historic local church in Arundel is St Nicholas. **l. 7 pre-baroque** Baroque refers to an ornate style that existed roughly between 1580 and 1680. The style of the tomb, which was carved in the preceding period, was much plainer. **l. 27 thronged the glass** The stained glass windows of the church are made resplendent by the sun's rays. **l. 33 an unarmorial age** People who gaze at the tomb now know nothing about the coats of arms, the family mottoes stated thereon, and the lineage of great families with their proud traditions.

Questions: Poems 181 to 183

(a) Each poem is concerned with the enduring quality of love; yet each makes a different point. What focus does each poem take?

(b) In each poem, is your strongest impression of the beloved, the lover, or the nature of love? Why?

(c) Which poets comment on the quality of life in their particular generation?

Poems 184 to 186

The strong images of these poems strike a sombre note.

184. *Erosion*

See the note on modernist juxtaposition (p. 508).
l. 4 scarp An escarpment; the steep face of a cliff.

185. *In a Station of the Metro*

See the notes on ellipsis (p. 498), modernist juxtaposition (p. 508), and imagist poetry (p. 506).
Metro The Paris subway.

186. *Domination of Black*

See the note on symbol (p. 505).

Stevens's poem assumes a dream-like quality of vivid impression and indefinable statement. Colours, shapes, and sounds interweave, accumulating emotional impact as a pattern evolves. The final domination of black is the expression of a deep despairing anxiety. **l. 8 hemlocks** A species of evergreen that burns vigorously with bright flames. **l. 10 peacocks** Birds noted for their gorgeously coloured, fan-shaped tail plumage and their startling and incongruously raucous voice. The peacock is traditionally associated with an elegant lifestyle.

How does Stevens achieve such a strong cumulative effect in this poem? How would you describe the mood of the poem?

Questions: Poems 184 to 186

    (a) What do you take to be each poet's attitude toward the situation presented?

    (b) Each poem evokes a specific locale. How do the treatments of these locales differ?

    (c) Which poems rely more on literal imagery and which on figurative imagery? How does the kind of imagery used affect the reader's response?

Poem 187

Shelley's ode makes a philosophic statement by describing his response to nature.

187. *Ode to the West Wind*

See the notes on apostrophe (p. 492), the ode (p. 512), the sonnet (p. 522), and terza rima (p. 527).

l. 18 Angels Here, in the original Greek sense of 'messengers.' **l. 21 Maenad** A female worshipper in the wild rituals of Dionysus, the Greek god of wine and sensual ecstasy. **l. 31 coil** A gently curling motion; a softly splashing sound. **l. 32 pumice** Hardened lava. **Baiae** A port near Naples in Roman times. **ll. 33-34** The Mediterranean Sea dreams of the Roman towers that it once mirrored at Baiae, whose ruins it now partially covers. **l. 57 lyre** The instrument that accompanied song or recitation in Greece; also, the wind-harp, a stringed instrument that made music when set in the wind. It became a favourite Romantic symbol for poetic inspiration. **l. 63** Shelley's passionate arguments for social and religious liberty had been denounced or ignored in England.

Questions: Poem 187

    (a) What does autumn mean to Shelley?

    (b) What specific events does Shelley associate with autumn?

    (c) Describe the range of tones that you find in the poem.

    (d) Comment on the effectiveness of combining the terza rima and the sonnet as a vehicle for the content.

Poems 188 to 191

These nature poems focus on the autumn season.

189. *The Mowing*

See the notes on the lyric (p. 509) and sonnet (p. 522).

l. 4 cicadae Large insects indigenous to hot climates and famed for the piercing sound of their persistent chorus. **l. 8** Three species of plants commonly found in fields. **l. 11 cordial** Both in the sense of 'friendly' and 'a beverage reputed to be good for the heart.'

In what way is the harvested crop more than just fodder for the animals?

191. *Stopping by Woods on a Snowy Evening*

Frost has achieved a *tour de force* in this short lyric, possibly the best-known poem in American literature. The poem can be read simply as a response to a lovely experience or as a symbolic representation of musings on life and the ever-present recognition of the inevitability of death. The language and images are both natural and subtle. The interesting interlocking of the simple rhyme pattern from stanza to stanza achieves a flowing continuity, while the rhythms of the phrasing, the combinations of pleasing sounds, and the repetition in the final two lines make the poem easily memorable. What details does Frost not bother to mention in his vignette?

Questions: Poems 188 to 191

    (a) What basic impressions are common to all four poems? What differences, if any, do you find in the treatment of the themes?

    (b) Compare the treatment of nature in this group of poems with the treatment of nature in 'Ode to the West Wind.'

Poems 192 to 195

Each of these poems celebrates a beloved.

445

192. *Plucking the Rushes*

Waley's translation captures the quality, characteristic of Chinese poetry, of relying as much upon omission as upon what is said.

193. *The River-Merchant's Wife: A Letter*

Translated from a Japanese version of the original Chinese. Chinese poetry frequently evokes the emotional overtones of a concrete situation by means of suggestion and understatement. **l. 5 Chokan** A village in China near Nanjing.

194. *A Birthday*

This poem represents the poet in her most joyful mood, in which she uses bright pictorial imagery to convey her spiritual state. **l. 6 halcyon** Calm; the halcyon or kingfisher is believed to bring peaceful weather at its breeding time. **l. 10 vair** The fur of a type of squirrel, used to trim garments in medieval times; the word may also be used here in its heraldic sense of parti-coloured.

Questions: Poems 192 to 195

   (a)   No two of these love poems treat love in the same way. What is the particular situation and atmosphere in each poem?

   (b)   Which poem(s) do you find most appealing? Why?

Poems 196 to 200

The following poems are accounts of unconventional behaviour and feelings of toughness.

196. *Accidentally Broke*

In what way is this poem like a haiku? See the note on the haiku (p. 498).

197. *On the Move*

Gunn has drawn on the philosophy of the French existentialists, who argued that one cannot find a set of values unless one creates them from moment to moment through whole-hearted action. **l. 5 their** The birds'. **l. 7 baffled sense** Human beings have confused, obscure instincts and cannot express them exactly in words. The following stanza describes the attempt to express them in violent movement. **l. 24 the taken routes** People choose the routes they will take without knowledge of where they lead, and they stake their future on the choice. **l. 30 valueless** Without defined values.

198. *The Hitchhiker*
l. 8 the famous resort Probably the Banff Springs Hotel. What implication is Newlove making in the last two lines of the poem?

200. *The Fights*
l. 5 slues Turns forcibly aside. **l. 6 A thin gillette's width** For many years Gillette, the manufacturer of razor blades, sponsored broadcasts of sporting events, including boxing. **l. 31 long count** A trick used by a dishonest referee. When the boxer he favours is knocked down, the referee counts more slowly than is legitimate, thus giving his favourite an advantage.

Question: Poems 196 to 200
(a) These poems portray outsiders and social rebels. To what extent are they presented sympathetically? To what extent are we intended to censure them?

Poems 201 and 202
A more or less jaundiced look at humanity is presented in these two poems.

201. *The Improved Binoculars*
See the note on extended metaphor (p. 505).
l. 11 auricle Something shaped like the external portion of the ear.

Questions: Poems 201 and 202
    (a)   What is the difference in tone in these two poems?
    (b)   What features create the particular tone of each poem?

Poems 203 to 205

These three poems look toward the future.

203. *The Fisherman*

Yeats tried for years to establish an Irish national literature. But the intrigues of Dublin public life and the riots of 1907 that greeted John Synge's play, *The Playboy of the Western World*, convinced him that the general public was not a deserving audience. Here he explains his resolve to write more directly and candidly, with a new kind of reader in mind. **l. 4 Connemara** A rugged district in County Galway, Ireland. **l. 12 reality** Parallel to 'What I had hoped' in line 10. **ll. 13-24** Most of the references in these lines are to local personalities; in the heat of Yeats's invective, they become types of the philistine and the rogue. **l. 14 the dead man** The playwright John Synge, who had died five years earlier. See p. 35. **ll. 33-34** A reference to fly-fishing.

205. *Selections* from the 'Rubaiyat of Omar Khayyam of Naishapur'

Omar Khayyam (Omar the Tentmaker), a Persian mathematician and poet of the eleventh century, wrote some five hundred rubais or quatrains. Although most were self-contained epigrams, they were held together by a philosophy of pleasure and a melancholy awareness of death's finality. These stanzas are excerpts from the first edition of Fitzgerald's free translation, made in 1859. **l. 20 Sultan Mahmud** Sultan of Ghazni (971?-1029), in what is now Afghanistan.

Questions: Poems 203 to 205
    (a)   What hope is expressed in each poem?
    (b)   What causes for despair are recognized in each poem?

Poems 206 and 207

These two poems focus on the issue of death.

206. *Dirge Without Music*

Millay has been accused of wearing her heart on her sleeve. Is that a fault? Do you find that this poem refutes or supports the claim?

207. *And Death Shall Have No Dominion*

See the notes on consonance (p. 525), near-rhyme (p. 511), and transferred epithet (p. 527).

The prose sense of this poem is relatively simple: though people die, they shall be raised at the end of time. This theme, which Thomas states in the first line of the poem, is developed in rich and powerful variations through to the last line. It is an expansion and re-affirmation of Revelation 20: 13: 'And the sea gave up the dead which were in it; and death and hell delivered up the dead which were in them.' Thomas's imagination was steeped in the Bible; his prophetic tone and many of his cadences derive from the same source.

The tone and mood of the poem progress from the explosive harshness of the first stanza, through the brutal imagery of torture in the second, to the more mellow affirmation of the final stanza. The title is drawn from Romans 6: 9: 'Knowing that Christ being raised from the dead dieth no more; death hath no more dominion over him.' **ll. 5-8** What parallels can you find with poem 157 (p. 255)? **l. 6 go mad** Become insane; leave this existence while insane. **l. 12 windily** A serious pun. The word refers back to the 'winding of the sea,' suggesting both the movement of the sea and the shroud in which the dead are buried at sea. **l. 16 unicorn evils** The unicorn is often symbolic of Christ. Note the force of the paradox.

Questions: Poem 206 and 207

    (a)   Contrast the attitudes and moods of the poets as they contemplate death.

    (b)   Comment on the rhythms of the two poems.

Poems 208 to 210

The following poems look back on history.

208. *The Isles of Greece* from *Don Juan*

See the note on ottava rima (p. 512).

Byron wrote the sixteen-canto poetic fantasy *Don Juan* before the war in which Greece gained her independence from Turkey. This selection from Canto III displays his deep admiration for Greece, an admiration which led him to join in the struggle for freedom. **l. 2 Sappho** A woman from the Greek island of Lesbos, who wrote lyric poetry in about 600 B. C. **l. 4 Delos** A small island in the Aegean, supposed to have been summoned from the sea by Neptune. It was said to be the birthplace of Phoebus Apollo, the god of the sun and of music, poetry, and prophecy. **l. 7 Marathon** A plain about twenty-two miles from Athens and the scene of a victory of the Athenians over the Persians in 490 B. C. Before the victory, a messenger ran 150 miles from Athens to Sparta in forty-eight hours to convey a request for help; the modern marathon race perpetuates the memory of the feat. **l. 13 A king** Xerxes (c. 519-465 B. C.), king of the Persians. **l. 14 Salamis** The Greeks defeated Xerxes in 480 B. C. in a naval battle just off the island of Salamis near Attica. **ll. 22-24 A remnant . . . Thermopylae** In 480 B. C. Leonidas and three hundred Spartans heroically held off the forces of Xerxes at the pass of Thermopylae between Thessaly and Greece.

209. *All That's Past*

See the note on alliteration (p. 525).

Contrast the philosophy and tone of this poem with those of the preceding poem. Observe de la Mare's control of vowels and consonants, particularly in the first stanza. **l. 24 amaranth** An imaginary flower that never fades.

210. *Echo*

See the note on near-rhyme (p. 511).

An example of de la Mare's ability to evoke the mysterious, fearful world of the troubled mind.

Questions: Poems 208 to 210

    (a)   Which of the poems discuss the passage of time in purely personal terms? Which discuss it in larger terms?

    (b)   Do the poems in this grouping that make abstract statements succeed in holding your interest? Why or why not?

Poems 211 to 214

These poems speak of mortality and immortality.

211. *Death the Leveller*

See the note on metonymy (p. 510).

This is a song from Shirley's play, *The Contention of Ajax and Ulysses.* In the early and middle seventeenth century, many writers gave voice to the disillusionment and sense of transience that had replaced the heroic self-confidence of the Elizabethans.

212. *What Thou Lovest Well Remains* from *The Cantos*

See the note on modernist poetry (p. 510) and the biography of Ezra Pound (p. 478).

This selection from Canto LXXXI, *The Cantos* is a particularly powerful section, written while Pound was imprisoned. Here he is examining his life to see what has been 'vanity' and what will endure. **l. 8 Elysium** The dwelling place of blessed souls after death. **l. 11 centaur** A mythical creature, half man, half horse. **l. 18 Paquin** A house of French fashion design. **l. 19** Pound finds the green world that he can see from his prison outdoes his most elegant work. **l. 20** A rhythmic paraphrase of l. 6 of Chaucer's 'Balade de Bon Conseyl.' **l. 30 Rathe** Bent on; anxious to; offering advice to. **niggard** Stingy. **l. 36 Blunt** Wilfrid Scawen Blunt (1840-1922) was a poet, politician, and explorer who was opposed to British Imperialism. Pound refers to his interchanges with Blunt as a generous-spirited commerce with the past and example of action that will endure.

213. *Song* from *Cymbeline*

From Act IV, scene 2, ll. 258-281.

The lament at the supposed death of Imogen, the heroine of the play, who had disguised herself as a boy. **l. 11 Physic** Medical knowledge. **l. 14 thunder-stone** Thunderbolt. **l. 18 Consign to thee** Submit to the same terms as you do; sign, together with you, a contract. **l. 19 exorciser** Here, one who conjures up evil spirits. **l. 21 unlaid** Not set at rest. **l. 23 consummation** Completion of life.

214. *Song*

A song from the comedy, *Summer's Last Will and Testament* (1600). The plagues at the end of the sixteenth century killed great numbers. Here, the anxiety of people confronted with death is intensified by the sophisticated, elusive rhythms, and by liturgical and popular phrases expressing resignation. **l. 10 Phisick** The art of medicine. **l. 19. Helens** Helen of Troy's. In the classical revival of the Renaissance, Helen of Troy became a conventional symbol of beauty. **l. 23 Hector** The most valiant Trojan leader in the war against the Greeks. **l. 26** Bells were rung in the streets of London to warn people to stay indoors as the bodies of the dead were taken to burial during a plague. **l. 29** What is the effect of the change of rhythm? **l. 36 degree** Social rank.

Questions: Poems 211 to 214

    (a)   How has each poet used concrete images to realize his theme?

    (b)   It has been said that a lyric poem cannot achieve an effect akin to catharsis in tragedy. On the basis of these poems would you support or oppose this statement?

Poem 215

The implications of the poem refer back to the whole selection of poems in this anthology.

215. *I Give You the End of a Golden String*

l. 4 Jerusalem New Jerusalem, the heavenly city of God (Revelation 21: 2, 10).

Biographies

a time, Professor of Poetry at Oxford. An idealist, he wrote to pass on his conviction that the pursuit of a broad enlightened mind was the highest form of human endeavour. His deep philosophic melancholy resulted from religious doubts and disillusionment with what he saw as the low calibre of national life. His active social conscience led him in later years to devote more energy to literary, religious, and social criticism than to poetry.

DOVER BEACH p. 130

ATWOOD, Margaret (b. 1939)

Born in Ottawa, Atwood has lived in several areas of Canada, including both urban areas and complete wilderness. She worked at various occupations before becoming one of Canada's foremost literary figures. She is an active spokesperson for several human rights and environmental groups. Poet, novelist, and critic, she is both forceful and incisive in her writing. The well-knit development of the poems, together with the exceptionally vivid and intimate imagery, aptly convey her comments on the realities of human existence.

BACKDROP ADDRESSES COWBOY p. 84

THOUGHTS FROM UNDERGROUND from *The Journals of Susanna Moodie* p. 192

THE IMMIGRANTS from *The Journals of Susanna Moodie* p. 194

AUDEN, Wystan Hugh (1907-73)

Auden was one of a group of English poets who became interested in Marxism during the depression of the 1930s. He later became an American citizen, less radical politically, and an adherent of the Anglo-Catholic faith. He is noted for his wit and verbal skill.

THE UNKNOWN CITIZEN p. 30

AS I WALKED OUT ONE EVENING p. 156

AVISON, Margaret (b. 1918)

Avison began publishing her poems in various periodicals while living in Toronto, Ontario in 1939. She has since published several collections of her poems. They combine unusually vivid visual and conceptual impressions that move with detachment between

455

immediate detail and the cosmic order. Her later work reflects her profound religious convictions.

THE SWIMMER'S MOMENT p. 128

BARAKA, Imamu Amiri (b. 1934)

Baraka is the name chosen by the American LeRoi Jones, after he became involved in the militant black nationalist movement in the 1960s. He is a poet, playwright, short-story writer, and novelist. He also ran a periodical, established a publishing firm, and founded and directed the Black Arts Repertory Theatre/School.

SOS p. 275

BELLOC, Hilaire (1870-1953)

Born in France and educated in England, Belloc was a prolific writer of essays, travel books, and children's stories. His wit and zest for life won attention for his controversial opinions and his defence of Roman Catholicism.

ON HIS BOOKS p. 77

JIM p. 77

BENNETT, Louise (b. 1919)

A Jamaican, Louise Bennett has lectured widely in the United States and the United Kingdom, acted in repertory theatre in England, and taught at the University of the West Indies. She has chosen to write her poetry in the picturesque dialect of the Jamaican people, reflecting their joys and sorrows, frequently wicked wit, religious beliefs, and philosophies of life. Her popular work is considered a major influence on the 'dub' poets, whose dialect poetry is important in the development of Jamaican culture today.

BANS O' KILLING p. 202

BERRY, Wendell (b. 1934)

Berry's main interests are the history and ecology of his native state of Kentucky. His first book was a long poem in praise of John F. Kennedy.

THE PEACE OF WILD THINGS p. 282

456

BIRNEY, Earle (b. 1904)

Birney was a Professor of English at the University of Toronto and the University of British Columbia. He wrote *Turvey*, a highly successful humorous novel of army life, and several volumes of poetry. Much of his poetry is experimental, and it often has a strong sense of irony.

DAVID p. 175

BLAKE, William (1757-1827)

Blake, apprenticed as a child to a London engraver, later illustrated his poetry with his own distinctive engravings. He moved from clear, apparently simple lyrics to darker satirical poems and complex symbolic prophecies. A revolutionary thinker, he believed that divine love pervaded the world but could be known only in the human imagination, that the usual contrast between good and evil was inadequate, and that external authority should be disregarded.

THE TYGER p. 114 and p. 116

THE SICK ROSE p. 158

LONDON p. 281

I GIVE YOU THE END OF A GOLDEN STRING p. 333

BORSON, Roo (b. 1952)

Born in California, but living and writing mostly in Vancouver and Toronto, Borson has published several books of poetry. She uses commonplace events and people as her subjects and, using a series of striking tableaux, imbues the reader with a sense of revelation.

TALK p. 224

BRECHT, Bertolt (1898-1956)

Brecht's plays and poetry express with wit and passion his deep concern for the working class. A Marxist, he fled his native Germany during the period of Nazi domination, but returned to live in East Berlin after World War II. His drama became internationally important in that it utilized new forms designed to suit the political themes. His poems are couched in unrhymed speech rhythms that convey his message with clarity and conviction.

QUESTIONS FROM A WORKER WHO READS p. 279

BRINGHURST, Robert (b. 1946)

Fluently multilingual, Robert Bringhurst was brought up in the Canadian Rocky Mountains and the western United States. He uses biblical stories, myths, and legends as a framework for his lengthy poems, and frequently uses images of mountains and stone for an underlying impression of endurance. In these poems, he is able to convey a sense of twentieth-century immediacy as he injects his own fresh viewpoints into the original stories.

DEUTERONOMY p. 105

BROWNING, Elizabeth Barrett (1806-61)

Elizabeth Barrett led the retired life of a semi-invalid until her romantic elopement from London to Italy with Robert Browning. Her literary reputation depends largely upon her love sonnets and her letters to her husband.

SONNET: HOW DO I LOVE THEE? p. 49

BROWNING, Robert (1812-89)

As a believer in progress, liberty, and the individual's struggle for self-fulfilment, Browning appealed to the optimistic spirit of Victorian England. He wrote large-scale poetic dramas, short lyrics, and the remarkable dramatic monologues for which he perfected the poetic form. His frequently gnarled style is both vigorous and compressed. Browning societies were formed where he read and explained his own poetry to fashionable audiences. After his elopement with Elizabeth Barrett he lived for a long time in Italy, and the influence of the Renaissance on his work is quite evident.

HOME THOUGHTS FROM ABROAD p. 209

MY LAST DUCHESS p. 265

BURNS, Robert (1759-96)

Burns, a Scottish farmer burdened by poverty, had a great capacity for enjoying life. His aim was to fix in writing the sung and spoken tradition of the people and return it to them as living literature. His poetry, which won him acceptance in the intellectual community of Edinburgh, reflects the robust humour, tenderness, and love of liberty of the Scottish people.

THE BRAW WOOER p. 154

BYRON, George Gordon (6th Baron) (1788-1824)

Wealthy, handsome, and unconventional, Lord Byron became a notorious romantic hero in England and finally escaped gossip by living in Europe. Passionately dedicated to the concept of freedom, he died in the Greek struggle for independence from Turkey. He wrote serious love lyrics, satirical poems, and reflective cantos on historical subjects, but it was his brooding, disillusioned hero, typified in Childe Harold, that had a profound influence on European literary thought.

SHE WALKS IN BEAUTY p. 235

THE ISLES OF GREECE from *Don Juan* p. 324

CAMPBELL, Wilfred (1858-1918)

Following a career as an ordained minister in New Brunswick and Ontario, Campbell later became a civil servant in Ottawa. Like the Confederation poets, amongst whom he is often included, he shows the influence of England's Romantic poets in his loving portrayal of nature and his concern over changing values in a world where science was challenging accepted beliefs.

INDIAN SUMMER p. 303

CARROLL, Lewis (1832-98)

Lewis Carroll was the pseudonym of Charles Lutwidge Dodgson, a mathematician, writer, and ordained dean of the church. His famous fantasies for children, *Alice's Adventures in Wonderland* and *Through the Looking Glass and What Alice Found There*, and his humorous poems such as *The Hunting of the Snark*, have become standard sources of literary allusion.

THE MAD GARDENER'S SONG p. 54

CAUSLEY, Charles (b. 1917)

Causley grew up in Cornwall, England. He served in the Royal Navy for four years and taught school for a time before launching into a career with the British Broadcasting Corporation. The ballad stanza form that he so frequently uses and his evocative images combine to create particularly haunting impressions.

NURSERY RHYME OF INNOCENCE AND EXPERIENCE p. 80

CHAUCER, Geoffrey (1340?-1400)

As well as being a writer, Chaucer held various administrative and diplomatic posts in the service of King Edward III and King Richard II. In his professional capacity, like all the members of the upper classes in England since the time of the Norman Conquest, he spoke and wrote in French. But he chose to write his long narrative poems in the London dialect, and in doing so, gained acceptance for English as a literary language. Shrewd and loving in his insight into human nature, possessing a rich and varied humour, he ranks with the great authors of the world.

LINES from the Prologue to the *Canterbury Tales* p. 109

THE WIF OF BATHE from the Prologue to the *Canterbury Tales* p. 220

COHEN, Leonard (b. 1934)

Poet, novelist, and songwriter, Leonard Cohen was born in Montreal, and has lived intermittently in Greece, California, New York, and Montreal. His questioning of love, faith, and personal direction found a response in the young people of the 1960s, making him one of the most popular writers of the time. The emotional tenor of his work ranges from tender delicacy to despair, or an ecstatic desire for a union of the spirit and the body.

SUZANNE TAKES YOU DOWN p. 228

GO BY BROOKS p. 308

COLERIDGE, Samuel Taylor (1772-1834)

Although Coleridge's life was marred by poverty, poor health, and an addiction to opium, his mind teemed with ideas and projects. His contributions to poetry, philosophy, and literary criticism were original and stimulating, but the variety of his interests frequently prevented him from finishing projects. He wrote his greatest poetry — unique for its mysterious, charged atmosphere — during the period of his friendship with Wordsworth.

KUBLA KHAN p. 237

CORNFORD, Frances (1886-1960)

Frances Cornford, the granddaughter of Charles Darwin, lived in Cambridge, England, where she befriended many young poets including Rupert Brooke and Thom Gunn. She wrote unaffectedly on simple themes, imparting to them a pleasingly original flavour.
TO A FAT LADY SEEN FROM A TRAIN p. 13

CORTÁZAR, Julio (1914-1984)

Cortázar was an Argentinian novelist, short-story writer, and literary critic who lived most of his life in exile as a translator in Paris. His writings, in which an aura of the surreal is imposed on everyday life, convey a sense of foreboding.
THE LINES OF THE HAND p. 57

CREELEY, Robert (b. 1926)

Creeley is a Professor of English who was one of the founders of what has come to be known as 'The Black Mountain' movement in American writing. In his poems, many of which have a tinge of William Carlos Williams, an unexpected statement about a concrete situation is charged with emotion.
THE FARM p. 210

CROZIER, Lorna (b. 1948)

Crozier published under the name of Lorna Uher until 1981. She has spent most of her life in the prairies. In addition to being a writer she has been a teacher and a director of communications for the Saskatchewan government.
THE CHILD WHO WALKS BACKWARDS p. 267

CUMMINGS, Edward Estlin (1894-1962)

Cummings's experimental verse, in which he adroitly manipulates form, syntax, typography, and sound patterns, was considered eccentric rather than serious until later experimental poets came on the scene. Cummings usually gives a wry but wistful twist to his recognition of the various personal problems that afflict average human beings.
ANYONE LIVED IN A PRETTY HOW TOWN p. 102
SOMEWHERE I HAVE NEVER TRAVELLED, GLADLY BEYOND p. 236

DANTE, Alighieri (1265-1321)

Dante was involved in the bitter political feuds of medieval Florence; as a result of antagonizing the Pope in one such feud, he was banished to spend the last twenty years of his life in relative obscurity in Northern Italy and Paris. The penalty, if he returned, was to be death by burning. He wrote his most famous work, *The Divine Comedy*, during this exile. Sublime, brilliant, gracious, and grim in turn, it is both personal and topical. It is one of the great works of European literature.

THE INFERNO, CANTO THIRD from *The Divine Comedy* p. 239

DEKKER, Thomas (1570?-1632?)

Dekker's many plays, poems, and tracts present a vivid picture of London in his time. Although he suffered from poverty and was imprisoned for debt, his works, which express his sympathy for the poor and oppressed, are marked by a sunny simplicity.

GOLDEN SLUMBERS p. 173

DE LA MARE, Walter (1873-1956)

Walter de la Mare, an English poet, novelist, and writer of short stories, is chiefly noted for his unique blend of reality and fantasy, and the whimsical haunting effects created by the musical quality of his writing. He is one of the comparatively few twentieth-century poets of note who adopted the traditional techniques of previous centuries.

THE SONG OF THE MAD PRINCE p. 52
ALL THAT'S PAST p. 326
ECHO p. 327

DICKINSON, Emily (1830-86)

Emily Dickinson lived a secluded life in her father's home in Massachusetts. Her poetry, in which her profound thoughts are masked by an apparent simplicity, was first published after her death. The innovations in her imagery and rhyme make many of her poems miniature *tours de force*.

I TASTE A LIQUOR NEVER BREWED p. 8

DOBSON, Austin (1840-1921)

Dobson, an English poet and man of letters, was educated in England and France. He is best known for his biographies of eighteenth-century literary figures, and for his light verse, characterized by his use of French verse forms.

DONNE, John (1573-1631)

Donne forfeited his career as secretary to Sir Thomas Egerton, Keeper of the Great Seal, by secretly marrying Anne More, Lady Egerton's niece. For this indiscretion he was dismissed from his position and imprisoned. After his wife's death, he entered the Church and won fame for the passionate, rhetorical sermons he preached as Dean of St Paul's. He created the metaphysical style in poetry, which influenced many writers in the seventeenth and twentieth centuries. Donne wrote most frequently about love; his early poems were written in praise of women, the later ones in praise of God.

DRYDEN, John (1631-1700)

A versatile man of letters, Dryden became Poet Laureate under Charles II. After joining the Roman Catholic Church, however, he lost his public honours and lived his later years in poverty. His occasional and satirical verse, poetic dramas, translations, and literary criticism had a wide influence on eighteenth-century writers. He made the heroic couplet a vehicle for witty and urbane comment.

ELIOT, Thomas Stearns (1888-1965)

T. S. Eliot was born in St Louis and became a British subject in 1927. In the poems written before 1930, when his *Ash Wednesday* appeared, he expressed frustration with what he saw as a hypocritical, sterile society. The term 'Ash-Can School' was applied to his poetry by his detractors. After his conversion to Anglo-Catholicism, his beliefs grew less pessimistic. His revolutionary techniques, substantially derived from those of Ezra Pound, had a far-reaching influence on contemporary poets.

THE LOVE SONG OF J. ALFRED PRUFROCK p. 40

THE HOLLOW MEN p. 245

FITZGERALD, Edward (1809-83)

Fitzgerald, a friend of Tennyson and many other Victorian writers, is remembered chiefly for his poetic version of the *Rubaiyat*, which he composed from existing translations in several languages.

SELECTIONS from the *Rubaiyat of Omar Khayyam of Naishapur* p. 320

FROST, Robert (1875-1963)

Although Frost's poetry has a basically American flavour, reflecting the years he spent in teaching, editing a newspaper, and running a farm in New England, the first recognition of his poetry came from Britain. He grew to be accepted as the quiet voice of rural and peaceable America, while retaining an individualist's approach to life. Geniality, rural speech patterns, and wry humour mark much of his poetry.

THE ROAD NOT TAKEN p. 21

STOPPING BY WOODS ON A SNOWY EVENING p. 304

GHOSE, Zulfikar (b. 1935)

Born in Pakistan, Ghose emigrated to England as a young man, eventually working as the cricket correspondent for *The Observer* and a teacher. He moved to the United States in 1969, where he became a Professor of English.

THIS LANDSCAPE, THESE PEOPLE p. 199

GINSBERG, Allen (b. 1926)

Born in New Jersey, Ginsberg was a deeply troubled young man. He travelled throughout the world, suffering all manner of horrifying experiences, but survived to write some of the best work of the 'Beat' generation. His first major publication, *Howl and Other Poems*, was confiscated as obscene, but was later cleared of the charges. With unconstrained language and flowing cadences, he pours out his anguished perceptions and his will to survive.

A SUPERMARKET IN CALIFORNIA p. 75

GOLDSMITH, Oliver (1728-74)

Author of a well-loved novel, *The Vicar of Wakefield*, and the amusing comedy *She Stoops to Conquer*, Goldsmith was a member of an important group of eighteenth-century writers and artists that included the famous Dr Johnson. Shy and undemonstrative as a person, he expresses in his writing a warmth and gentle charm.

THE VILLAGE MASTER from *The Deserted Village* p. 27

GUNN, Thom (b. 1929)

Educated at Cambridge University, England, Gunn later emigrated to California. His poetry reveals his intuitive understanding of the primitive and the violent aspects of life. He has created in some poems a personal myth of the black-jacketed motorcycle rider as a kind of modern hero, rootless, but constantly pushing into the unknown in search of values.

ON THE MOVE p. 310

HARDY, Thomas (1840-1928)

Hardy was a promising architect before he discovered his talent for writing. Relatively traditional in form, his novels are set in 'Wessex' — his native Dorsetshire. They reveal his belief that fate pursues its course relentlessly, indifferent to human suffering. His poems also reveal his human sympathy and deep awareness of the ironies of life, but they break away from Victorian diction and methods of poetic organization.

GREAT THINGS p. 250

IN TIME OF 'THE BREAKING OF NATIONS' p. 290

HEANEY, Seamus (b. 1939)

Heaney was brought up on a farm in County Derry, Ireland, and attended Queen's University, Belfast, where he later taught for a time. His work includes poetry that recaptures both the physical and wondering responses to his early experiences.

THE RAILWAY CHILDREN p. 211

HERBERT, George (1593-1633)

Herbert renounced an academic career at Cambridge University to become a parson in rural England. His metaphysical poems, concerned chiefly with his personal faith, are noted for their unusual form and elaborate, ingenious metaphors.

VIRTUE p. 254

HERRICK, Robert (1591-1674)

Herrick wrote bright lyrics celebrating the joys of simple pastoral life, adopting the classical theme of *carpe diem* — taste the pleasures of life before they fade. After his appointment as a clergyman in Devonshire he turned to religious subjects.

A SWEET DISORDER p. 231

HODGSON, Ralph (1871-1962)

An English poet who moved to the United States, Hodgson wrote simple melodic poetry that often expressed his feeling of comradeship with the inarticulate and oppressed. Many of his poems have animals as their subjects.

REASON HAS MOONS p. 171

HOPKINS, Gerard Manley (1844-89)

Hopkins became a Jesuit novice at the age of twenty-two. He suppressed his desire to write poetry and learn the Welsh language: to him poems were forms of self-indulgence. An understanding superior, however, advised him to cultivate his aesthetic talents. Influenced by Welsh and Anglo-Saxon poetry, Hopkins developed an energetic vocabulary that drew upon alliteration, coined words, and rich sound patterns. The study of classical and Welsh metres led to the development of sprung rhythm. Many of Hopkins's poems reflect his ecstatic response to nature as a manifestation of God's love.

GOD'S GRANDEUR p. 187

HURRAHING IN HARVEST p. 188

HUGHES, Langston (1902–67)

Langston Hughes's first volume of poems was hailed as a revival of Black art in America. Essentially a city poet, he used the rhythms of jazz and blues to convey the sufferings of his people.

LITTLE GREEN TREE p. 37

SNAIL p. 174

HUGHES, Ted (b. 1930)

Hughes grew up in Yorkshire, England, and began writing poetry that reflected the brooding wildness of the moors. His gained acclaim, however, when he published some poetry during an extended visit in the United States. He has been Poet Laurette of England since 1984. Many of his poems express the defiance and independence of animals or men who live by their immediate instincts.

HAWK ROOSTING p. 213

ISSA (1763–1828)

Issa became an established haiku writer and leader of a school for haiku writers in Tokyo (Edo at that time). He gave his unique imprint to the haiku form that had been developed by many illustrious predecessors over the centuries. His haiku are amongst the most loved of the tens of thousands that exist, conveying a sense of humanity and irony that can be traced to the tragedies that dogged his life.

YOU HEAR THAT FAT FROG p. 33

MY GRUMBLING WIFE p. 34

CLIMBING MOUNT FUJI p. 174

JARRELL, Randall (1914-65)

Randall Jarrell, poet, professor, critic, and editor, was born in Nashville, Tennessee. His experiences in World War II are responsible for many of his best-known poems, although he is by no means simply a war poet.

THE DEATH OF THE BALL TURRET GUNNER p. 86

JILES, Paulette (b. 1943)

Born in Salem, Missouri, Paulette Jiles spent her early years moving around the southern and midwestern United States; she attended six elementary schools and three high schools. She moved to Toronto in the late sixties, and has lived in the far-north and British Columbia. Her poetry possesses a personal kind of vitality with tough, unsentimental images.

WATERLOO EXPRESS p. 20

JOHNSTON, George (b. 1913)

George Johnston's portrayal of the suburban lives of ordinary people is whimsical, but by no means superficial. He was a Professor of English at Carleton University, Ottawa. His style of composing is unusual: he composes his lines and commits them to memory, completing the whole poem before setting any words down on paper.

WAR ON THE PERIPHERY p. 91

JONSON, Benjamin (1572-1637)

Jonson's rambunctious spirit, which led to his being imprisoned on two occasions, is evident in his lively play *The Alchemist*. Generally speaking, however, his writing exhibits a painstaking care and rigorous scholarship, which are often contrasted with the more free-wheeling genius of Shakespeare. The civilized grace of his lyrics made them models for the Cavalier poets at court.

HYMN TO DIANA p. 172

JOYCE, James (1882-1941)

Joyce spent most of his life as a voluntary exile from his native Dublin, for he believed that the Irish people could not forget their religious prejudices sufficiently to appreciate art. His originality emerges most strongly in his novels, where he uses sound patterns and stream-of-consciousness techniques to portray character and evoke associative impressions.

THE HITHERANDTHITHERING WATERS OF from *Finnegan's Wake* p. 39

KEATS, John (1795-1821)

Keats abandoned the study of medicine in order to devote his life to poetry, becoming one of the great figures of the English Romantic movement. His poems are characterized by an intense yearning for beauty and an imaginative evocation of the sensuous. Never physically robust, he became seriously ill with tuberculosis at twenty-five, and died the following year.

ON FIRST LOOKING INTO CHAPMAN'S HOMER p. 67

ODE ON A GRECIAN URN p. 68

SONNET: WHEN I HAVE FEARS p. 70

KLEIN, Abraham Moses (1909-72)

Klein, a Montreal lawyer, reflected in his early poetry his absorption with Jewish history, philosophy, social conditions, and religious rites. In his later works, his emphasis shifted to French-Canadian themes.

AUTOBIOGRAPHICAL p. 196

KOCH, Kenneth (b. 1925)

Poet, anthologist, playwright, and Professor of English, Koch is a resident of New York City. He is well known in educational circles for his two books on helping students to appreciate and write poetry — *Rose, Where Did You Get That Red?* and *Wishes, Lies and Dreams*.

VARIATIONS ON A THEME BY WILLIAM CARLOS WILLIAMS p. 289

KOGAWA, Joy (b. 1935)

Born in British Columbia, Kogawa was interned with her family during World War II. She later moved to Ottawa and then Toronto. Her wartime experience is reflected without bitterness or resentment in a successful novel, *Obasan*. Her poetry catches vividly the more highly charged moments of her personal life.

WHAT DO I REMEMBER OF THE EVACUATION? p. 204

LAMPMAN, Archibald (1861-99)

Lampman, an Ottawa civil servant, cultivated his deep appreciation of nature on canoe trips and walking excursions. His reading of Keats and Wordsworth influenced his poetic style.

IN NOVEMBER p. 301

LARKIN, Philip (1922-85)

Larkin was an English university librarian and an authority on jazz. In poems that deliberately avoid a heroic style, he frequently explored the 'quiet desperation' beneath the surface of ordinary people's lives.

AN ARUNDEL TOMB p. 292

LAWRENCE, David Herbert (1885-1930)

Born and raised in an English coal-mining family, Lawrence became acutely sensitive to brutality and vitally concerned with human relationships. He travelled widely in Europe, the United States, and Australia, seeking both a climate that would help him in his struggle with tuberculosis and a society that would not shackle the elemental drives in human nature. His novels and poetry, which reflect his deep response to his experiences, explore the psychology of love and hate.

SNAKE p. 10

THE WHITE HORSE p. 212

LAYTON, Irving (b. 1912)

The poetry of this rambunctious Jewish writer from Montreal celebrates the sensual life, sees the poet as a prophetic hero, and pours scorn on all who would limit his absolute freedom. His vigorous imagery and speech cadences are frequently controlled by a painstaking craftsmanship.

THE IMPROVED BINOCULARS p. 316

LINDSAY, Vachel (1879-1931)

A native of Springfield, Illinois, Lindsay toured the country selling his poems and drawings. His more successful poetry gains its effect from his mastery of the rhythms of speech and jazz.

THE FLOWER-FED BUFFALOES p. 212

LI PO (701-762)

A Chinese poet whose verses are among the finest known, Li Po disregarded the honours and rewards offered by the emperor, seeking instead a life of adventure. He is said to have been drowned while attempting to kiss the moonlit water on which his boat was sailing.

THE RIVER-MERCHANT'S WIFE: A LETTER p. 305

LORCA, Federico García (1898-1936)

Born and raised in southern Spain, Lorca began the study of law but soon abandoned it for poetry and drama, becoming one of the country's greatest playwrights. Though he took little part in politics, he was shot by Fascist soldiers during the Spanish Civil War. His great poetic themes are love and death and their ritual expression in births, marriages, and funerals. He fuses sophisticated techniques with a style drawn from gypsy ballads, folk songs, and children's lyrics.

THE SIX STRINGS p. 63

LOWELL, Robert (1917-77)

Robert Lowell, probably the most talented poet of his New England family, lectured on poetry and creative writing. His early poetry relies on complex metaphors fused under great emotional pressure; in his later work he developed a more direct form of expression. Whether religious or autobiographical, his poems issue from a tragic sense of life.

HOME AFTER THREE MONTHS AWAY p. 98

MACEWEN, Gwendolyn (1941-1988)

A native of Toronto, MacEwen left school at eighteen years of age to devote herself to writing. She produced volumes of poetry, novels, plays, documentaries, translations of Greek literature, and children's books. The striking imagery in her poetry, often portraying aspects of everyday life, extends its reach into deeper concerns and broader implications.

1958 p. 225

MCGINLEY, Phyllis (1905-78)

An author of light humorous essays, verse, and children's books, Phyllis McGinley lived in New York and published in *The New Yorker* and other well-known magazines.

GIRL'S-EYE VIEW OF RELATIVES p. 96

MACKAY, Louis (1901-82)

A native of Hensall, Ontario, MacKay became a Professor of Classics, while maintaining a strong interest in Canadian literature. He wrote robustly satiric poetry.

THE ILL-TEMPERED LOVER p. 51

MACNEICE, Louis (1907-63)

Irish by birth, MacNeice became a Professor of Classics and an author and producer with the British Broadcasting Corporation. He wrote of the impact of concrete moments in everyday life, creating the impression of colloquial speech with his skillful use of pauses, changed rhythms, and word order.

SNOW p. 189

MARLOWE, Christopher (1564-93)

Marlowe epitomizes the man of the Renaissance. He was captivated by the physical world, sensual experiences, and spiritual and religious matters. He contributed to the development of Elizabethan drama with the rhetorical power of his blank verse and the great, confident sweep of his imagination. His unsolved murder in a tavern brawl cut short a career that might have ranked him amongst the greatest English writers of all time.

THE LAST HOUR OF FAUSTUS from *The Tragical History of Dr Faustus* p. 167

THE SHEPHERD TO HIS LOVE p. 283

MARQUIS, Don (1878-1937)

Marquis's columns in New York newspapers and his books such as *archy and mehitabel* made him popular as a satirist. In archy the cockroach, he created a voice for his raffish opinions on contemporary life.

CHEERIO MY DEARIO p. 148

MARVELL, Andrew (1621-78)

Marvell was employed for some years as a tutor to Lord Halifax's daughter and then to Oliver Cromwell's ward. He later entered politics and wrote violent satires against Charles II. His witty, humane lyrics were influenced by metaphysical poetry.

TO HIS COY MISTRESS p. 233

MASEFIELD, John (1878-1967)

An English author of poetry, plays, novels, literary studies, and children's literature, Masefield was Poet Laureate for many years. His long narrative poems and his sea poems are his best-known works today.

AN EPILOGUE p. 319

MAZUR, Gail (b. 1937)

Mazur was born in Cambridge, Massachusetts and continues to live there. She studied under Robert Lowell and has made poetry her life's work, publishing carefully crafted poems, becoming an editor, and giving readings throughout New England.

BASEBALL p. 14

MILLAY, Edna St Vincent (1892-1950)

Edna St Vincent Millay became popular in America during the 1920s as a high-spirited rebel. Her lyrics are direct emotional statements, often tinged with disillusionment. Amongst her best works are her love sonnets, which draw extensively on the resources of the great Elizabethan sequences.

DIRGE WITHOUT MUSIC p. 322

MILTON, John (1608-74)

Milton was a renowned scholar, polemicist, and poet in seventeenth-century England. Much of his work reveals his impassioned belief in individual, religious, and civil liberty. He experimented with the use of classical and medieval poetic forms — odes, elegies, pastorals, sonnets, epics, and poetic drama. His epic *Paradise Lost*, composed and dictated to his daughter after he became totally blind, ranks with Homer's *Iliad*, Vergil's *Aeneid*, and Dante's *The Divine Comedy* among the great poetic achievements in history.

ON HIS BLINDNESS p. 184

HAIL, HOLY LIGHT from *Paradise Lost*, Book III p. 185

MOORE, Marianne (1887-1972)

Moore was successively a teacher, librarian, and literary editor. Her highly experimental verse had a distinct influence on many of her contemporary American writers. She avoids stereotypic phrases and sentiments, sometimes creating jarring rhythms and an impression of deliberate distancing from both her subject and her audience.

SILENCE p. 223

MORTON, John Bingham (1893-1979)

J. B. Morton was best known for his satirical column written under the name 'Beachcomber' in a London newspaper. His publications include several biographies of famous Frenchmen, humorous stories, satire, and poetry.

THE DANCING CABMAN p. 147

MURRAY, Les A. (b. 1938)

Murray grew up in farming country on the southeast coast of Australia. He worked at several jobs, including translating from western European languages and working for the government. He has been a full-time writer since 1971.

AN ABSOLUTELY ORDINARY RAINBOW p. 259

NASHE, Thomas (1567-1601)

A writer of pamphlets, plays, and picturesque tales, Nashe took an active part against the Puritans in the ardent religious controversy of Elizabethan England.

SONG p. 332

NERUDA, Pablo (1904-73)

Pablo Neruda is considered the greatest Spanish-language poet of this century. Born in Chile, Neruda won recognition as a poet at the age of sixteen. He lived for many years as a bohemian student and writer and then accepted consular missions in South America, Europe, and the Far East. He entered Chilean politics as a member of the Communist Party, and when it was banned, spent years in exile, writing and publishing all the while.

WALKING AROUND p. 17

NETSILIK PEOPLE (INUIT)

The Netsilik people live in the archipelago region of the Canadian Arctic. These Inuit people have a unique culture that includes storytelling, song-making, poetry reciting, carving, and painting. Some of their stories and poems have been passed down by word of mouth over the generations. Until very recently they had no written form of language. Each and every person is expected to be able to make up oral poems on special occasions to share with the other members of their community. Their songs deal with the harshness of Arctic life and incidents of everyday family life.

HEAVEN AND HELL p. 112

NEWLOVE, John (b. 1938)

Newlove's origins in farming communities in Saskatchewan are reflected in many of his poems. In these poems he manages to convey a sense of a particular space in a moment of time. He also expresses concern over the early history of the West. His poems range from a mood of lovely lyricism to a matter-of-factness that gives the impression of a report.

THE HITCHHIKER p. 312

NICHOL, Barrie Phillip (1944-1988)

Born in Vancouver, Nichol spent most of his productive years in Toronto. He was an editor and an inventive writer, producing, as well as his lyric poetry, a considerable body of concrete and sound poetry that has been recognised internationally. He was a member of The Four Horsemen, a popular poetry-reading ensemble.

PRAYER p. 257

NOOTKA PEOPLE

A confederacy of Native Canadian people living on the northwest coast of British Columbia.

PLAINT AGAINST THE FOG p. 258

SONG TO BRING FAIR WEATHER p. 258

NOWLAN, Alden (1933-83)

A Maritimer and writer of poetry, a novel, plays, short stories, and articles, Nowlan wrote compassionately of people and creatures who suffer from society's inhumanity.

IT'S GOOD TO BE HERE p. 269

WEAKNESS p. 270

SATURDAY NIGHT p. 313

OKARA, Gabriel (b. 1921)

A native of Nigeria, Okara is one of the few African writers to write of African philosophy using a vernacular version of his native language, imagery, and symbolism. His work has been translated into several languages.

ONCE UPON A TIME p. 100

OLDS, Sharon (b. 1942)

A native of California, Sharon Olds has received many awards for her poetry. She conveys a sense of a normal person who is shocked or even horrified by the implications of everyday life experiences.

RITE OF PASSAGE p. 83

ONDAATJE, Michael (b. 1943)

Born in Sri Lanka, Ondaatje has become one of the most distinguished writers in Canadian history. His poetry, fiction, and plays are written in a highly personal voice that mirrors his inner life at the same time as it brings to life aspects of settings in a wide world of time and space. He not only uses film techniques in his writing, but has made several short art films.

TO A SAD DAUGHTER p. 93

OWEN, Wilfred (1893-1918)

Owen was born in Shropshire, England, and died in France one week before the armistice that ended World War I. A very sensitive and compassionate person, he spoke out against the suffering caused by war, achieving remarkable control in his verse in the few short years of his life.

STRANGE MEETING p. 88

PARKER, Dorothy (1893-1967)

A native of New Jersey, Dorothy Parker usually published her witty and sardonic short stories and verse in *Esquire* or *The New Yorker*. They were later collected and published as books.

INDIAN SUMMER p. 152

PATCHEN, Kenneth (1911-72)

Despite a spinal disability that kept him immobilized for thirty years, Patchen published scores of collections of poems, novels, plays, and unique, hand-lettered, hand-illustrated booklets. He was one of the poets who pioneered the 'public birth of Poetry-Jazz' in San Francisco and Los Angeles in the late 1950s. His work creates a surrealistic world where humour, bitterness, affection, and spiritual belief all have their place.

& SO THE LITTLE FIELDMOUSE SAID p. 127

PATTEN, Brian (b. 1946)

A Liverpudlian living in London, Patten has been very successful at poetry readings. In his poetry, his conversational style, applied to the little hard-edged vignettes of daily life, clutches at the heart.

YOU'D BETTER BELIEVE HIM p. 61

PICKTHALL, Marjorie (1883-1922)

Marjorie Pickthall was born in England, but lived much of her life in Toronto. Her poems and stories are often concerned with mystical Christianity, death, and haunting dreams of medieval times.
ST YVES' POOR p. 110

PLATH, Sylvia (1932-63)

Extremely intelligent and sensitive, Plath led a tortured life, ending in suicide, which she portrayed in the novel *The Bell Jar*. Her poetry veers from convincing fantasy into menacing nightmare.
MUSHROOMS p. 122

POPE, Alexander (1688-1744)

During his childhood Pope suffered a crippling disease. This handicap and the discrimination he suffered as a Roman Catholic in eighteenth-century England contributed to the bitterness with which he conducted his literary feuds. He brought the poetry of satire to a new level of brilliance and elegant irony. Through his verbal dexterity and his great skill in the use of rhetorical balance and antithesis he perfected the heroic couplet.
EPIGRAM p. 216

THE PROPER STUDY from *An Essay on Man* p. 217

POUND, Ezra (1885-1972)

Pound was always a controversial figure. In England he spearheaded a group, including T. S. Eliot, which sought to free modern poetry from Victorian conventions. He broadcasted Fascist propaganda from Italy during World War II and was confined to a mental hospital from 1945 to 1958. Pound's poetry is marked by sensitivity and flexible control in both cadence and language, and his translations of Anglo-Saxon, Chinese, and Greek works are among the finest in English literature.
SALUTATION p. 32

IN A STATION OF THE METRO p. 294

THE RIVER-MERCHANT'S WIFE: A LETTER p. 305

WHAT THOU LOVEST WELL REMAINS from Canto LXXXI,
   The Cantos p. 329

PRATT, Edwin John (1883-1964)

Pratt was a native of Newfoundland, but spent much of his adult life in Toronto where he was a Professor of English. He occupies a distinct niche in the Canadian literature of his time with his long narrative poems, usually about the sea, war, or the early history of Canada. His tales are swiftly paced and marked by an exuberant use of technical terms and catalogues in an epic vein. His lyrics frequently employ strikingly vivid images.

THE PRIZE CAT p. 215

EROSION p. 294

PURDY, Alfred (b. 1918)

Purdy, a native of Ontario, worked at odd jobs for years before becoming a professional writer. As a writer he travels widely and engages in poetry-reading tours. His work, which reflects both his sense of place and a kinship with a listening audience, is marked by a refreshing robustness.

DEPRESSION IN NAMU, B. C. p. 9

THE COUNTRY NORTH OF BELLEVILLE p. 142

MY '48 PONTIAC p. 145

RALEGH, Sir Walter (1552-1618)

Sir Walter Ralegh is popularly known for his position of favour in the court of Queen Elizabeth and his expeditions to the Americas. It is thought that he wrote his graceful lyrics in the Tower of London, where he was imprisoned and finally executed on a charge of conspiring against James I. Only about thirty of these lyrics have survived.

THE NYMPH'S REPLY p. 285

RALEIGH, Sir Walter Alexander (1861-1922)

Sir Walter was a distinguished Professor of English at various British universities. He is best known for his essays and literary criticism.

WISHES OF AN ELDERLY MAN AT A GARDEN PARTY p. 317

REANEY, James (b. 1926)

Reaney has been one of Canada's leading experimental poets, combining a scholarly knowledge of literature with a freewheeling, witty gift of invention. His work also includes a series of plays about events in early southern Ontario history, the libretto for several operas, and one children's book.

BRANWELL'S LAMENT from *A Suit of Nettles: June* p. 140

REED, Henry (b. 1914)

Reed served with the British Army and Foreign Office during World War II. He then became a freelance writer for the media in London, England. He is best known for his book of verse *A Map of Verona*.

NAMING OF PARTS p. 89

RITSOS, Yannis (b. 1909)

Author of over forty volumes of poetry and translations, Ritsos was imprisoned for long periods of time and had his books banned in his native Greece because of his leftist politics.

PENELOPE'S DESPAIR p. 36

ROBERTS, Sir Charles George Douglas (1860-1943)

Roberts was one of a group of writers who, in the 1890s, discovered the aesthetic potential of the Canadian landscape, as did the Group of Seven some years later in painting. He is also well known for his animal stories, and less well known for his 'transcendental' poetry in which individuals come face to face with the universe and God.

THE MOWING p. 302

ROBINSON, Edwin Arlington (1869-1935)

Robinson was one of the first American poets to break away from the stylized poetic diction of his forebears and use natural language in his verse. He portrayed individuals who adhered to a creed of human values rather than seeking prestige and power.

RICHARD CORY p. 264

ROCHESTER, John Wilmot, Earl of (1647-80)

Wilmot fell in and out of favour with Charles II because of the unbridled style of his life. During his later years he became religious. His witty and polished poetry is frequently quite obscene.

IMPROMPTU ON CHARLES II p. 32

ROETHKE, Theodore (1908-63)

Roethke lived the first part of his life in New England and the last years near Seattle. He wrote sensitive lyrics that drew on his detailed observations of nature to describe man's kinship with all forms of life. His work ranges from light, witty poems and poems in traditional forms to sustained, subtle verse, where the experimental forms create an almost surrealistic atmosphere.

A FIELD OF LIGHT p. 5

ROSENBLATT, Joe (b. 1933)

Born in Toronto, but living latterly in British Columbia, Rosenblatt has produced many volumes of highly original verse, chant poems, and collections of his drawings. His belief in the interconnectedness of human life with the world of animals, insects, and plants is expressed in a unique combination of technical language and a vocabulary resonant with mysticism.

NATURAL PRAYER p. 124

ROSSETTI, Christina (1830-94)

Born in England of Italian parentage, Christina Rossetti, along with her brother, Dante Gabriel Rossetti, was associated with the Pre-Raphaelite movement in England. This movement began when a group of poets and artists sought a way of life in which a concern for beauty and spiritual matters would replace the materialistic obsession of industrial England. Her poetry is pictorial and generally melancholy.

A BIRTHDAY p. 307

ROTTMANN, Larry (b. 1942)

Rottmann was born in Jefferson City, Missouri. He served in the Vietnam War and was deeply distressed by the atrocities committed and the suffering of the victims. In an effort to inform the

American public he and a group of his fellow soldiers published *The 25th Infantry Division in Viet Nam* and *The Indo-China Story*.
APO 96225 p. 86

SANDBURG, Carl (1878-1967)

.Sandburg, who spent much of his life in the general area of Chicago, was the author of a highly esteemed biography of Abraham Lincoln. In his poetry, he wrote repeatedly about industrial America. In championing the common people he developed a tough, powerful idiom to depict both the vitality and the brutal injustices of the society in which he lived.
NIGHT BELLS p. 173

SHAKESPEARE, William (1564-1616)

Shakespeare grew up in Stratford, married at eighteen, and later joined an acting company in London. His early plays were attempts to follow the accepted pattern of his predecessors and contemporaries. Within two decades, however, he had created the greatest body of drama ever written. His 154 sonnets, which for many years he showed only to friends, trace the course of an intimate friendship, the poet's discovery of his own genius, and his musings on time, death, and love.
SONNET XVIII: SHALL I COMPARE THEE TO A SUMMER'S DAY? p. 47
SONNET XXX: WHEN TO THE SESSIONS OF SWEET
    SILENT THOUGHT p. 48
SONNET LV: NOT MARBLE, NOR THE GILDED MONUMENTS p. 76
SONNET CXVI: LET ME NOT TO THE MARRIAGE OF TRUE MINDS p. 291
SONG From *Cymbeline* p. 331

SHELLEY, Percy Bysshe (1792-1822)

Shelley was expelled from Oxford for his pamphlet *The Necessity of Atheism*, and later left England to avoid public censure of his radical convictions in politics, morality, and religion. While living in Switzerland and Italy he wrote pantheistic lyrics of great beauty, portraying God and the natural universe as synonymous. He tried to sustain a tone of ecstatic elevation by deliberate imprecision of imagery, vowel music, and the repeated use of such words as 'soaring' and 'ethereal.' His lyrical drama, *Prometheus Unbound*, sums up his vision of freedom in which the human spirit is to triumph over all who would restrain it by force.

OZYMANDIAS p. 25

ODE TO THE WEST WIND p. 297

SHIRLEY, James (1596-1666)

Originally a priest in the Church of England, Shirley joined the Roman Catholic Church and became a teacher. He was also a popular playwright. His best-known poems are lyrics from his plays.

DEATH THE LEVELLER p. 328

SMITH, Arthur James Marshall (1902-80)

A native of Montreal, Smith spent his life in university teaching. His trenchant criticism during the thirties and forties set much more rigorous standards than Canadian poetry was attaining at the time. His own writing is disciplined and austere.

THE LONELY LAND p. 190

SMITH, Stevie (1902-1971)

Stevie Smith is a delightful and original English poet. She used echoes of past poets, childlike rhymes, and assonance to provide an exciting combination of gaiety and deep distress. Her own drawings reinforce the comic and harrowing elements of her poetry.

NOT WAVING BUT DROWNING p. 129

SOLT, Mary Ellen (b. 1920)

An American, Solt is a highly regarded member of an international group of concrete poets. Many of her poems use visual, often typographical forms to produce aesthetic expression.

FORSYTHIA p. 126

SPENDER, Stephen (b. 1909)

Spender was one of a group of politically radical English poets headed by W. H. Auden in the 1930s. His sense of urgency, sustained rhythms, and use of machine-age images frequently produce poetry that is vivid and exciting.

I THINK CONTINUALLY OF THOSE WHO WERE TRULY GREAT p. 249

SPENSER, Edmund (1552-99)

Spenser was one of the outstanding writers who made the Elizabethan period a landmark in the history of English literature. Like many other writers in the early development of English poetry, he was serving eighteen years as a political appointee in Ireland. His major work, an allegory entitled *The Faerie Queene*, intermingles themes of religion, love, and morality as it sweeps along with a rich texture of rhythm, sound, and pictorial images.

THE SHEPHEARDES LAMENT from *The Shepheardes Calender:*
December p. 138

STEVENS, Wallace (1879-1955)

An American insurance executive, Stevens published his first volume of poetry at the age of forty-four. He wrote frequently of the longing, anguish, and consolations of the religious skeptic, preferring to work through suggestive detail rather than by explicit statement. His sustained cadences make him one of the twentieth-century masters of formalist technique.

DOMINATION OF BLACK p. 295

SUCKLING, Sir John (1609-42)

Suckling, a gallant, witty Cavalier poet, fought for King Charles I in the Civil Wars and then fled to France where, in fear of poverty, he is said to have committed suicide. His songs, many of which were incorporated into his plays, display a flippant cynicism that masks his melancholy spirit.

THE CONSTANT LOVER p. 153

SWINBURNE, Algernon Charles (1837-1909)

Because Swinburne repudiated the moral and religious conventions of Victorian England, he was both scorned and venerated by his generation. His rich melodious verse recreates the pagan spirit of classical literature and mythology.

LINES From 'The Garden of Proserpine' p. 38

SYNGE, John Millington (1871-1909)

Synge depicts in his plays the realistic, comical, and mystical elements of the Irish character. He developed a lyrical, earthy style based on the dialect of the Aran Islands off the Irish coast.

AN OLD WOMAN'S LAMENTATIONS p. 35

TENNYSON, Alfred Lord (1809-92)

Tennyson's skill with imitative harmony, melodious language, and vivid phrasing made him a much-quoted poet during his lifetime and one of the best-known poets in English literature. In 1833 the death of his friend, Arthur Hallam, precipitated a period of religious doubt in his life. *In Memoriam* traces the gradual resolution of that doubt and the achievement of a mystical faith. His poetry mirrors the conflict in values of Victorian England.

ULYSSES p. 22

TEARS, IDLE TEARS p. 159

SELECTIONS from *In Memoriam* p. 160

TESSIMOND, A. S. J. (1902-62)

At the age of sixteen, Tessimond ran away to London from his home in Birkenhead. Failing to make a living there, he resumed his studies, took a university degree, and eventually became a writer of advertising copy. Much of his poetry deals with modern urban life in England.

CATS p. 214

THOMAS, Dylan (1914-53)

A Welshman with a remarkably fine voice for reading, Thomas achieved international fame and popularity during his wayward lifetime. His three recital tours of North America were hailed as literary events. A combined zest for life and an underlying feeling of stark tragedy pervade his works. These include volumes of poetry, autobiographical sketches, short stories, and a drama for voices. Using the rich idiom of Welsh speech, he developed

rhetorical rhythms and explosive, sensuous language. Artfully ambiguous diction and traditional symbols charged with private significance may at first obscure his meaning, but render his feelings with
precision.

FERN HILL p. 1
WELSH NIGHT from *Under Milk Wood* p. 170
AND DEATH SHALL HAVE NO DOMINION p. 323

THOMAS, Ronald Stuart (b. 1913)

A vicar in West Wales, Thomas writes of the poverty and dignity of
the people he serves. His cadences suggest something of the bleak-
ness of his native country.

A PEASANT p. 26

TSVETAYEVA, Marina (1892-1941)

The daughter of cultured parents living outside Moscow, Tsvetayeva was forced into exile during the Russian Revolution. There
she wrote poetry which many now consider to place her amongst
the major poets of the twentieth century. When she returned to the
Soviet her husband was executed, and later her son was killed in
war. She herself suffered from oppression and poverty until she
finally took her own life. The strength of her images and the tension created by her rhythms gives her work a deeply passionate
quality.

WE SHALL NOT ESCAPE HELL p. 227

TWAIN, Mark (1835-1910)

Mark Twain was the pseudonym of Samuel Clemens, a native of
Missouri. He worked for a time as a pilot on the Mississippi River
before becoming a newspaper editor and a writer of humorous
fiction. His best-known works are the novels *The Adventures of Tom
Sawyer* and *The Adventures of Huckleberry Finn*.

A MAN HIRED BY JOHN SMITH & CO. p. 56

VILLON, François (1431-1463?)

Although Villon lived the life of a vagabond and a thief in Paris, his poetry was well known and highly esteemed. It has continued to be appreciated and has been translated into many languages. Details of his life are known from his poems and police records.

AN OLD WOMAN'S LAMENTATIONS p. 35

WALLACE, Bronwen (1945-89)

A native of Kingston, Ontario, Wallace worked for a time at a centre for battered women and children. The pictorial sequences in her poems may reflect her interest in film-making.

COMMON MAGIC p. 261

WALLER, Edmund (1606-87)

A man of wealth and a parliamentarian, Waller was imprisoned for trying to capture London for Charles I and was later pardoned by Cromwell. He regained favour at the time of the Restoration. He was probably the first English poet to establish the heroic couplet as a major form. His lyric poetry is distinguished by an elegant simplicity.

GO, LOVELY ROSE p. 232

WHITMAN, Walt (1819-92)

Whitman was for some years an unsuccessful journalist in and around New York City. For a time during the Civil War he worked as a volunteer nurse in the Northern Army. His first poetry was published at his own expense. In his expansive free-verse form, which is often regarded as the beginning of modern poetry in America, he celebrates the spirit of democratic America and himself as its spokesperson.

SELECTIONS from *Song of Myself* p. 71

WILLIAMS, William Carlos (1883-1963)

A physician in a small New Jersey town, Williams was also an experimental writer. To avoid being 'poetic' in the sense of being artificial, he developed a conversational rhythm and diction, while constantly relating his ideas to the physical world.

THE ARTIST p. 62
RALEIGH WAS RIGHT p. 286
THE TERM p. 287
THIS IS JUST TO SAY p. 288

WILMOT, John, Earl of Rochester (1647-80)
See ROCHESTER, p. 480.

WORDSWORTH, William (1770-1850)
Wordsworth was the prime figure in the Romantic movement of English poetry. He and Coleridge expressed their radical beliefs about poetry in the preface to their *Lyrical Ballads*. Rejecting the artificial conventions of eighteenth-century poetry, Wordsworth undertook to write of common life exalted by powerful feeling. Reflecting on his boyhood in the English Lake District, he wrote of his belief that the spiritual education of the sensitive individual depended on the interaction of nature and the imagination.

THERE WAS A BOY from *The Prelude* p. 4
TINTERN ABBEY p. 132

YEATS, William Butler (1865-1939)
Yeats's colourful career included a prolonged and unhappy love affair, nationalistic activities during the Gaelic revival, assistance in founding the famous Abbey Theatre in Dublin, and lifelong experiments with magic and the occult. His lonely childhood was reflected in the languid rhythms and world-weary mood of such early lyrics as 'The Lake Isle of Innisfree.' Gradually, however, he forged a style whose racy idiomatic language and hard, sometimes brutal imagery, allowed him to move from controlled invective to poignant love poetry or to exalted philosophical reasoning. T. S. Eliot called him the greatest lyric poet of the century.

THE LAKE ISLE OF INNISFREE p. 208
THE CHOICE from 'A Dialogue of Self and Soul' p. 252
THE FISHERMAN p. 318

ZIEROTH, Dale (b. 1946)

A native of Manitoba, Zieroth worked for a time in media and education in Toronto and for a time for the National Parks in the Canadian Rockies. His deceptively simple style creates considerable intensity as he presents his concerns about the land and its inhabitants.

COYOTE PUP MEETS THE CRAZY PEOPLE IN KOOTENAY
NATIONAL PARK p. 271

Glossary of Terms
Used in the Discussion of Poetry

Although talking about poetry must never be taken for experiencing it, a fuller understanding of the components of poetry allows what may have been a vague appreciation to become a rich response. It is for this reason that the following comments have been included. Each of the sections on IMAGERY (p. 501), RHYTHM (p. 515), and SOUND (p. 524) discusses a range of inter-connected terms that are easier to approach as a group. Some titles of books useful for further study have been indicated in the bibliography (p. 529).

ACCENTUAL VERSE *See* RHYTHM (p. 521).

ALLEGORY *See* IMAGERY (p. 506).

ALLITERATION *See* SOUND (p. 525).

ALLUSION Allusion is an undeveloped reference to some figure, place, or event outside the immediate framework of the subject discussed. It may be historical, biblical, mythological, or literary. In poetry such as the Homeric epics, where a listening audience may be taxed by the details of an unfolding story, allusions to matters of common background are used to provide a reassuring atmosphere of familiarity. An allusion may also enrich a poem by inducing the reader, at the mention of a proper noun or strategic phrase, to recall an entire story. The reader is then expected to apply its significant features to the subject being discussed, without there being any actual digression at the surface level of the poem.

When Milton mentions the Orphean lyre in 'Hail, Holy Light' (p. 185) from *Paradise Lost*, he invokes the whole story of Orpheus and Eurydice. Allusion may even be used for comic effect, as in the poem 'Cheerio My Deario' (p. 148). Archy refers to Cleopatra and King Tutankhamun in his description of Mehitabel, the alley cat.

Modernist Allusion. Modernist allusion not only refers to earlier history or literature, but frequently incorporates the actual phrases of earlier writing. Thus a modernist writer may weave into the texture of a poem a fragment from Shakespeare, Dante, or a state document of the Renaissance. The intention is usually to give a double perspective on the subject of the poem, whether by providing an ironic contrast, by reinforcing some element of that subject, or by suggesting the continuity of human experience.

In 'The Hollow Men' (p. 245), Eliot juxtaposes a re-worded nursery rhyme, 'Here we go round the prickly pear,' and a quotation from the Lord's Prayer, 'For Thine is the Kingdom.' The combination of allusions is neither blasphemy nor plagiarism, for Eliot is deliberately taking our minds back to the certainty and hope of the Christian prayer. The effect is like a double exposure on film: the confusion and anger of the speaker, mouthing fragments of a nursery rhyme, are superimposed upon the 'peace which passeth all understanding' of Christian devotion. The allusions are ironic, for serenity is incongruously suggested amidst great suffering and deprivation.

AMBIGUITY The expression of an idea in such a way that more than one meaning may be attributed to it. Although in straightforward exposition ambiguity can give rise to undesirable confusion, its deliberate use in literature adds a rich complexity. Poets in particular use words to suggest two or more equally suitable senses in a given context, or to convey a basic meaning accompanied by a variety of overtones. The last two lines of 'Fern Hill' (p. 1) by Dylan Thomas suggest simultaneously the ideas of youth and decay, freedom and subjection to inexorable laws, and enjoyment of new experiences and decline into death:

> *Time held me green and dying*
> *Though I sang in my chains like the sea.*

AMPHIBRACH A foot having one unaccented, one accented, and one unaccented syllable (e.g., stăccátŏ). For a fuller discussion of metre, see RHYTHM (p. 515).

ANAPAEST A foot having two unaccented syllables and one accented syllable (e.g., ă sŭrpríse). For a fuller discussion of metre, see RHYTHM (p. 515).

ANTITHESIS Two adjoining phrases, clauses, or sentences of more or less parallel grammatical structure but of contrasting meaning are said to be in antithesis. The device is often used in couplets, with antithesis occurring either between lines or between halves of one line. Pope used it with virtuosity in 'The Proper Study' from *An Essay on Man* (p. 217):

> *Created half to rise, and half to fall;*
> *Great Lord of all things, yet a prey to all.*

APOSTROPHE A direct greeting or appeal to a person, usually not present, or to an object or abstraction, usually personified. The device suggests the close involvement of the poet with the subject apostrophized.

In 'Ode on a Grecian Urn' (p. 68) Keats apostrophizes the urn as 'Thou still unravish'd bride of quietness.'

In the invocation to *Paradise Lost* Milton addresses the heavenly muse:

> *O Spirit, that dost prefer*
> *Before all temples th' upright heart and pure,*
> *Instruct me.*

ARCHETYPE Literally, the original model from which a pattern is formed. The term has been used by many literary critics in the twentieth century to describe any image, plot, or character type that appears and reappears in many forms, particularly in religion, mythology, or literature. The term was originally adopted in Carl Jung's depth psychology to describe the images that are found in the 'collective unconscious.' Such images recur, he argued, in the thoughts and dreams of all people, generating powerful responses that well up from beneath a person's rational nature. Hence these visions appear to be one of the fundamental forms, or 'primordial images' through which the unconscious expresses itself.

The work of many writers generates these archetypal responses. A typical example of an archetypal image is the cycle of day and night, the seasons, life and death; of an archetypal character, the hero-saviour; and of an archetypal plot, the purifying journey. A modern-day application of an archetype is 'You'd Better Believe Him' (p. 61).

ASSONANCE *See* SOUND (p. 525).

BALLAD The *traditional ballad* is a simple narrative poem composed to be sung. As early as the eleventh or twelfth century, travelling minstrels in Europe were composing and singing stories of romance and tragedy. By the fifteenth century, such tales were being composed in increasing numbers for enthusiastic audiences of people who had a taste for violent tales of love and revenge, grimly realistic tales of war and treachery, and tales of the supernatural. Also popular were riddles and stories of humorous escapades and of practical jokes.

Although some of these ancient ballads became fixed in print over the succeeding centuries, many continued to be passed on by word of mouth in various dialects. Thus various versions of ballads exist. Some were collected and adapted by later enthusiasts, such as Sir Walter Scott.

The ancient ballads are simple narratives, fraught with strong emotions or crude humour about well-known personages or people of high degree. Stark imagery, homely detail, alliteration, direct speech, and sudden transitions from one idea, event, or setting to the next make them fast-moving, powerful poems. Frequently so many details have been omitted that the ballad begins near the climax of the plot. Lines and phrases are repeated, often with slight variations.

The usual *ballad stanza* consists of four lines: the first and third lines are in iambic tetrameter, occasionally rhyming, and the second and fourth in iambic trimeter, usually rhyming.

Starting in the eighteenth century, many poets, admiring the simplicity of the traditional ballads, imitated them in a more polished and sophisticated style. Probably the most famous of these *literary ballads* are those of Sir Walter Scott and William Wordsworth.

The influence of the ballad form is still strong in the popular songs of North America and the Caribbean. Some modern folk ballads, such as 'John Henry' (p. 276), preserve the strong story line and bare emotion of their predecessors, incorporating a contemporary dialect or using colloquial speech and slang. Modern literary ballads, such as Auden's 'As I Walked Out One Evening' (p. 156), dispense with conventional phrases and develop only a few of the traditional ballad features, thereby emphasizing the mood and message of the poem rather than its story. By sophisticated means, the literary ballad achieves self-conscious simplicity and power.

BLANK VERSE A series of unrhymed lines of poetry, almost always in iambic pentameter. Although there is no conventional division into stanzas, the lines are often grouped in verse paragraphs to mark the development of thought. Elizabethan poets and dramatists used blank verse because of its resemblance to unrhymed classical poetry. It also has great advantages for reproducing normal English speech rhythms. Of all regular metrical patterns, it is the most flexible; in the hands of a master, it can be used to achieve effects of sustained power, as in Tennyson's 'Ulysses' (p. 22). *See also* RHYTHM (p. 515).

CADENCE *See* RHYTHM (p. 518).

CAESURA A pause in the metre of a verse line. It not only provides variety in the rhythm of the line, but may subtly direct the reader's attention to what immediately follows the pause. In scansion it is indicated by the mark //. *See* RHYTHM (p. 520).

CANTO One of the major sections or divisions of a long poem. Dante's *The Divine Comedy* is divided into 100 cantos. See *The Inferno*, Canto Third (p. 239).

CLIMAX The effect of fulfilment that may be achieved at the end of a series when its elements are arranged in a scale of ascending importance. The series may be one of words, images, ideas, incidents, emotional responses, or rhythms. Consider the list of infinitives in the last line of 'Ulysses' (p. 22) and the accumulation of ideas in 'What Thou Lovest Well Remains' (p. 329).

COMPARISON *See* IMAGERY (p. 502).

CONCEIT An ingenious or far-fetched comparison, in which subject and object often have no apparent similarity. In the *Petrarchan conceit* the subject — frequently the poet's beloved — is compared at length to something more or less appropriate, such as a garden, star, or season of the year. See Shakespeare's Sonnets XVIII (p. 47) and CXVI (p. 291), and Spenser's 'The Shepheardes Lament' (p. 138). In the *metaphysical conceit*, the comparison is apparently inappropriate; yet the startling, involved, and often wittily impudent analogies are justified in a successful conceit. See Donne's 'A Valediction: Forbidding Mourning' (p. 164) and Herbert's 'Virtue' (p. 254).

CONCRETE POETRY A generic term applied to experimental poetry that had a community of international practitioners after World War II. In general, there are three kinds of concrete poetry: visual, sound, and kinetic. The poets frequently break away from conventional grammatical structures and spelling patterns, and even standard human sound patterns. The poems may approach visual or musical art forms, but they remain poems in intent. See 'Natural Prayer' (p. 124) and 'Forsythia' (p. 126).

CONNOTATION The *denotation* of a word or phrase is its specific meaning, independent of its emotional colouring or associations. The word 'cat,' for instance, denotes a specific domestic animal.

The *connotation* of a word or phrase is the body of implications that it may carry, the unstated associations that it awakens in the mind of the reader as a result of the reader's previous encounters with it in a variety of other contexts. Such associations may be completely personal, or common to a number of people who speak the same language. For example, 'Jake is ferret-faced' evokes a picture of the general contour of Jake's features; but it also connotes an element of viciousness.

495

CONSONANCE *See* SOUND (p. 525).

CONVENTION A device, style, or theme that has become familiar, and is, therefore, in spite of its apparent artificiality, recognized and accepted as an instrument of literary expression. To this extent, most of the techniques of language and versification in poetry may be said to be conventions. We accept the soliloquy, for instance, as a stylistic convention by means of which a dramatist can convey the thoughts of one of the characters. In the same way, we accept, as a thematic convention, the pastoral with its idealized picture of country life. Thus, any convention demands of the reader a 'willing suspension of disbelief.'

COUNTERPOINT *See* RHYTHM (p. 517).

COUPLET Two consecutive rhyming lines in the same metre. The couplet is a suitable medium for expressing one idea or image concisely, as in the conclusion of a Shakespearean sonnet (p. 523). It is especially effective for epigrams:

> *I am His Highness' dog at Kew;*
> *Pray tell me, sir, whose dog are you?*
>   ALEXANDER POPE, Epigram (p. 216)

The *heroic couplet* expresses a self-contained thought in two rhyming lines of iambic pentameter. Relying also on end-stopped lines, parallel structure, and the caesura, Dryden, Pope, and other eighteenth-century poets achieved striking epigrammatic effects:

> *In squandering wealth was his peculiar art;*
> *Nothing went unrewarded but desert.*
>   JOHN DRYDEN, Zimri (p. 219)

DACTYL A foot having one accented syllable followed by two unaccented syllables (e.g., lázĭlў). For a fuller discussion of metre, see RHYTHM (p. 515).

DENOTATION *See* CONNOTATION (p. 495).

DIDACTIC POETRY Poetry written to persuade the reader of the rightness of a particular point of view, usually moral, religious, or political. A good poem can be thoroughly didactic, as 'To Every Thing There Is a Season' (p. 104) and 'Bans O' Killing' (p. 202); have a mildly didactic purpose, as 'Nursery Rhyme of Innocence and Experience' (p. 80); or be apparently without didactic intent, as, according to some readers, 'Stopping by Woods on a Snowy Evening' (p. 304). Didactic poetry that disregards the artistic demands of the poem in the interest of moralizing is distasteful to most readers.

DIMETER A verse of two feet. For a fuller discussion of metre, see RHYTHM (p. 515).

DRAMATIC IRONY *See* IRONY (p. 507).

DRAMATIC MONOLOGUE A form of dramatic poetry in which a situation is presented through the medium of a sustained speech made by one character to a silent audience of one or more persons. The progressive revelation of the nature of the speaker, who may be either a historical or imaginary person, is the major source of interest. This focal character's personality and past are unmasked by the gestures and manner of speech, and by the implied reactions and comments of the person or persons being addressed.

The circumstances that bring together the speaker and audience have an intrinsic interest and tension, but they also provide an artistic framework, setting, and motivation for psychological analysis. In 'My Last Duchess' (p. 265), for example, Browning has chosen a meeting between the widowed Duke and an envoy sent to negotiate a new marriage. At the beginning of the poem the two men have just entered a gallery in the Duke's home. At the end of the poem they are leaving together.

Arnold's 'Dover Beach' is not considered a dramatic monologue. Although the poem has a speaker, listener, setting, and attitude toward life, there is no set of circumstances creating dramatic tension; nor is there a revelation of the facets of the speaker's life as a source of major interest.

497

DRAMATIC POETRY Poetry that creates a situation involving dramatic tension or emotional conflict between characters. It employs dialogue extensively or exclusively and is frequently suitable for stage presentations. The poet creates one or more characters and reveals their natures by means of their individual responses. Such poetry may occur in poetic drama such as *The Tragical History of Dr Faustus* (p. 167) or *Under Milk Wood* (p. 170), or it may be an independent poem such as 'My Last Duchess' (p. 265), which employs many of the same techniques of characterization and revelation as the drama. The excerpt from the Book of Job (p. 117) may be discussed in terms of dramatic poetry, since it represents the words of the Lord revealing His nature, rather than the direct comments of the poet upon the Divine nature.

DUB POETRY Developed in the 1940s in Jamaica, dub poetry is very much a part of the oral and folk tradition. It uses the idiom and syntax of West Indian vernacular as an authentic language to convey the attitudes, feelings, and cultural awareness of the Caribbean people. See 'Bans O' Killing' (p. 202).

ELEGY A poem of lament or of sober meditation. The subject is a mournful event (usually the death of a person), regret for the past, or pessimistic fears for the future. The poems of *In Memoriam* (p. 160) deal extensively with these themes. The diction and syntax of an elegy are highly stylized and the expression is grave and controlled.

ELLIPSIS A figure of speech in which customary grammatical elements are omitted from the text to create a desired effect, as in the condensation of Pound's poem (p. 294):

The apparition of these faces in the crowd;
Petals on a wet, black bough.

Hopkins produces a strong, unanalytical impression using ellipsis in 'God's Grandeur' (p. 187): 'There lives the dearest freshness deep down things.'

END-STOPPED LINE A line of poetry that ends with a pause. *See* RHYTHM (p. 520).

ENGLISH SONNET *See* SONNET (p. 523).

ENJAMBMENT The device of continuing the sense and cadence of one line of poetry into the next without a pause between the two lines. *See* RHYTHM (p. 520).

EPIC A long narrative poem with a serious theme of national or universal significance, recounting heroic deeds of the past in a consistently dignified style.

The unifying theme emerges from the culture of a particular period, although the events dealt with may be mythical or historical. Embodying many of the ideals of their society, epic heroes, though fallible, perform deeds requiring great courage and superhuman strength.

Certain conventions are common to most epics. The poet generally opens by stating the theme and asking a Muse for inspiration. The poem then plunges *in medias res* (into the middle of the action), leaving the necessary exposition to follow in later portions of the epic. Throughout the poem elements of the supernatural and divine intervention play an important part. The poet includes lists of warriors, ships, events; puts long stylized speeches into the mouths of the main characters; and makes frequent use of the *epic simile* (p. 503). Frequently a recurring proper name is associated with a particular adjective. For example, in *The Odyssey* the name 'Ulysses' is usually linked with an adjective meaning 'of many wiles'; such an adjective is often called a *Homeric epithet*. The excerpt 'Hail, Holy Light' (p. 185) from *Paradise Lost* contains several of the features mentioned.

Other examples of famous epics are Homer's *The Iliad* and *The Odyssey*, Vergil's *Aeneid*, the Old English poem *Beowulf*, and Spenser's *The Faerie Queene*.

EPIC SIMILE *See* IMAGERY (p. 503).

EPIGRAM A brief, memorable, often witty poem. Pope's 'Epigram' (p. 216) is an example. The term has also come to denote a concise and memorable statement in prose; for example, 'A little sincerity is a dangerous thing, and a great deal of it is absolutely fatal.' — Oscar Wilde.

EXTENDED METAPHOR *See* IMAGERY (p. 505).

FABLE A brief tale in prose or verse that illustrates a moral. The moral is often explicitly stated at the end. In its usual form, the fable satirizes some aspects of human nature by picturing animals with those characteristics. 'You'd Better Believe Him' (p. 61) has the subtitle 'A Fable.'

FALLING FOOT A foot, such as the trochee or the dactyl, that begins with an accented syllable and ends with an unaccented syllable. For a fuller discussion of metre, see RHYTHM (p. 515).

FEMININE ENDING The ending of a line of poetry in which the final syllable is unaccented. For a fuller discussion of metre, see RHYTHM (p. 515).

FEMININE RHYME A rhyme in which the final syllables are unaccented. The final accented syllable and all subsequent unaccented syllables must rhyme (e.g., showing — going). For a fuller discussion of rhyme, see SOUND (p. 524).

FIGURES OF SPEECH A comprehensive term for certain technical devices used in poetry. The term includes various types of metaphorical language such as simile (p. 503), metaphor (p. 503), personification (p. 514), metonymy (p. 510), and synechdoche (p. 526), as well as rhetorical devices such as transferred epithet (p. 527), and hypberbole (p. 501).

FOOT *See* RHYTHM (p. 515).

FREE VERSE *See* RHYTHM (p. 520).

HAIKU (or *hokku*) A short Japanese poem evolved from the *tanka* (p. 527). It has been popular for centuries, and is still popular today.

In the haiku, an apparently simple image evokes a thoughtful response from the reader, the form of the poem being so designed that a change of point of view is achieved. Presenting an unlimited range of moods, haiku usually refer to a season of the year or a time of day, the reference establishing a set of associations for the specific text.

The English version of the haiku consists of three unrhymed lines containing five, seven, and five syllables. See 'You Hear That Fat Frog' (p. 33), 'My Grumbling Wife' (p. 34), and 'Climbing Mount Fuji' (p. 174).

HEROIC COUPLET Two rhyming lines of iambic pentameter that express a self-contained thought. For a fuller discussion of the COUPLET, see p. 496.

HEXAMETER A verse line of six feet. For a fuller discussion of metre, see RHYTHM (p. 515).

HOMERIC EPITHET *See* EPIC (p. 499).

HOMERIC SIMILE *See* IMAGERY (p. 503).

HYPERBOLE Extravagant exaggeration for comic or dramatic effect. Marvell uses hyperbole to describe the woman in 'To His Coy Mistress' (p. 233).

IAMBIC PENTAMETER A verse line of five iambs. The most common line in English poetry from about 1550 to 1900, especially in poetry of some length or seriousness. *See also* RHYTHM (p. 515) and BLANK VERSE (p. 494).

IAMBUS or IAMB A foot having one unaccented syllable and one accented (e.g., tŏ bé). For a fuller discussion of metre, see RHYTHM (p. 515).

IMAGERY The *imagery* of a poem is a collective term for the individual images it contains, as well as others it may suggest. An *image* is a representation, in memory or in imagination, of some aspect of the external, sensory world. Since the experience represented in the image is shared by the writer and reader, the reader becomes a participant rather than an outside observer.

In the critical discussion of poetry, the term 'image' is often applied to the word or phrase that evokes such a representation. In Arnold's 'Dover Beach' the phrase 'the grating roar of pebbles' creates an aural, visual, and tactile image. 'Dover Beach' (p. 130) includes imagery of the sea and of music.

Comparison. Imagery can be used in two ways: *literally*, for straightforward description of the external world, and *figuratively*, for making the expression of something abstract, vague, or hackneyed as concrete and compelling as possible. A line from 'The Love Song of J. Alfred Prufrock' (p. 40) illustrates the difference in usage. Eliot speaks of 'The yellow fog that rubs its back upon the window-panes.' The first image, 'yellow fog,' and the third, 'window-panes,' are both used literally; they evoke details of the scene that Eliot is actually describing. The second image, 'rubs its back,' is employed figuratively to make vivid the motion of the fog by comparing it to the movement of a cat. (It is interesting to note the shift in the corresponding figurative image in Eliot's next line, 'The yellow smoke that rubs its muzzle on the window-panes.')

Figurative images always involve comparisons or resemblances and are not found exclusively in poetry. One rarely completes a sentence in ordinary prose or conversation without resorting to comparisons that flesh out the thoughts. The phrase 'by any stretch of the imagination,' for example, compares the immaterial attribute 'imagination' to a substance with the physical quality of elasticity.

There are two elements in every comparison: the *subject*, of which the poet is speaking, and the *object*, with which the subject is compared. (Subject and object are sometimes referred to as *tenor* and *vehicle* respectively.) A person might say, 'I'm as poor as a church mouse.' The subject is the penniless speaker; the object is the underfed church mouse.

In this case the comparison is *explicit* because the point of similarity, poverty, is openly stated. If the point of similarity or the object of comparison were no more than implied, the comparison would be *implicit*. The metaphor 'He was burning with rage' makes an implicit comparison between subject (a man) and object (a fire).

Simile. A simile is the most straightforward kind of comparison. By means of the words 'like' or 'as' it compares the subject to some object more familiar or gripping, for example, 'O my Luve's like a red, red rose.'

A simile often restricts the *connotations* (p. 495) of its object, selecting the one feature common to subject and object and underlining it. When Mazur says in the poem 'Baseball' (p. 14) 'Our guys look like Sennett cops,' she is not suggesting that the baseball players' uniforms could be mistaken for police uniforms; she is explicitly pointing out that clumsy, stupid incompetence is the relevant common feature of the baseball players and the Mack Sennett cops of silent film.

Some fairly direct comparisons using the verb 'to be' occasionally omit the word 'like' or 'as.' For example, 'He was a whirlwind' could be used instead of 'He was like a whirlwind.' It makes little difference whether the resulting comparison is considered an incomplete simile or a metaphor. Technically speaking, however, it is a metaphor.

The Homeric or *Epic simile* is an elaborate form of simile in which the comparison is expanded upon in detail, for its own sake, so as to produce a picture complete in itself. The details are added for artistic and emotional effect, and do not necessarily correspond to features in the subject illustrated. In many epic similes the object is introduced by 'as when' or 'just as,' and the subject is tied back in by 'so' or 'thus.'

Metaphor. A metaphor compares the subject and object implicitly, without using 'like' or 'as.' Either the point of similarity is implied:

I think continually of those who were truly great.
Who, from the womb, remembered the soul's history
Through corridors of light *where* the hours are suns.
    STEPHEN SPENDER, I Think Continually
    of Those Who Were Truly Great (p. 249)

or the object of the comparison is implied:

Tyger! Tyger! burning *bright!*
    WILLIAM BLAKE, The Tyger (p. 116)

In either case, the effect of the omission is twofold: it involves readers more closely by leading them to complete the comparison in their own imagination; and it multiplies the connotations of the object.

In the metaphor 'Tyger! Tyger! burning bright,' the image of a tiger and the image of a burning fire are set side by side in our minds. As we find the readiest connection between the images (the bright colours found in both the flames and the tiger's eyes and fur), a flash of insight links the two images. The comparison is etched into our minds, for we have, in a sense, participated in creating the poem. In 'Fern Hill' (p. 1) and Shakespeare's 'Sonnet XXX: When to the Sessions of Sweet Silent Thought' (p. 48), a series of such flashes lights up the poems.

Another source of strength in a metaphor is its refusal to be confined to a single meaning. In Blake's poem, the tiger is compared to a flame 'burning bright,' and we see the beast in our mind's eye. But at once, the word 'burning' suggests more than that; the tiger is not only bright as fire, but menacing as fire and untameable as fire. Blake has found a metaphor so telling that its connotations are as powerful as its primary meaning.

A metaphor, then, begins by presenting one meaning that is more or less common to all readers and concludes by suggesting much more. By making its comparison implicitly, it invites us to complete it for ourselves and so make it fully our own. The more sensitive a reader is, the more complex the response. As well, different readers may have different combinations of responses.

Occasionally a poem is governed by a general metaphor from which a succession of individual images takes its origin. For example, in Shakespeare's 'Sonnet XXX: When to the Sessions of Sweet Silent Thought' (p. 48), four or five comparisons are derived from commerce, the object of the governing metaphor. This development of an image is often referred to as an *extended metaphor*. Allegory, discussed more fully on p. 506, is a special kind of extended metaphor.

For a discussion of other forms of metaphor, see CONCEIT (p. 495), METONYMY (p. 510), PERSONIFICATION (p. 514), and SYNECHDOCHE (p. 526).

Symbol. In a symbol, the customary techniques of literary comparison are reversed. Instead of beginning with the subject to be discussed, and then comparing that subject to an object, the poet leaves the subject unstated and examines the physical properties of the object so closely that it takes on a number of deeper meanings. Symbols are particularly effective when a poet wishes to discuss abstract and complex subjects without sounding vague or pretentious in the process.

Blake's poem 'The Tyger' creates a symbol of compelling power in order to pose a highly metaphysical question in concrete terms. The energy, beauty, and destructiveness of the tiger, suggested by 'burning bright,' lead the reader to contemplate all the forces of evil and untamed energy in the world. When Blake asks, 'Did He who made the Lamb make thee?'; the question expands to cosmic proportions. At the same time as our mind is becoming engrossed in such speculations, however, the tiger remains a tiger in the mind's eye. For modern applications of symbol see Mazur's 'Baseball' (p. 14), Plath's 'Mushrooms' (p. 122), Rosenblatt's 'Natural Prayer' (p. 124), Solt's 'Forsythia' (p. 126), and Stevens's 'Domination of Black' (p. 295).

There are two classes of symbols: *traditional* and *private*. *Traditional symbols* are widely used and are immediately understood. Over the years a number of traditional symbols have come into being, each having acquired great richness of suggestion, and having become, in effect, a kind of archetype. Among these archetypes are the rose, the star, the mountain top, the journey, towers, the eagle, and the colour green. At various times, however, poets invest these symbols with different primary meanings, for example, the star has signified perfect beauty, human aspirations, and divine guidance.

Private symbols have wholly personal meanings derived from the poet's individual experiences and beliefs. Sometimes poets succeed in conveying the wealth of meaning and association that their private symbols have for them. Sometimes, however, readers feel that the symbols have remained private, and add nothing to the poem. Some readers respond with pleasure to the symbols in 'The Hollow Men' (p. 245) while others find they have no reference to common experience and therefore have no significance for them.

Allegory. A special form of extended metaphor in which abstract ideas are personified and presented in a sustained narrative. Frequently the personifications represent virtues and vices and a journey provides the thread of continuity. Thus the allegory moves on two levels of interest: one, the surface story, the other, the allegorical revelation of truth. Bunyan's *Pilgrim's Progress*, Melville's *Moby Dick*, Faulkner's *A Fable*, Spenser's *Faerie Queene*, and Golding's *Lord of the Flies* are all allegories. Dante's *The Divine Comedy* (p. 239) is grounded in this approach.

IMAGIST POETRY A type of short poem that emerged in Britian and the United States in the early decades of the twentieth century. It reflected the influence of ancient Chinese poetry, classical Greek poetry, the Japanese haiku, and comtemporary French poetry. The outstanding characteristics include the starkness of images, an absence of surrounding detail, and an irregular, but musical, cadence. Ezra Pound, D. H. Lawrence, and Wallace Stevens have all written this type of poetry.

IMITATIVE HARMONY *See* SOUND (p. 525).

IMITATIVE RHYTHM *See* SOUND (p. 525).

INTERNAL RHYME Rhyme between the final word in a line and an earlier word in the line as in Belloc's 'On His Books' (p. 77): 'When I am *dead*, I hope it may be *said*.' In a wider usage, it is a rhyme between any two words in a line. For a fuller discussion of rhyme, see SOUND (p. 524).

INVECTIVE A direct and often overstated denunciation of follies or vices. If handled with a degree of finesse, invective can become a liberating expression of anger for writer and reader alike, as in 'Sir Penny' (p. 28), 'The Ill-Tempered Lover' (p. 51), and 'Zimri' (p. 219). If the speaker appears heavy-handed or self-righteous, however, the words can degenerate into an ineffective tirade.

IRONY The presentation of a character, incident, or idea in such a way as to suggest two points of view at one and the same time. Irony may exist in a number of contrasts: between the words of a speaker and the speaker's actual attitude, between the understanding of a speaker and what observers know to be true, or between what is expected and what is realized in retrospect to have been true. Pope's 'The Proper Study' (p. 217) uses irony as a basic technique, as does Auden's 'The Unknown Citizen' (p. 30). In the latter, the citizen's exemplary lifestyle resulted in his being ignored and forgotten; whereas, if he had been any kind of scoundrel, he would have been newsworthy. In 'Zimri' (p. 219), Dryden makes a series of ironic comments about Zimri, whom he is ridiculing. For example, Dryden writes: 'He had his jest, and they had his estate.'

Dramatic Irony. Dramatic irony occurs in a play when the audience perceives a significant aspect of a speech or situation that is not understood by the characters involved. In *Macbeth*, for example, Duncan speaks these words on his arrival at Cawdor:

This castle hath a pleasant seat; the air
Nimbly and sweetly recommends itself
Unto our gentle senses.

The dramatic irony is intense; for the theatre audience knows that the castle will be the scene of Duncan's murder.

In the dramatic monologue, 'My Last Duchess' (p. 265), the duke points to a piece of sculpture and says:

Notice, Neptune, though,
Taming a sea-horse, thought a rarity,
Which Claus of Innsbruck cast in bronze for me!

He is unaware that he is revealing his own nature as a sinister tyrant who looks on a wife as one of the *objets d'art* he collects.

JUXTAPOSITION The device of placing side by side, without comment, elements that would normally not be associated. These may be words, images, ideas, or quotations; in every instance, the elements that have been juxtaposed on the page are intended to be united by an act of the reader's imagination.

In 'Erosion' (p. 294), Pratt juxtaposes the effects of the erosion of the sea on the cliffs with the effect of sea disasters etched on the face of a woman; the effect is telling.

Modernist Juxtaposition. In modernist juxtaposition, possibly under the influence of French and Chinese poetry, the elements tend to be juxtaposed with greater starkness than they were previously, and tend to be drawn from widely separated contexts. A justly famous example of this starkness is Pound's 'In a Station of the Metro.' It began as a thirty-line description of several girls glimpsed in a Paris subway station. In the final version, the two most important images are juxtaposed — and that is the entire poem:

The apparition of these faces in the crowd;
Petals on a wet, black bough.

The conclusion of 'The Hollow Men' (p. 245) illustrates the distance that can exist between juxtaposed elements. Fragments of a nursery rhyme, philosophic exposition, and the Lord's Prayer are placed side by side to convey the complex state of mind in which the speaker finds himself. For a fuller discussion of these lines, see p. 491.

Later examples of the technique can be traced in the work of such poets as Theodore Roethke (p. 5).

LIMERICK A limerick is a verse form used for comic effect, usually composed of five lines rhyming *aabba* with the first, second and third lines trimeters, while the third and fourth are dimeters. The dominant rhythm is anapaestic. See Mark Twain's limerick (p. 56).

LYRIC The word 'lyric' is derived from a Greek term that referred to poetry accompanied by the music of the lyre. The phrase 'lyric poetry' is sometimes used loosely to apply to most, if not all, short poems, including sonnets, songs, odes, triolets, as well as poems not in conventional forms. It is probably more useful however, to restrict the meaning of the term to a short poem, whether regular or irregular in form, distinguished by its intense personal feeling and unified by the poet's consistent response to an incident or an idea. Such a lyric frequently exhibits a graceful, fluid rhythm and an evocative pattern of sound.

Lyrics are sometimes classified by their approach to the subject. The *descriptive lyric*, the most objective of the lyrical forms, describes some natural object or some event without stressing the poet's reaction to it. Sir Charles G. D. Robert's 'The Mowing' (p. 302) is an example.

The *reflective* or *meditative lyric* often starts from some concrete object or situation, moves through the poet's reaction, and attains a conviction or attitude of more universal application. The poems from *In Memoriam* (p. 160) are among the many examples of reflective lyrics in this book.

MASCULINE ENDING The ending of a line in which the last syllable is accented. For a fuller discussion of metre, see RHYTHM (p. 515).

MASCULINE RHYME A rhyme in which the final or only syllables are accented (e.g., ago — show). For a fuller discussion of rhyme, see SOUND (p. 524).

METAPHOR *See* IMAGERY (p. 503).

METAPHORICAL LANGUAGE A comprehensive term applied to all the figures of speech in which one idea is presented in terms of another; for example, metaphor, simile, metonymy. *See* IMAGERY (p. 501).

METAPHYSICAL POETRY A term generally used to refer to the work of a group of seventeenth-century poets including John Donne, George Herbert, Henry Vaughan, and Andrew Marvell. Metaphysical poetry is characterized by its regular use of irony (p. 507), paradox (p. 512), and conceits (p. 495). Its major subjects are sexual love and religious devotion. These subjects were treated in a way that required intellectual contemplation, rather than relying on the sensuous appeal that Elizabethan poets used when they dealt with them.

The perceptions of life presented by the metaphysical poets were extremely complex, but they were expressed in apparently simple language and commonplace imagery, the latter often drawn from the world of science that was opening up to them at that time. As a result, the poetry often acquired a quality of intellectual vigour, subtlety, and daring.

METONYMY A special kind of metaphor in which a sign is substituted for the thing signified (The *pen* is mightier than the *sword*); a container for the thing contained (the *kettle* is boiling); a cause for an effect ('When I consider how my *light* is spent'). Occasionally the reverse procedure is followed, as in the reference to reading Shakespeare rather than reading the plays of Shakespeare.

METRE *See* RHYTHM (p. 516).

METRICAL VERSE *See* RHYTHM (p. 515).

MILTONIC SONNET *See* SONNET (p. 523).

MODERNIST POETRY A term adopted by some critics to designate much of the poetry written between 1915 and about 1950. Like 'Elizabethan' or 'Romantic,' it is a useful label with which to identify literature of a given period that exhibits certain general characteristics. The term is not synonymous with 'modern.'

The writing of poetry changes with the passage of time, just as society changes. A particular vision of the world becomes popular and is expressed in a certain way by a group of poets. Gradually it looses hold on people's imagination and is replaced by a new vision and another poetic mode. Not all poets in a given period reflect the same vision and mode.

After World War I, the optimistic view enshrined in popular thought seemed to be passing away. Many young writers were growing bitterly disillusioned with society. In England a group of adventurous poetic rebels led by Ezra Pound and T. S. Eliot set themselves the heroic task of reappraising the traditions and values of Western civilization. They took stock of contemporary society in Europe and North America and presented their analysis in a poetry of radical technique.

Eliot's *The Waste Land*, published in 1922, was an instantaneous scandal. Its philosophy grated on open nerve-ends, while its technique was so revolutionary that Eliot was accused of playing an elaborate joke. Both Eliot and Pound continued to write, however, and their 'modernist' techniques were taken up by other young poets. Appreciation of their daring language and metaphors was reinforced by the posthumous publication in 1918 of the poetry of Gerard Manley Hopkins, who had died forty years earlier.

Such poets as W. B. Yeats and E. E. Cummings profited immensely from the modernist revolution, while Robert Frost, Walter de la Mare, and others continued using the more traditional methods.

More recently media, technology, and the concept of the global village have further affected the structure, language, and imagery of poetry. See CONCRETE POETRY (p. 495) and DUB POETRY (p. 498) for examples of developments after modernism.

MONOMETER A rare verse line of only one foot. For a fuller discussion of metre, see RHYTHM (p. 515).

NARRATIVE POETRY Poetry that is primarily concerned with the relating of events and experiences rather than with the dramatic interplay of characters or the poet's individual response to events or experiences.

NEAR-RHYME Also referred to as 'half-rhyme' and 'slant-rhyme.' It is the repetition of the consonant sound, but not the preceding vowel, in the final accented syllables. See SOUND (p. 525).

OCTAVE The first eight lines of a Petrarchan sonnet. *See* SONNET (p. 522).

ODE An elaborate lyric that celebrates a serious theme. The original Greek ode, as exemplified in Pindar, followed a strict form. In English literature, however, the term is used more loosely to refer to any poem, often inspired by an important occasion, expressing lofty ideas and exalted feelings. Some conventions of the original form may be retained. Keats's 'Ode on a Grecian Urn' (p. 68) and Shelley's 'Ode to the West Wind' (p. 297) are well-known examples of the English ode.

ONOMATOPOEIA The use of words that imitate sounds. *See* SOUND (p. 525).

OTTAVA RIMA A stanza pattern having eight iambic pentameter lines rhyming *abababcc*. It has been credited to Boccaccio and used effectively by Spenser, Milton, Keats, and Byron. See 'The Isles of Greece' (p. 324).

PARADOX A statement that at first appears to be contradictory, but on further consideration appears to be justified. For example, John Donne in his poem 'Death' (p. 166), reversing the point usually made, says that death is the 'slave to fate, chance, kings, and desperate men.' He goes on to say 'death shall be no more! Death, thou shalt die!' By means of this self-contradictory statement the reader is more than usually involved in the thought and feelings of the poet.

On a larger scale, a paradox may be the awareness that a truth consists of two opposing elements. In 'Fern Hill' (p. 1), Thomas is expressing the paradox that a young person, in the process of growing up, is moving closer to death. In 'The Tyger' (p. 116), Blake is exploring the paradox that innocence and daemonic energy both exist in a world created by God.

PARODY A satire on a literary style or a particular work of literature that exaggerates its characteristic features, usually applying them to an inappropriate subject. 'Variations on a Theme by William Carlos Williams' by Kenneth Koch (p. 289), for example, is a parody of Williams's poem 'This Is Just to Say' (p. 288).

PASTORAL A highly conventionalized form of literary expression, usually in poetry, which presents life in an idealized rural setting.

People living in a complicated or artificial society frequently exhibit what might be called 'the pastoral impulse,' a longing for a gentle country setting in which they could be more fully themselves. Poets frequently create such a setting when expressing their views of life. In fact, a coherent pastoral tradition extends from the poetry of Greece and Rome to that of the Renaissance and the seventeenth century.

In expressing the pastoral impulse, such poets as Theocritus and Vergil evolved a series of conventions. The Greek poets' favourite pastoral landscape was Arcadia, a name that has become synonymous with rural peace and contentment. The heroes were graceful shepherds (hence 'pastoral,' from the Latin *pastor*, shepherd), with few problems beyond making themselves sufficiently amiable to their charming companions. They danced, indulged in singing matches, serenaded their lovers, and played at being rustics in a serene landscape, with the livestock grazing at a discreet distance.

No one supposes that life in the country was ever like that; but pastoral poets are not speaking of real life. They merely conjure up the innocence and simple dignity we feel we should ideally possess.

Pastoral poems can be enjoyed for their own sake, as graceful fantasies. They can also be the means of posing certain searching questions about life and human nature. Spenser's *The Shepheardes Calender* (p. 138) falls within the formal pastoral tradition; Wordsworth's 'There Was a Boy' (p. 4) and Thomas's 'Fern Hill' (p. 1) illustrate later developments. See also 'The Shepherd to His Love' (p. 283), 'The Nymph's Reply' (p. 285), and 'Raleigh Was Right' (p. 286).

PENTAMETER A verse line of five feet. For a fuller discussion of metre, see RHYTHM (p. 515).

PERSONA A poetic personality adopted by a poet that may or may not resemble the poet's everyday character. See Keats's 'Sonnet: When I Have Fears' (p. 70), Whitman's *Song of Myself* (p. 71), and Browning's 'My Last Duchess' (p. 265).

PERSONIFICATION In the metaphorical figure of speech known as personification, the poet attributes human characteristics to an abstract idea or an inanimate object, often by depicting it as engaged in some typically human action: 'Death lays his icy hands on kings.'

PETRARCHAN SONNET *See* SONNET (p. 522).

PORTMANTEAU WORD A composite word made up of parts of real words, and intended to convey, by an elaborate pun, a blend of the meanings of all the words that can be recognized in it. The technique was developed to its limit in *Finnegan's Wake* (p. 39).

PROSODY A term that encompasses the technical principles of poetry, including metre and rhythm, rhyme, and other effects of sound and stanza forms.

PUN A play on words of similar sound, in which one word is used with two or more different meanings. At present the device is generally used for humorous or witty effects, as in Belloc's 'On His Books' (p. 77): 'His sins were scarlet, but his books were read.' A pun can also occur in a serious context, as when, in 'Virtue' (p. 254), George Herbert uses both the words 'fall' and 'die' to provide two very different, but interactive, references.

PYRRHIC A rare foot of two unstressed syllables (e.g., ĭn thĕ). For a fuller discussion of metre, see RHYTHM (p. 515).

QUANTITATIVE VERSE *See* RHYTHM (p. 521).

QUATRAIN A stanza of four lines.

RHYME *See* SOUND (p. 524).

RHYTHM At its most basic level in poetry, rhythm is the ordered succession in time of stronger and weaker elements of speech sounds, alternating with moments of silence to form a pattern. On a larger scale, the rhythm of poetry is established by syntax, grouping of words, length of lines, stanza form, and even combination of stanzas. These aspects of poetry are closely allied to music. Prose also achieves rhythmic effects, although its patterns are usually not so readily discernible.

Rhythm and pattern are not limited to language and music. From one point of view, they are the modes by which we apprehend our experience: the relationships depicted in art; and the discernment of the cycles of life and death, the seasons, day and night, and even our daily routines.

Metrical verse. Until this century metrical verse was by far the most common form of rhythm in English poetry. The *strong* and *weak* elements in metrical verse consist of the stressed and unstressed syllables of words, pronounced as we say them in daily speech. Metrical rhythm is then created by the succession of stressed and unstressed syllables following one another in regular or predictable measures, referred to as *feet.* For other forms of poetic rhythm see the notes on FREE VERSE (p. 520), ACCENTUAL VERSE (p. 521), SYLLABIC VERSE (p. 521), and QUANTITATIVE VERSE (p. 521).

The Foot. The basic unit of metrical rhythm. It is a group of stressed and unstressed syllables that recurs in a recognizable pattern.

The following feet have two syllables:

An *iambus* (or *iamb*) has one unaccented syllable followed by one accented syllable, e.g., tŏ bé. This is the most common foot in English poetry.

A *trochee* has one accented syllable followed by one unaccented syllable, e.g., lázy̆. It creates a sing-song effect when used as a steady rhythm and consequently is used more often as a variant than as a basic pattern. It is frequently used as a strong opening foot in an iambic line.

A *spondee* has two accented syllables, e.g., fát mén. It is used in English only as a variant or to slow the pace.

A *pyrrhic*, which is seldom used in English poetry, has two unaccented syllables, e.g., ĭn thĕ.

The following feet have three syllables:

An *anapaest* has two unaccented syllables followed by one accented syllable, e.g., ă sŭrpríse. The preponderance of unaccented syllables tends to lighten the line.

A *dactyl* has one accented syllable followed by two unaccented syllables, e.g., lázĭlў. It is generally used as a variant foot.

An *amphibrach* is a sequence of one unaccented syllable, one accented syllable, and another unaccented syllable, e.g., stăccátŏ.

The term *rising foot* is applied to a foot in which stress falls on the final syllable (tŏ bé), and the term *falling foot* to a foot in which the stress comes at the beginning, e.g., béĭng.

If the final foot of a line is *rising*, as in:

The hills and leafless forests slow / lў yiéld,

the ending is termed *masculine*. An ending with an unstressed final syllable is termed *feminine*. The latter can be used to create an effect of hesitation, or of pensive brooding:

When I first reached this / cóuntrў.

Metre. The metre of a line is determined by the number and nature of its feet. The following terms are used to indicate the number of feet in each line:

monometer — one foot	*tetrameter* — four feet
dimeter — two feet	*pentameter* — five feet
trimeter — three feet	*hexameter* — six feet

A second term is added to describe the basic foot in the line. Thus, a line of three trochees is a trochaic trimeter; a line of six iambs is an iambic hexameter. Successive lines are seldom completely regular, however. Sometimes the rhythm of a poem may be so varied that its metre is not immediately apparent.

Scansion. In scansion, which is the analysis of the metre of a poem, the syllables that are stressed when the lines are spoken naturally are marked by an oblique stroke, called an *ictus*:

The hílls and léafless fórests slówly yiéld.

The remaining syllables are marked as unstressed, or weak:

Thĕ hílls ănd léaflĕss fórĕsts slówlў yiéld.

The lines are then marked off into their component feet. Normally a foot has as its nucleus one stressed syllable:

Thĕ hílls / ănd léaf / lĕss fór / ĕsts slów / lў yiéld.

As this line contains five iambs, it is an iambic pentameter. The predominant foot establishes the metre of a line, although any other foot may be interposed as a variant.

The attempt to write completely regular English verse tends to result in something deadly to read. Each line of such doggerel jogs along at the same pace. That a good poem can vary, within the metre, from limpid grace to rushing energy, is due to two other essential features of the rhythm of natural speech: syncopation (sometimes known as counterpoint) and cadence.

Syncopation or *counterpoint* can be readily understood if we examine a well-known line from *Hamlet*. If the line were mechanically scanned as iambic pentameter, we would have this result:

Tŏ bé / ŏr nót / tŏ bé / thăt ís / thĕ qués / tiŏn.

Speaking the line with these stresses we would hear:

To BE *or* NOT *to* BE, *that* IS *the* QUES*tion.*

Obviously this mechanical scansion makes nonsense of the line. While the precise intonation of the line might vary, we would normally hear it spoken in this manner:

To BE *or* NOT *to be,* THAT *is the* QUES*tion.*

Notice what has taken place. What would have been the fourth metrical iamb, 'thăt ís,' is spoken as a trochee 'THAT is.' In other words, a trochee in speech stress has been counterpointed or mounted upon the iambic metre. Similarly, in the third foot, a pyrrhic has been mounted on the iambic metre. Other instances of syncopation might show an anapaest counterpointed on a dactyl, or a spondee upon a trochaic metre. The effect is like syncopation in music.

Cadence. Another way to create interesting rhythms is by means of cadence. Cadence is the product of three elements: the natural grouping of words, the length and syntax of sentences, and the speed of the line.

If we think again of Hamlet's speech, we find that yet another factor, the natural *grouping* of the words, affects our spoken version of it. As it stands, the line is spoken in approximately this manner:

To BE *or* NOT *to be,* THAT *is the* QUES*tion.*

But when Hamlet speaks the words, he does not simply trundle the words out one after another. He pauses over some and clusters others together. He groups the words into their natural phrases. The line might be spoken in this manner:

To BE / *or* NOT *to be,* // THAT / *is the* QUES*tion.*

The words in every piece of poetry can be grouped in this way. Skilful grouping by the poet will add dignity to the meaning of words, give them lightness and crispness, or even create an ironic effect by giving the opposite impression to what the words intend.

On a larger scale than the grouping of phrases, cadence is determined by the nature of each *sentence unit* within the poem. Consider this passage from Milton's 'Hail, Holy Light' from *Paradise Lost* (p. 185):

Thee I revisit now with bolder wing,
Escaped the Stygian Pool, though long detained

> *In that obscure sojourn, while in my flight,*
> *Through utter and through middle darkness borne,*
> *With other notes than to th' Orphean lyre*
> *I sung of Chaos and the eternal Night,*
> *Taught by the Heavenly Muse to venture down*
> *The dark descent, and up to reascend,*
> *Though hard and rare: thee I revisit safe*
> *And feel thy sovran vital lamp.*

The sense of a sustained ordeal, final arrival, and mighty exaltation is achieved, not only by the length of the sentence, but also by the welding together of its syntactical parts. The succession of lines remains an indivisible unit. The length and structure of Milton's periodic sentences convey in themselves the grandeur of his theme.

Compare the effect of those lines with the following passage from 'A Field of Light' by Theodore Roethke (p. 5):

> *The dirt left my hand, visitor.*
> *I could feel the mare's nose.*
> *A path went walking.*
> *The sun glittered on a small rapids.*
> *Some morning thing came, beating its wings.*
> *The great elm filled with birds.*

Each of the six lines is a short sentence, using the simple syntactical structure of subject, verb, and object. The cadence, as a result, spurts, pauses, and bursts ahead again; the effect is breathless wonder. Roethke has shaped his sentence units as deliberately as Milton did. They are entirely different, however, because they have such a different function.

One of Alexander Pope's technical gifts was the ability to increase or retard the *speed* of a line at will. He composed the following lines in *An Essay on Criticism* to demonstrate how the speed of a line should reinforce the sense:

> *When Ajax strives some rock's vast weight to throw,*
> *The line too labours, and the words move slow:*

> *Not so, when swift Camilla scours the plain,*
> *Flies o'er th'unbending corn, and skims along the main.*

In comparing the first and second couplets, which move at such different rates of speed, notice these points: the relation between the last letter of one word and the first letter of the next; the predominant vowel sounds; the predominant foot; the placing of monosyllables and polysyllables. Notice also the additional problem Pope set himself in the fourth line, which is nevertheless the swiftest.

Another factor in the speed of the line is the position of the *caesura*, or pause. In the first two lines quoted, Pope has used caesuras to retard the movement.

Pauses also occur at the conclusion of every line in the passage, creating *end-stopped* lines. Most poets rely at times on *enjambment*, the continuation of the sense and cadence of one line into the next, so that the reader does not pause between the two lines. The result is termed a *run-on* line. The massively proportioned sentence from *Paradise Lost* (p. 518) owes much of its power to the four run-on lines that buttress it.

Free Verse. While the tradition of metrically based rhythm has been dominant in English poetry for at least four centuries, rhythm can be handled in other ways. Free verse is one common alternative. It differs from more traditional verse in the methods it uses to establish the rhythmic pattern of a poem. Without imposing a regular metre, pre-determined lengths for the lines, or a fixed form for each stanza, it develops its pattern of rhythm and cadence in response to the immediate needs of the poem. Its resources, therefore, are as variable as those of language itself.

Free verse is difficult to use well, for it demands a knowledge of regular forms, sensitivity to word values, and a well-developed sense of rhythm from the poet who must, in effect, create a new form for each poem. Although free verse in English is as old as the poetry of the Authorized Version of the Bible, modern poets have seized on its unlimited possibilities for experimentation and complexity:

I celebrate myself, and sing myself,
And what I assume you shall assume,
And every atom belonging to me as good belongs to you.

I loafe and invite my soul,
I lean and loafe at my ease observing a spear of summer grass.
        WALT WHITMAN, *Song of Myself* [1](p. 71)

Accentual Verse was the rhythm used by Anglo-Saxon poets. It is based on the number of stressed syllables in each line. The number of unstressed syllables and the proximity of stressed syllables to each other may vary.

Sprung Rhythm. Gerard Manley Hopkins developed a refinement of accentual rhythm that he termed *sprung rhythm*. The number of stresses in the line remains constant, and each foot begins with a stress. A foot may consist of a single stressed syllable or of a stressed syllable followed by one, two, or three unstressed syllables. Here are the opening lines of 'Hurrahing in Harvest' (p. 188), showing Hopkins's own scansion of the sprung rhythm:

Summer énds now; now, bárbarous in béauty, the stóoks aríse

Aróund: up abóve, what wínd-walks! what lóvely beháviour

Of silk-sack clóuds! has wílder, wílful-wávier

Méal-drift móulded ever and mélted acróss skíes?

Quantitative Verse is another alternative to metrical rhythm. It is derived from classical poetry and is based on the length of time required to utter a syllable, long vowels and stressed syllables taking more time than short vowels and unstressed syllables. The various classical verse forms had a fixed number of long and short syllables for each foot, but the English language, with its natural accentual stresses does not lend itself to the set classical patterns.

Syllabic Verse is an uncommon alternative to metrical rhythm in which each line contains a pre-determined number of syllables, the rhythm being provided by the normal accentuation of speech. Corresponding lines in successive stanzas normally contain the same number of syllables. The form was used extensively by Marianne Moore.

RISING FOOT A foot, such as the iambus or the anapest, which begins with an unaccented syllable and ends with an accented syllable. For a fuller discussion of metre, see RHYTHM (p. 515).

RUN-ON LINE A line whose sense and cadence continue into the next line without pause. *See* RHYTHM (p. 520).

SATIRE Ridicule directed against a vice or folly in a contemporary person or institution offensive to the writer. It may range from gentle mockery to bitter attack. See 'The Unknown Citizen' (p. 30) and 'Zimri' (p. 219).

SCANSION *See* RHYTHM (p. 517).

SESTET The final six lines of a Petrarchan sonnet. *See* SONNET (below).

SIMILE *See* IMAGERY (p. 503).

SLANT-RHYME *See* SOUND (p. 525).

SONNET A poem in which a theme or subject is developed within a strict form, normally of fourteen iambic pentameter lines. Its concentration makes it ideal for meditation on love and death, descriptions of nature and states of mind, compliments, or invective. The thought pattern follows the divisions of the structure very closely, each division making its own distinct contribution. Conceits and a reliance on metaphor add richness to the content and style. There are four traditional patterns for English sonnets.

The Italian or Petrarchan Sonnet. In the fourteenth century, Petrarch, an Italian poet, made the form famous by writing a sequence of love sonnets. The Italian sonnet consists of an *octave* or *octet* (eight lines) that describes the subject or introduces a problem, and a *sestet* (six lines) that comments on it or resolves it. Two quatrains, each rhyming *abba* constitute the octave. Ordinarily, the first quatrain introduces the subject, while the second provides a more specific elaboration. Two *tercets*, rhyming in various ways, *cde cde*, or *cdc dcd*, constitute the sestet. The first tercet is usually the link that provides continuity within the form. The final tercet makes a climactic statement. The transition from octave to sestet is sometimes referred to as the *volta*. See Elizabeth Barrett Browning's 'Sonnet: How Do I Love Thee?' (p. 49), Keats's 'On First Looking into Chapman's Homer' (p. 67), and Hopkins's 'God's Grandeur' (p. 187) and 'Hurrahing in Harvest' (p. 188).

The Shakespearean, Elizabethan, or English Sonnet. English sonneteers contributed to the evolution of both theme and form. The Shakespearean sonnets, embracing a variety of moods and themes, were written exclusively in a form that consisted of three quatrains with independent rhymes, concluding with a rhyming couplet (*abab*, *cdcd*, *efef*, *gg*). The quatrains may provide three examples of the theme, with the couplet offering a conclusion; or they may provide three metaphorical statements of the theme, with the couplet offering a final statement. The first quatrain may introduce the subject, while the second and third both present a more detailed treatment. A pause before the couplet sets it off, to establish an epigrammatic quality or a touch of novelty. Later poets, such as Donne and Keats, used this version, although the Italian sonnet retained popularity. Donne extended the scope of the sonnet to include religious themes. The trend to greater freedom continued. See Shakespeare's sonnets (pp. 47, 48, 76, 291) and Keats's 'Sonnet: When I Have Fears' (p. 70).

The Spenserian Sonnet. Spenser's *Amoretti*, a sequence of love sonnets, established an interlocking rhyme pattern of *abab*, *bcbc*, *cdcd*, *ee*. The Spenserian sonnet is a form midway between the restrictions of the Petrarchan and the greater liberty of the Shakespearean sonnets.

The Miltonic Sonnet. The Miltonic sonnet follows the basic Italian form, with one very important development: the thought of the octave often flows freely into the sestet. Milton also made the sonnet powerful enough for passionate statements of political and moral opinion. His poem 'On His Blindness' (p. 184) is an example of this form.

Some poets have used the sonnet as a basis from which to develop a wide variety of structural patterns. In his 'Ode to the West Wind' (p. 297), for example, Shelley used fourteen-line units composed of four tercets and a final couplet. Keats, in his 'Ode on a Grecian Urn' (p. 68), used a stanza form that was a ten-line adaptation of the sonnet form — a quatrain followed by two tercets. Other poets may substitute assonance for rhyme or even dispense with rhyme completely.

SOUND Words, the basic units of speech, are combinations of sounds. Normally, they are linked together according to conventional structures of grammar and syntax to convey meaning. The sounds themselves, however, may also convey impressions, just as the background music in a film may convey a sense of harshness, pleasantness, languor, or tension. Intervals of silence in the midst of sounds allow momentary opportunities for the listener to make sense of the sounds and conjure up further associations. Orchestrating sounds can help listeners associate images, recall ideas, and determine emphasis. Some of the techniques for utilizing sound are grouped below.

Rhyme (also *Rime*). Rhyme occurs when there is an identical sound in the monosyllables or final stressed syllables of two or more words, and in any of the unstressed syllables that may follow.

When final stressed syllables rhyme, the rhyme is called *masculine* (e.g., mark — bark). When the rhyming words ends with unstressed syllables, the rhyme is called *feminine* (e.g., shaken — taken). A *polysyllabic* rhyme can give a comic or lugubrious effect, as in the title of Marquis's 'Cheerio My Deario' (p. 148).

Internal Rhyme. Internal rhyme usually occurs between a final word of a line and an earlier word in the same line. In a wider usage, it occurs between any two words in a line. Sylvia Plath uses internal rhyme in 'Mushrooms' (p. 122): 'Soft fists insist on.'

Assonance and Consonance. Assonance occurs when the vowels of two stressed syllables sound alike, but not the consonants following the vowels (e.g., trees — leaves).

In *consonance* the consonants agree (especially the final consonants), but the vowels differ (e.g., acquire — air).

When modern poets use consonance at line endings it is called *near-* or *slant-rhyme.* Wilfred Owen in 'Strange Meeting' (p. 88) rhymes 'escape' with 'scooped' and 'groaned' with 'groined.' Dylan Thomas in 'And Death Shall Have No Dominion' (p. 323) uses the freer slant-rhyme. He rhymes 'moon' with 'gone' and 'ears' with 'sea-shores,' which contains assonance between '*EA*rs' and 's*EA*,' and partial consonance between 'ea*RS*' and 'seasho*RES*.'

Alliteration. Alliteration is the repetition of the initial letter or sound of words in close proximity (e.g., '*sh*ining from *sh*ook foil').

A wider use of the term includes alliteration between the first letters of stressed syllables, whether or not they occur at the beginning of a word. An example can be found in 'Hurrahing in Harvest' (p. 188): 'These things, these things were *h*ere and but the be*h*older.' Alliteration is often used when the poet wishes to create a strong association between words. The effect is both musical and unifying.

Onomatopoeia. Onomatopoeia occurs when the sound of a word suggests its meaning (e.g., 'whisper' or 'plop').

Imitative Rhythm. Imitative rhythm is found in entire phrases or lines, where the cadence imitates the movement described.

> *I sprang to the stirrup, and Joris and he,*
> *I galloped, Dirk galloped, we galloped all three.*
> > ROBERT BROWNING, How They Brought the
> > Good News from Ghent to Aix

Imitative Harmony unites onomatopoeia and imitative rhythm so that sound and cadence together suggest the sense, as in Lawrence's 'Snake' (p. 10):

He reached down from a fissure in the earth-wall in the gloom
And trailed his yellow-brown slackness soft-bellied down, over the edge of
the stone trough
And rested his throat upon the stone bottom,
And where the water had dripped from the tap, in a small clearness,
He sipped with his straight mouth,
Softly drank through his straight gums, into his slack long body.
Silently.

SOUND POETRY Sound poetry relies on the suggestive powers of or-
chestrated or structured human sounds, rather than on syntax, to
convey meaning. For example, a poem by The Four Horsemen, a
sound-poetry performance group, plays upon the sounds of the
word 'milk' to convey a host of images associated with milk. Sometimes electronic devices such as synthesizers, echo chambers, or
other non-vocal sounds are used for additional effect. 'Natural
Prayer' (p. 124) is an example of a sound poem. *See also* CONCRETE
POETRY (p. 495).

SPEED *See* RHYTHM (p. 519).

SPENSERIAN SONNET *See* SONNET (p. 523).

SPONDEE A foot having two accented syllables (e.g., fát mén). For a
fuller discussion of metre, see RHYTHM (p. 515).

SPRUNG RHYTHM *See* RHYTHM (p. 521).

STANZA A stanza is a unit of verse lines with certain formal characteristics that are repeated throughout a poem. The TERCET (p. 527) and
the QUATRAIN (p. 514) are among the simpler forms.

SYMBOL *See* IMAGERY (p. 505).

SYNCOPATION *See* RHYTHM (p. 517).

SYNECHDOCHE A form of metonymy in which the significant part is
used for the whole, or a genus for a species. Thus sailors are often

referred to as 'hands.' The recent tendency is to allow the term 'metonymy' to assume the function of both metonymy and synechdoche.

TANKA An ancient form of Japanese poetry. The English version consists of thirty-one syllables arranged in five lines of 5, 7, 5, 7, and 7 syllables. Its early tradition was courtly, with elevated language and themes of love, nature, travel, lamentations and felicitations. Some consider the *haiku* (p. 500) to have been derived from the tanka. Yosano Akiko, author of 'You Never Touch' (p. 50), is a modern practitioner of the tanka form.

TERCET A stanza of three lines, usually rhyming.

TERZA RIMA A series of tercets, normally in iambic pentameter, with interlocking rhymes *aba*, *bcb*, *cdc*, and so on. The form lends itself to the development of a quickly moving series of little scenes. Dante uses it in *The Divine Comedy* (p. 239), and Shelley in his 'Ode to the West Wind' (p. 297).

TETRAMETER A verse line of four feet. For a fuller discussion of metre, see RHYTHM (p. 515).

TRANSFERRED EPITHET An adjective or adverb that is transferred from the word it naturally modifies to another word, normally nearby. For example:

And as I was green *and carefree, famous among the barns*
About the happy *yard*
        DYLAN THOMAS, Fern Hill (p. 1)

Here the device conveys the child's happy confusion of sense impressions and subjective feelings.

TRIMETER A verse line of three feet. For a fuller discussion of metre, see RHYTHM (p. 515).

TRIOLET A light, carefree poem of eight lines with only two rhymes (*abaaabab*). See 'A Kiss' (p. 46) and 'Girl's-Eye View of Relatives' (p. 96).

TROCHEE A foot having one accented syllable followed by one unaccented syllable (e.g., lázў). For a fuller discussion of metre, see RHYTHM (p. 515).

VERSE FORMS The formal structures that poems may take, in whole or in part. There are innumerable combinations of rhymes and line lengths, and varying lengths of stanza. Some of the best-known verse forms are the couplet, quatrain, sonnet, terza rima, and triolet.

VOLTA A term used to indicate the turn of thought in a sonnet. *See* SONNET (p. 523).

WIT The framing, in vivid and memorable language, of unexpected parallels, incongruous juxtapositions, and paradoxes. Wit relies, for its stylistic sparkle, upon balanced constructions, deft phrasing, and a knowing, often ironic, tone. It is frequently epigrammatic. Its tendency is less to reveal deep truths about a subject than to impress us with the play of an urbane and agile mind, one that is sometimes willing to be less than fair with the subject for the pleasure of setting it in an unexpected perspective. Varieties of wit can be appreciated in 'To His Coy Mistress' (p. 233), 'Zimri' (p. 219), and 'Wishes of an Elderly Man at a Garden Party' (p. 317).

A Selected Bibliography

Criticism

CLEANTH BROOKS & ROBERT PENN WARREN: *Understanding Poetry*; Holt, Rinehart and Winston.

JOHN CIARDI & MILLER WILLIAMS: *How Does a Poem Mean?*; Houghton Mifflin Company.

HUGH KENNER: *The Art of Poetry*; Holt, Rinehart and Winston.

GEOFFREY N. LEECH: *A Linguistic Guide to English Poetry*; Longman Group.

WINIFRED NOWOTTNY: *The Language Poets Use*; The Athlone Press.

PHILIP DAVIES ROBERTS: *How Poetry Works*; Penguin Books.

M. L. ROSENTHAL & SALLY M. GALL: *The Modern Poetic Sequence*; Oxford University Press.

References for Literary Terms

M. H. ABRAMS: *A Glossary of Literary Terms*; Holt, Rinehart and Winston.

SYLVAN BARNET and others: *A Dictionary of Literary Terms*; Little, Brown and Company.

BABETTE DEUTSCH: *Poetry Handbook: A Dictionary of Terms*; Grosset and Dunlap.

ALEX PREMINGER ET AL: *The Princeton Encyclopedia of Poetry and Poetics*; Princeton University Press.

W. F. THRALL, ADDISON HIBBARD & C. HUGH HOLMAN: *A Handbook to Literature*; The Odyssey Press.

Index of Authors

The poem numbers are given in parentheses.

535

Index of Titles

Untitled poems, such as sonnets, may be found under the first line of the poem. The poem numbers are given in parentheses.

Index of Subjects, Moods, and Attitudes

References are to the poem numbers. The listing is by no means exhaustive.

Index of Genres

References are to the poem numbers. This listing cannot, by the nature of literature, be definitive. Poems that have some features of a genre but lack other essential features may be listed, not as typical representatives, but as bearing an interesting relationship to the genre. Categories such as lyric poetry and free verse are not included since so many poems could be listed under these headings.

Ballad
The Twa Corbies, ANONYMOUS (41); Sir Patrick Spens, ANONYMOUS (42); Nursery Rhyme of Innocence and Experience, CHARLES CAUSLEY (55); As I Walked Out One Evening, W. H. AUDEN (96); John Henry, ANONYMOUS (171)

Blank Verse
There Was a Boy, WILLIAM WORDSWORTH (2); Ulysses, ALFRED LORD TENNYSON (13); Strange Meeting, WILFRED OWEN (60); Tintern Abbey, WILLIAM WORDSWORTH (86); The Last Hour of Faustus, CHRISTOPHER MARLOWE (102); Hail, Holy Light, JOHN MILTON (112)

Concrete Poetry
Natural Prayer, JOE ROSENBLATT (80); Forsythia, MARY ELLEN SOLT (81)

Dialect Poems
An Old Woman's Lamentations, J. M. SYNGE (23); The Twa Corbies, ANONYMOUS (41); Sir Patrick Spens, ANONYMOUS (42); Lines from the Prologue to the *Canterbury Tales*, GEOFFREY CHAUCER (71); The Braw Wooer, ROBERT BURNS (95); Bans O' Killing, LOUISE BENNETT (121); The Wif of Bathe, GEOFFREY CHAUCER (137); John Henry, ANONYMOUS (171)

Drama
The Last Hour of Faustus, CHRISTOPHER MARLOWE (102); Welsh Night, DYLAN THOMAS (103)

Dramatic Monologue
My Last Duchess, ROBERT BROWNING (164)

Dub Poetry
Bans O' Killing, LOUISE BENNETT (121)

Elegy
The Song of the Mad Prince, WALTER DE LA MARE (36); The Shepheardes Lament, EDMUND SPENSER (87); Branwell's Lament, JAMES REANEY (88); My '48 Pontiac, AL PURDY (90); *In Memoriam* (Selections), ALFRED LORD TENNYSON (99); Dirge Without Music, EDNA ST VINCENT MILLAY (206); Song from *Cymbeline*, WILLIAM SHAKESPEARE (213); Song, THOMAS NASHE (214)

Epic
Hail, Holy Light, JOHN MILTON (112)

Epigram
Impromptu on Charles II, JOHN WILMOT, EARL OF ROCHESTER (19); On His Books, HILAIRE BELLOC (53); Epigram, ALEXANDER POPE (134)

Fable
You'd Better Believe Him, BRIAN PATTEN (43)

Haiku
You Hear That Fat Frog, ISSA (21); My Grumbling Wife, ISSA (22); Climbing Mount Fuji, ISSA (109); Accidentally Broke, ISHIKAWA TAKUBOKU (196)

Heroic Couplet
The Village Master, OLIVER GOLDSMITH (16); Lines from the Prologue to the *Canterbury Tales*, GEOFFREY CHAUCER (71); The Proper Study, ALEXANDER POPE (135); Zimri, JOHN DRYDEN (136); The Wif of Bathe, GEOFFREY CHAUCER (137); My Last Duchess, ROBERT BROWNING (164)

Imagist Poetry

The Farm, ROBERT CREELEY (126); The White Horse, D. H. LAWRENCE (128); The Term, WILLIAM CARLOS WILLIAMS (178); This Is Just to Say, WILLIAM CARLOS WILLIAMS (179); In a Station of the Metro, EZRA POUND (185)

Limerick

A Man Hired by John Smith and Co., MARK TWAIN (39)

Longer Poems

The Love Song of J. Alfred Prufrock, T. S. ELIOT (28); *Song of Myself* (Selections), WALT WHITMAN (50); Jim, HILAIRE BELLOC (54); Tintern Abbey, WILLIAM WORDSWORTH (86); *In Memoriam* (Selections), ALFRED LORD TENNYSON (99); David, EARLE BIRNEY (110); *The Inferno*, Canto Third, DANTE (151); The Hollow Men, T. S. ELIOT (152)

Narratives

Jim, HILAIRE BELLOC (54); Deuteronomy, ROBERT BRINGHURST (70); David, EARLE BIRNEY (110); *The Inferno, Canto Third*, DANTE (151)

Odes

Ode on a Grecian Urn, JOHN KEATS (48); Ode to the West Wind, PERCY BYSSHE SHELLEY (187)

Parody

Variations on a Theme by William Carlos Williams, KENNETH KOCH (180)

Pastoral Poetry

The Shepheardes Lament, EDMUND SPENSER (87); Branwell's Lament, JAMES REANEY (88); The Shepherd to His Love, CHRISTOPHER MARLOWE (175); The Nymph's Reply, SIR WALTER RALEGH (176); Raleigh Was Right, WILLIAM CARLOS WILLIAMS (177)

Chronological Index

References are to the poem numbers. In borderline cases, the poets have been placed in categories according to the period in which they wrote their best-known poems and the distinguishing characteristics of those poems.

Pre-Renaissance (Before 1500)

I Know Where I'm Going, ANONYMOUS (10); Sir Penny, ANONYMOUS (17); An Old Woman's Lamentations, J. M. SYNGE (AFTER FRANÇOIS VILLON) (23); Western Wind, ANONYMOUS (30); The Twa Corbies, ANONYMOUS (41); Sir Patrick Spens, ANONYMOUS (42); To Every Thing There Is a Season, THE BIBLE (KING JAMES VERSION) (69); Lines from the Prologue to the *Canterbury Tales*, GEOFFREY CHAUCER (71); Then the Lord Answered Job Out of the Whirlwind, THE BIBLE (KING JAMES VERSION) (75); The Wif of Bathe, GEOFFREY CHAUCER (137); *The Inferno, Canto Third*, DANTE (151); Though I Speak with the Tongues of Men and of Angels, THE BIBLE (KING JAMES VERSION) (157); Plucking the Rushes, ANONYMOUS (192); The River-Merchant's Wife: A Letter, LI PO (A VERSION BY EZRA POUND) (193)

Renaissance (1550-1650)

Sonnet XVIII: Shall I Compare Thee to a Summer's Day, WILLIAM SHAKESPEARE (31); Sonnet XXX: When to the Sessions to Sweet Silent Thought, WILLIAM SHAKESPEARE (32); Tom O' Bedlam's Song, ANONYMOUS (37); Sonnet LV: Not Marble, Nor the Gilded Monuments, WILLIAM SHAKESPEARE (52); The Shepheardes Lament, EDMUND SPENSER (87); The Constant Lover, SIR JOHN SUCKLING (94); A Valediction: Forbidding Mourning, JOHN DONNE (100); Death, JOHN DONNE (101); The Last Hour of Faustus, CHRISTOPHER MARLOWE (102); Hymn to Diana, BEN JONSON (105); Golden Slumbers, THOMAS DEKKER (106); A Sweet Disorder, ROBERT HERRICK (146); Go Lovely Rose, EDMUND WALLER (146); Virtue, GEORGE HERBERT (156); The Shepherd to His Love, CHRISTOPHER MARLOWE (175); The Nymph's Reply, SIR WALTER RALEGH (176); Sonnet CXVI: Let Me Not to the

Modern (1900-1945)

Contemporary (1945-Present)

Acknowledgements

The publishers and editors are grateful for permission to reproduce the copyright material by the following authors.

MILTON ACORN: 'I've Tasted My Blood,' 'The Fights.' From *Dig Up My Heart: Selected Poems 1952-1983* by Milton Acorn. Used by permission of the Canadian Publishers, McClelland and Stewart, Toronto.

YOSANO AKIKO: 'You Never Touch' by Yosano Akiko from *The Penguin Book of Japanese Verse*, translated by Geoffrey Bownas and Anthony Thwaite (Penguin Books, 1964), copyright © Geoffrey Bownas and Anthony Thwaite, 1964. Reproduced by permission of Penguin Books Ltd.

JACK ANDERSON: 'Going to Norway' from *City Joys*. Reprinted by permission of the author.

MARTIN ARMSTRONG: 'Mrs Reece Laughs' from *Collected Poems*. Reprinted by permission of Peters Fraser & Dunlop Group Ltd.

MARGARET ATWOOD: 'Backdrop Addresses Cowboy' from *The Animals in that Country* by Margaret Atwood, copyright © Oxford University Press Canada 1968.
'Thoughts from Underground,' 'The Immigrants' from *The Journals of Susanna Moodie* by Margaret Atwood, copyright © Oxford University Press Canada 1970.

W. H. AUDEN: 'As I Walked Out One Evening,' 'The Unknown Citizen.' Reprinted by permission of Faber and Faber Ltd. from *Collected Poems* by W. H. Auden.

MARGARET AVISON: 'The Swimmer's Moment' from *Winter Sun/The Dumbfounding* by Margaret Avison. Used by permission of the Canadian Publishers, McClelland and Stewart, Toronto.

IMAMU AMIRI BARAKA: 'SOS' from *Black Magic Poetry 1961-1967*. Reprinted by permission of Sterling Lord Literistic, Inc. Copyright © 1969 by Amiri Baraka (LeRoi Jones).

ULLI BEIER: 'Lullaby' from *African Poetry*, edited by Ulli Beier. Cambridge University Press.

563

HILAIRE BELLOC: 'On His Books' from *Sonnets and Verses* by Hilaire Belloc, reprinted by permission of A. D. Peters and Co. Ltd.
'Jim' by Hilaire Belloc from *Cautionary Tales for Children* by permission of Gerald Duckworth.

LOUISE BENNETT: 'Bans O' Killing.' Reprinted by permission of the author.

WENDELL BERRY: 'The Peace of Wild Things' from *Openings*, copyright © 1968 by Wendell Berry, reprinted by permission of Harcourt Brace Jovanovich, Inc.

JOHN BERRYMAN: Excerpt from *The Dream Songs* by John Berryman. Copyright © 1959, 1962, 1963, 1964 by John Berryman. Reprinted by permission of Farrar, Straus and Giroux, Inc.

EARLE BIRNEY: 'David' from *The Collected Poems of Earle Birney* by Earle Birney. Used by permission of the Canadian Publishers, McClelland and Stewart, Toronto.

ROO BORSON: 'Talk' from *A Sad Device*. Reprinted by permission of the author.

BERTOLT BRECHT: 'Questions from a Worker Who Reads' by Bertolt Brecht, translated by Michael Hamburger, from *Poems 1913-1956*. Reprinted with permission of Methuen London.

ROBERT BRINGHURST: 'Deuteronomy' from *The Beauty of the Weapons* by Robert Bringhurst. Used by permission of the Canadian Publishers, McClelland and Stewart, Toronto.

CHARLES CAUSLEY: 'Nursery Rhyme of Innocence and Experience' from *Collected Poems* by Charles Causley. Reprinted by permission of Macmillan.

LEONARD COHEN: 'Go by Brooks' from *The Spice Box of Earth*. 'Suzanne Takes You Down' from *Leonard Cohen Selected Poems*. Used by permission of the Canadian Publishers, McClelland and Stewart, Toronto.

FRANCES CORNFORD: 'To a Fat Lady Seen from a Train' from *Collected Poems*. The Cresset Press.

JULIO CORTÁZAR: 'The Lines of the Hand' from *Cronopois and Famas* by Julio Cortázar, translated by Paul Blackburn. Copyright © 1969 by Random House, Inc. Reprinted by permission of Pantheon Books, a Division of Random House, Inc.

ROBERT CREELEY: 'The Farm' by Robert Creeley, from *Collected Poems 1945-1975*. Reprinted by permission of the University of California Press. © 1983 The Regents of the University of California.

LORNA CROZIER: 'The Child Who Walks Backwards' from *The Garden Going on Without Us* by Lorna Crozier. Used by permission of the Canadian Publishers, McClelland and Stewart, Toronto.

E. E. CUMMINGS: 'Anyone Lived in a Pretty How Town' is reprinted from *Complete Poems 1913-1962*, by E. E. Cummings, by permission of Liveright Publishing Corporation. Copyright © 1923, 1925, 1931, 1935, 1938, 1939, 1940, 1944, 1945, 1946, 1947, 1948, 1949, 1950, 1951, 1952, 1953, 1954, 1955, 1956, 1957, 1958, 1959, 1960, 1961, 1962 by the Trustees for the E. E. Cummings Trust. Copyright © 1961, 1963, 1968 by Marion Moorehouse Cummings.

'Somewhere I Have Never Travelled, Gladly Beyond' reprinted from *ViVa*, poems by E. E. Cummings, edited by George James Firmage, by permission of Liveright Publishing Corporation. Copyright © 1931, 1959 by E. E. Cummings. Copyright © 1979, 1973 by the Trustees for the E. E. Cummings Trust. Copyright © 1979, 1973 by George James Firmage.

DANTE: *The Inferno, Canto Third*, by Dante, translated by John Ciardi. Reprinted by permission of Judith H. Ciardi.

WALTER DE LA MARE: 'All That's Past,' 'Echo,' 'The Song of the Mad Prince' reprinted by permission of the Literary Trustees of Walter de la Mare and The Society of Authors as their representative.

FRANCES DENSMORE: 'Plaint Against the Fog,' 'Song to Bring Fair Weather' by Nootka, translated by Frances Densmore, from *American and Indian Prose and Poetry*, edited by Margaret Astrov. Copyright 1964, by Margot Astrov. Reprinted by permission of the Putnam Publishing Group.

EMILY DICKINSON: 'I Taste a Liquor Never Brewed,' 'The Last Night That She Lived,' 'Within My Garden, Rides a Bird.' Reprinted by permission of the publishers and the Trustees of Amherst College from *The Poems of Emily Dickinson*, edited by Thomas H. Johnson, Cambridge Mass.: The Belknap Press of Harvard University Press, Copyright 1951, © 1955, 1979, 1983 by The President and Fellows of Harvard College.

'Within My Garden, Rides a Bird' and 'A Route of Evanescence' from *The Complete Poems of Emily Dickinson* by Emily Dickinson. Copyright 1929 by Martha Dickinson Bianchi: copyright © renewed 1957 by Mary L. Hampson. By permission of Little, Brown and Company.

ELIZABETH DREW: 'The Continuity of Poetry.' Reprinted from *Discovering Poetry* by Elizabeth Drew, with the permission of W. W. Norton & Company, Inc. Copyright 1933 by W. W. Norton & Company, Inc. Copyright renewed 1961 by Elizabeth Drew.

T. S. ELIOT: 'The Love Song of J. Alfred Prufrock,' 'The Hollow Men.' Reprinted by permission of Faber and Faber Ltd. from *Collected Poems 1909-1962* by T. S. Eliot.

EDWARD FIELD: 'Heaven and Hell' from *Songs and Stories of the Netsilik Eskimos*, translated by Edward Field. Reprinted by permission of the heirs of Knud Rasmussen.

ROBERT FROST: 'Stopping by Woods on a Snowy Evening,' 'The Road Not Taken' from *The Poetry of Robert Frost* edited by Edward Connery Lathem. Copyright © 1969 by Holt, Rinehart and Winston, Inc. Copyright © 1962 by Robert Frost. Copyright © 1975 by Lesley Frost Ballantine. Reprinted by permission of Henry Holt and Company, Inc.
'The Investment,' 'The Pasture.' Copyright 1928, 1930 by Holt, Rinehart and Winston and renewed 1956, 1958 by Robert Frost. Reprinted from *The Poetry of Robert Frost* edited by Edward Connery Lathem, by permission of Henry Holt and Company, Inc.

ZULKIFAR GHOSE: 'This Landscape, These People.' Reprinted from *The Loss of India* by permission of the author.

ALLEN GINSBERG: 'A Supermarket in California' by Allen Ginsberg. Copyright © 1955 by Allen Ginsberg. From *Collected Poems 1947-1980* by Allen Ginsberg. Reprinted by permission of Harper & Row, Publishers, Inc.

THOM GUNN: 'On the Move.' Reprinted by permission of Faber and Faber Ltd. from *The Sense of Movement* by Thom Gunn.

THOMAS HARDY: 'Great Things,' and 'In Time of "The Breaking of Nations." ' Reprinted from *Collected Poems of Thomas Hardy*, published by Macmillan & Co. Ltd.

SEAMUS HEANEY: 'The Railway Children.' Reprinted by permission of Faber and Faber Ltd. from *Station Island* by Seamus Heaney.

RALPH HODGSON: 'Reason Has Moons' from *Collected Poems* by Ralph Hodgson © Ralph Hodgson. Reprinted by permission of Macmillan of Canada, a Division of Canada Publishing Corporation.

LANGSTON HUGHES: 'Little Green Tree,' 'Snail.' Reprinted from *Selected Poems of Langston Hughes* by permission of Alfred A. Knopf, Inc. 'Little Green Tree' copyright 1948 by Alfred A. Knopf, Inc. 'Snail' copyright 1947 by Langston Hughes.

TED HUGHES: 'Hawk Roosting.' Reprinted by permission of Faber and Faber Ltd. from *Lupercal* by Ted Hughes.

ISSA: 'Climbing Mount Fuji,' 'My Grumbling Wife' from *Introduction to Haiku* by Harold G. Henderson. Copyright © 1958 by Harold G. Henderson. Reprinted by permission of Doubleday, a division of Bantam, Doubleday, Dell Publishing Group, Inc.
'My Grumbling Wife' by Issa, translated by Harry Behn, from *Haiku Harvest Series IV*. Reprinted by permission of Peter Pauper Press, Inc.
'You Hear That Fat Frog' by Issa, translated by Peter Beilenson, from *A Haiku Garland*. Reprinted by permission of Peter Pauper Press, Inc.

RANDALL JARRELL: 'The Death of the Ball Turret Gunner' from *The Complete Poems* by Randall Jarrell. Copyright 1945 by Mrs Randall Jarrell. Copyright renewed © 1972 by Mrs Randall Jarrell. Reprinted by permission of Farrar, Straus and Giroux, Inc.

PAULETTE JILES: 'Waterloo Express' from *Waterloo Express* (Toronto: House of Anansi Press, 1973). Reprinted by permission.

GEORGE JOHNSTON: 'War on the Periphery.' Reprinted by permission; © 1951, 1979, The New Yorker Magazine, Inc.

JAMES JOYCE: 'The Hitherandthithering Waters Of' from *Finnegan's Wake* by James Joyce. Copyright renewed © 1967 by George Joyce and Lucia Joyce. All rights reserved. Reprinted by permission of Viking Penguin Inc.

ABRAHAM KLEIN: 'Autobiographical' from *A. M. Klein: Complete Poetry*, edited by Zailig Pollock, University of Toronto Press. Reprinted by permission of University of Toronto Press.

KENNETH KOCH: 'Variations on a Theme by William Carlos Williams' from *Thank You and Other Poems*. Copyright © Kenneth Koch, 1985.

JOY KOGAWA: 'What Do I Remember of the Evacuation?' From *A Choice of Dreams* by Joy Kogawa. Used by permission of the Canadian Publishers, McClelland and Stewart, Toronto.

PHILIP LARKIN: 'An Arundel Tomb.' Reprinted by permission of Faber and Faber Ltd. from *The Whitsun Weddings* by Philip Larkin.

D. H. LAWRENCE: 'Snake' from *The Complete Poems of D. H. Lawrence*. Reprinted with permission of Laurence Pollinger Ltd. and the Estate of Mrs. Frieda Lawrence Ravagli.

'The White Horse' from *The Complete Poems of D. H. Lawrence*, edited by Vivian de Sola Pinto and F. Warren Roberts. Copyright © 1964, 1971 by Angelo Ravagli and C. M. Weekley, Executors of the Estate of D. H. Lawrence. All rights reserved. Reprinted by permission of Viking Penguin Inc.

IRVING LAYTON: 'The Improved Binoculars' from *A Wild Peculiar Joy* by Irving Layton. Used by permission of the Canadian Publishers, McClelland and Stewart, Toronto.

FEDERICO GARCÍA LORCA: 'The Six Strings' by Federico García Lorca, translated by Donald Hall. Reprinted by permission of Faber and Faber Ltd. from *The Rattle Bag*, edited by Seamus Heaney and Ted Hughes.

ROBERT LOWELL: 'Home After Three Months Away' from *Life Studies* by Robert Lowell. Copyright © 1956, 1959 by Robert Lowell. Reprinted by permission of Farrar, Straus and Giroux, Inc.

GWENDOLYN MACEWEN: '1958' from *Afterworlds* by Gwendolyn MacEwen. Used by permission of the Canadian Publishers, McClelland and Stewart, Toronto.

PHYLLIS MCGINLEY: 'Girl's-Eye View of Relatives' from *Times Three* by Phyllis McGinley. Copyright © 1957 by Phyllis McGinley, renewed © 1985 by Phyllis Hayden Blake. All rights reserved. Reprinted by permission of Viking Penguin Inc.

LOUIS MACKAY: 'The Ill-Tempered Lover' from *The Ill-Tempered Lover* by Louis MacKay. Reprinted by permission of McGraw-Hill Ryerson Limited.

568

LOUIS MACNEICE: 'Snow.' Reprinted by permission of Faber and Faber Ltd. from *The Collected Poems of Louis MacNeice*.

DON MARQUIS: 'Cheerio My Deario' by Don Marquis from *archy and mehitabel*. Copyright 1927 by Doubleday, a division of Bantam, Doubleday, Dell Publishing Group, Inc. Reprinted by permission of the publisher.

JOHN MASEFIELD: 'An Epilogue.' Reprinted by permission of Macmillan Publishing Company from *Selected Poems: Anniversary Edition* by John Masefield (New York: Macmillan, 1978), and permission of the Society of Authors as the literary representative of the Estate of John Masefield.

GAIL MAZUR: 'Baseball' from *Nightfire,* reprinted by permission of the author.

EDNA ST VINCENT MILLAY: 'Dirge Without Music' by Edna St Vincent Millay. From *Collected Poems*, Harper & Row. Copyright © 1928, 1955 by Edna St Vincent Millay and Norma Millay Ellis. Reprinted by permission.

MARIANNE MOORE: 'Silence' reprinted with permission of Macmillan Publishing Company from *Collected Poems* by Marianne Moore. Copyright 1935 by Marianne Moore, renewed 1963 by Marianne Moore and T. S. Eliot.
Lines from 'The Mind Is an Enchanting Thing.' Reprinted with permission of Macmillan Publishing Company from *Collected Poems* by Marianne Moore. Copyright 1944, and renewed 1972, by Marianne Moore.

J. B. MORTON: 'The Dancing Cabman.' Reprinted by permission of A. D. Peters and Co. Ltd.

LES MURRAY: 'An Absolutely Ordinary Rainbow' by Les Murray from *The Vernacular Republic*. Copyright © 1982 by Les Murray. Reprinted by permission of Persea Books, Inc.

PABLO NERUDA: 'Walking Around' by Pablo Neruda, translated by Ben Belitt. Reprinted by permission of Grove Press, a division of Wheatland Corporation. Copyright © 1961 by Ben Belitt.

JOHN NEWLOVE: 'The Hitchhiker' from *The Fatman: Selected Poems 1962-1972* by John Newlove. Used by permission of the Canadian Publishers, McClelland and Stewart, Toronto.

569

bpNICHOL: 'Prayer' from *Art Facts*, published in 1989 by Chax Press, Tucson, Arizona, U.S.A. Reprinted by permission of Ellie Nichol and Chax Press.

ALDEN NOWLAN: 'It's Good to Be Here,' 'Weakness' from *An Exchange of Gifts* by Alden Nowlan. Reprinted by permission of Irwin Publishing Inc., Toronto, Canada.
'Saturday Night' by Alden Nowlan. Reprinted by permission of Claudine Nowlan.

GABRIEL OKARA: 'Once Upon a Time.' Reprinted with permission from *Pergamon Poets II: Poetry from Africa*, edited by Sergeant, © 1968, Pergamon Press.

SHARON OLDS: 'Rite of Passage' from *The Dead and the Living* by Sharon Olds. Copyright © 1983 by Sharon Olds. Reprinted by permission of Alfred A. Knopf, Inc.

MICHAEL ONDAATJE: 'To a Sad Daughter' by Michael Ondaatje from *Secular Love*. Reprinted by permission.

WILFRED OWEN: 'Strange Meeting' from *The Collected Poems of Wilfred Owen*, edited by C. D. Lewis, published by Chatto & Windus. Reprinted with permission of the publisher and the Estate of Wilfred Owen.

DOROTHY PARKER: 'Indian Summer' from *The Portable Dorothy Parker* by Dorothy Parker. Copyright 1928, renewed © 1956 by Dorothy Parker. All rights reserved. Reprinted by permission of Viking Penguin Inc.

KENNETH PATCHEN: '& So the Little Fieldmouse Said' by Kenneth Patchen, *Hurrah for Anything*. Copyright © 1946, 1957, 1958 by Kenneth Patchen. Reprinted by permission of New Directions Publishing Corporation.

BRIAN PATTEN: 'You'd Better Believe Him' by Brian Patten from *Notes to the Hurrying Man*. Reprinted by permission of Unwin Hyman Ltd.

SYLVIA PLATH: 'Mushrooms' from *Collected Poems* by Sylvia Plath, copyright Ted Hughes 1967 and 1981, published by Faber and Faber, London, by permission of Olwyn Hughes.

EZRA POUND: 'The River-Merchant's Wife: A Letter' by Li Po, translated by Ezra Pound. 'In a Station of the Metro,' 'Salutation' by Ezra Pound, from *Personae*. Copyright 1926 by Ezra Pound. Reprinted by permission of New Directions Publishing Corporation. 'What Thou Lovest Well Remains.' Reprinted by permission of Faber and Faber Ltd. from *The Cantos of Ezra Pound*.

E. J. PRATT: 'Erosion,' 'The Prize Cat' from *E. J. Pratt: Complete Poems* by E. J. Pratt, edited by Sandra Djwa and R. G. Moyles. Copyright 1989 by University of Toronto Press. Reprinted by permission of University of Toronto Press.

AL PURDY: 'Depression in Namu, B. C.' from *Collected Poems* by Al Purdy. 'My '48 Pontiac' from *Wild Grape Wine* by Al Purdy. 'The Country North of Belleville' from *Cariboo Horses* by Al Purdy. Used by permission of the Canadian Publishers, McClelland and Stewart, Toronto.

JAMES REANEY: For permission to reprint 'Branwell's Lament,' from *A Suite of Nettles*, copyright Canada, 1958, by James Reaney, thanks are due to the author and the Macmillan Company of Canada.

HENRY REED: 'Naming of Parts' from *A Map of Verona* by Henry Reed, published by Jonathan Cape Ltd. Reprinted by permission of the Estate of Henry Reed.

YANNIS RITSOS: 'Penelope's Despair' by Yannis Ritsos, translated by Nikos Stangos, The Times Literary Supplement, August 21, 1970. © Times Newspapers Ltd. 1985.

SIR CHARLES G. D. ROBERTS: 'The Mowing' by Sir Charles G. D. Roberts. Reprinted by permission of Lady Joan Roberts.

THEODORE ROETHKE: 'A Field of Light' by Theodore Roethke. Copyright 1951 by The Tiger's Eye. From *The Collected Poems of Theodore Roethke*. Reprinted by permission of Doubleday, a division of Bantam, Doubleday, Dell Publishing Group, Inc.

JOE ROSENBLATT: 'Natural Prayer' from *Poetry Hotel: Selected Poems 1963-85* by Joe Rosenblatt. Used by permission of the Canadian Publishers, McClelland and Stewart, Toronto.

M. L. ROSENTHAL: 'Poetry and Ordinary Experience' from *Poetry and the Common Life* by M. L. Rosenthal. Reprinted by permission of the author. All rights reserved.

LARRY ROTTMANN: 'APO 96225' by Larry Rottmann. Reprinted by permission of the author.

CARL SANDBURG: 'Night Bells' from *The Complete Poems of Carl Sandburg*, Revised and Expanded Edition, copyright 1950 by Carl Sandburg and renewed 1978 by Margaret Sandburg, Helga Sandburg Crile, and Janet Sandburg, reprinted by permission of Harcourt Brace Jovanovich, Inc.

'Whiffs of the Ohio River at Cincinnati' from *Good Morning, America*, copyright 1928 and renewed 1965 by Carl Sandburg, reprinted by permission of Harcourt Brace Jovanovich, Inc.

A. J. M. SMITH: 'The Lonely Land' from *The Classic Shade* by A. J. M. Smith. Used by permission of the Canadian Publishers, McClelland and Stewart, Toronto.

STEVIE SMITH: 'Not Waving But Drowning' from *The Collected Poems of Stevie Smith*, published by Penguin Modern Classics. Used by permission of James MacGibbon.

MARY ELLEN SOLT: 'Forsythia' from *Flowers in Concrete* by Mary Ellen Solt. Reprinted by permission of the author.

STEPHEN SPENDER: 'I Think Continually of Those Who Were Truly Great.' Reprinted by permission of Faber and Faber Ltd. from *Collected Poems* by Stephen Spender.

WALLACE STEVENS: 'Domination of Black' and 'Sunday Morning.' Copyright 1923 and renewed 1951 by Wallace Stevens. Reprinted from *The Collected Poems of Wallace Stevens*, by permission of Alfred A. Knopf, Inc.

DYLAN THOMAS: 'And Death Shall Have No Dominion,' 'Fern Hill' from *The Poems*. 'Welsh Night' from *Under Milk Wood*. Used by permission of J. M. Dent and Sons.

R. S. THOMAS: 'A Peasant' from *Song at the Year's Turning* by R. S. Thomas. Reprinted by permission of Grafton Books, a division of the Collins Publishing Group.

MARINA TSVETAEVA: 'We Shall Not Escape Hell,' by Marina Tsvetaeva, translated by Elaine Feinstein, from *Selected Poems of Tsvetaeva*. Reprinted by permission of Olwyn Hughes.

ARTHUR WALEY: 'Plucking the Rushes' from *170 Chinese Poems*, translated by Arthur Waley. Reprinted by permission of Constable Publishers.

BRONWEN WALLACE: 'Common Magic' by Bronwen Wallace is reprinted from *Common Magic* by permission of Oberon Press.

GEORGE WHICHER: 'Sir Penny,' translated by George Whicher, *The Goliard Poets*. Copyright 1949 by George Whicher. Reprinted by permission of New Directions Publishing Corporation.

WILLIAM CARLOS WILLIAMS: 'Raleigh Was Right' by William Carlos Williams, *Collected Later Poems*. Copyright 1944 by William Carlos Williams. 'The Artist' by William Carlos Williams, *Pictures from Brueghel*. Copyright 1953 by William Carlos Williams. First printed in *The New Yorker*. 'The Term,' 'This Is Just to Say' by William Carlos Williams, *Collected Poems, Volume I: 1909-1939*. Copyright 1938 by New Directions Publishing Corporation. All poems by William Carlos Williams are reprinted by permission of New Directions Publishing Corporation.

WILLIAM BUTLER YEATS: 'The Choice,' 'The Fisherman,' 'The Lake Isle of Innisfree' from *The Collected Poems of W. B. Yeats* by W. B. Yeats. Reprinted by permission of A. P. Watt Limited on behalf of Michael B. Yeats and Macmillan London Ltd.

DALE ZIEROTH: 'Coyote Pup Meets the Crazy People in Kootenay National Park' from *Mid-River* (Toronto: House of Anansi Press, 1981). Reprinted by permission.

'Good Morning Blues.' New words and new music arrangement by Huddie Ledbetter. Edited with new additional material by Alan Lomax. TRO — © Copyright 1959 (renewed) Folkways Music Publishers, Inc., New York, N. Y. Used by permission.

Every effort has been made to determine and contact copyright owners. In the case of any omissions, the publisher will be pleased to make suitable acknowledgements in future editions.